TEACHER JOB SATISFACTION

THE GARLAND BIBLIOGRAPHIES
IN CONTEMPORARY EDUCATION
(*Advisory Editor*: Joseph M. McCarthy)
(Vol. 7)

GARLAND REFERENCE LIBRARY
OF SOCIAL SCIENCE
(Vol. 448)

THE GARLAND BIBLIOGRAPHIES IN CONTEMPORARY EDUCATION

Advisory Editor:
Joseph M. McCarthy

1. *Issues in Adult Basic Education*
   by Darlene Russ-Eft, David P. Rubin, and Rachel E. Holmen

2. *Contemporary Approaches to Moral Education*
   by James Leming

3. *Teacher Effectiveness*
   by Marjorie Powell and Joseph W. Beard

4. *Higher Education Finance*
   by Edward R. Hines and John R. McCarthy

5. *Teacher Attitudes*
   by Marjorie Powell and Joseph W. Beard

6. *Textbooks in School and Society*
   by Arthur Woodward, David L. Elliott, and Kathleen Carter Nagel

7. *Teacher Job Satisfaction*
   by Paula E. Lester

TEACHER JOB SATISFACTION
*An Annotated Bibliography and
Guide to Research*

Paula E. Lester

GARLAND PUBLISHING, INC. • NEW YORK & LONDON
1988

© 1988 Paula E. Lester
All rights reserved

Library of Congress Cataloging-in-Publication Data

Lester, Paula E.
  Teacher job satisfaction: an annotated bibliography and guide to research / Paula E. Lester.
    p.   cm. — (The Garland bibliographies in contemporary education ; vol. 7) (Garland reference library of social science ; vol. 448)
  Bibliography: p.
  Includes index.
  ISBN 0-8240-8922-7 (alk. paper)
  1. Teachers—Job satisfaction—Bibliography. 2. Teachers—Job stress—Bibliography. 3. Teachers participation in administration—Bibliography. I. Title. II. Series: Garland bibliographies in contemporary education; vol. 7. III. Series: Garland reference library of social science; vol. 448.
  Z5814.T3L46   1988   [LB2840]   016.371'0023—dc19
  88-9768   CIP

Printed on acid-free, 250-year-life paper
Manufactured in the United States of America

CONTENTS

Introduction: Teacher Job Satisfaction   vii

I.	BEGINNING TEACHERS	3
II.	ELEMENTARY SCHOOL TEACHERS	15
III.	SECONDARY SCHOOL TEACHERS	33
IV.	SUBJECT AREA TEACHERS	47
V.	COLLEGE TEACHERS	75
VI.	TEACHER MOTIVATION	115
VII.	TEACHER ADMINISTRATOR RELATIONSHIP	129
VIII.	TEACHER STRESS AND BURNOUT	157
IX.	TEACHING	201

Author Index   239
Title Index   253
Subject Index   305

INTRODUCTION:

TEACHER JOB SATISFACTION

Teacher job satisfaction has been a subject of study and interest for many years. The current number and variety of studies reflect a continuing interest. Some studies are purely descriptive, providing information about the present levels of job satisfaction/dissatisfaction. Other studies focus on describing job satisfaction among teachers in various geographic locations and at different levels within school districts. Still other studies investigate those factors that affect teachers' job satisfaction and the choice to enter or leave the profession. Among all the varied efforts to describe existing levels of job satisfaction, their sources and effects, a considerable body of knowledge exists about teachers. This bibliography attempts to review that large field for the years 1975 through 1986 to identify all the sources of information, and to list documents that discuss research on teacher job satisfaction. The bibliography does not include an assessment of the quality of the research reported in the listed documents; there are variations in the research methods and the veracity of the resulting information. However, the value of the bibliography is in its comprehensiveness. Users of the bibliography can locate the listed studies and then evaluate the studies using criteria relevant to their individual purposes.

1. STRUCTURE OF BIBLIOGRAPHY

Topics Covered

The bibliography includes studies of the job satisfaction of elementary, secondary school, and college teachers. Within these three broad groups, some studies investigate the job satisfaction of groups of teachers, e.g., teacher groups defined by subject area taught, such as special education, physical education, or English; or by personal and demographic characteristics, such as age, sex, length of service, school size, and grade level. Other studies that focus on the negative aspects of teachers' job satisfaction, teacher stress and burnout, are also included in the bibliography. The bibliography includes studies of beginning teachers' job satisfaction and preservice and inservice teacher education programs. In addition to many descriptive studies, the bibliography includes studies of factors that influence teachers' job satisfaction and dissatisfaction.

Studies with varied methodologies are included in the bibliography. Many of the studies are based on teachers' descriptions of their attitudes or results of questionnaires that measure their attitudes toward one or more aspects of their job. Some studies focus solely on the job satisfaction of teachers while others compare the levels of teacher job satisfaction with the job satisfaction of other groups, such as administrators, nurses, or the police. Studies of teacher job satisfaction in foreign countries are included. Some studies present a picture of teachers' job satisfaction at a specific point in time, while other studies describe teachers' career choice and career changes over a period of time. Still other studies describe the development of instruments to assess teacher job satisfaction and teacher stress and burnout.

Entries in the bibliography have been divided into nine general categories. Each category is described in Section 3 of this introduction, with illustrations of entries. In addition, each entry has been assigned from one to five subject terms that are listed in the subject index. The author index and title index also list each entry in the bibliography. The questionnaires cited in each entry are also listed in the subject index.

Topics Not Covered

With the focus on elementary and secondary education, the bibliography does not include studies which focus exclusively on organizational climate.

Introduction: Teacher Job Satisfaction ix

A more general category of documents is excluded from the bibliography: conference papers that are not available through some normal distribution source, such as ERIC or a university publications department.

Sources of Reference

Six major index systems were reviewed to locate documents to be included in the bibliography: <u>Education Index</u>, <u>Dissertation Abstracts</u>, <u>Psychological Abstracts</u>, <u>Sociological Abstracts</u> and both <u>Resources in Education</u> (RIE) and <u>Current Index to Journals in Education</u> (CIJE) of the Educational Resources Information Center (ERIC) system. The ERIC system, federally funded, makes documents available that would not otherwise obtain broad distribution. The system solicits documents from a variety of sources, including presenters at national and regional conferences and researchers in a variety of institutions. Documents are screened for appropriateness, copied onto microfiche, and announced in <u>Resources in Education</u> (RIE) or, if they have been published, <u>Current Index to Journals of Education</u> (CIJE). Both <u>RIE</u> and <u>CIJE</u> are monthly publications distributed to subscribers, usually organizations that also subscribe to the microfiche collection. The microfiche are distributed to libraries around the country and other institutions subscribing to the ERIC microfiche collection, such as state departments of education, county or regional education agencies (e.g., BOCES and intermediate school districts) and large local school districts. Many documents that would be available only in limited numbers or for a limited period of time, such as evaluation reports of specific educational programs, become accessible through the ERIC system.

Different research terms were used in the six systems, because the classification systems and the labels for classes of documents differ among the systems. The search began with the 1975 volume of each index and continued through the 1986 issues.

Types of Documents Included

The majority of the documents in the bibliography are research reports. These include technical reports describing results and methodologies as well as executive summaries of the research findings. The level of technical detail varies among these reports; some were written as final technical reports while others were written to communicate results to educators and other persons interested in teaching.

Some of the documents listed in the bibliography are reviews of research. Reviews may list and describe several studies or they may compile the information from several studies selected because of their focus on a single aspect of teachers' job satisfaction. They are often a helpful source of initial information about a specific area of study, but may not include all documents related to that specific area of study.

2. HISTORY OF RESEARCH ON TEACHER JOB SATISFACTION

Topics Studied

Herzberg, Mausner, Peterson, and Capwell (1957) have analyzed fifty years of research on job attitudes. They conclude that multiple characteristics of job satisfaction exist, because workers in any given position can be affected by many factors. They further conclude that the type of survey used affects the clustering of multiple characteristics. For example, surveys measuring worker dissatisfaction identify different factors than do surveys measuring worker satisfaction.

Hoppock (1935) compared the 100 most satisfied teachers and the 100 least satisfied teachers and found six factors: (a) security, (b) loyalty, (c) the teacher's social and economic status in the group, (d) the reaction of the teacher to distasteful situations, (e) the composition of the job, and (f) the teacher's judgment of others.

Vroom (1964) provides a review of the literature. Supervision, the work group, job content, promotional opportunities, wages, and hours of work are reported as possible factors affecting job satisfaction.

Athanasiou (1969) claims that job satisfaction cannot be explained solely by knowledge of the work role: "Personality factors in interaction with environmental factors might reasonably be expected to account for more variance in the prediction of job satisfaction than either one alone" (p. 70).

Sergiovanni (1969) states that teachers obtain satisfaction from activities that center upon the work itself.

Introduction: Teacher Job Satisfaction

He reports achievement, recognition, and responsibility as three sources of job satisfaction.

Hilgert (1971) had workers rank order ten job factors, from most important to least important. The most important factor contributing to job satisfaction was found to be good supervision, and the least important factor was good pay.

Coughlan (1971) developed an instrument to measure teacher attitude toward specific aspects of the work environment. The factors identified are: (a) board functioning, (b) system administration, (c) work load, (d) materials and equipment, (e) buildings and facilities, (f) principal relations, (g) colleague reactions, (h) community relations, (i) instructional program, (j) student development, (k) performance appraisal, (l) financial autonomy, and (m) professional autonomy.

Chung (1972) reports studies linking job content, the work group, promotional opportunity, reward, performance, supervision, and the physical environment to job satisfaction. Nicholson and Miljus (1972) describe job satisfaction in terms of promotional opportunities, participative supervision, interaction with peers, varied duties, and high pay.

Stone and Porter (1975) studied the relationship among job characteristics and workers' attitudes. The job characteristics utilized in this study are (a) variety, (b) autonomy, (c) task identity, (d) feedback, (e) friendship opportunities, (f) dealing with others, and (g) the prestige of the job. The variables from the study are: (a) organizational commitment, (b) job duties, (c) salary, (d) organizational effectiveness, (e) supervision, (f) promotion, (g) co-workers, (h) work itself, and (i) pay. The researchers found that "the job an individual holds is associated not only with the attitudes about the work itself, but also relates to other attitudes as well" (p. 64).

Katzell and Yankelovich (1975) discuss the following strategies for improving job satisfaction: (a) pay people more, (b) give people work that uses their skills, (c) provide helpful supervision, (d) provide harmonious work groups, (e) provide opportunities for mobility, (f) give people a chance to take part in decisions that affect them, and (g) improve working conditions.

Kaufman (1978) studied industrial arts teachers at the university level and investigated (a) the work environment (promotion, tenure, salary, job security, medical and life benefits, and retirement benefits), (b) supervisory traits, and (c) colleagues, in an attempt to identify several variables that influence job satisfaction.

The terms intrinsic and extrinsic factors, satisfiers and dissatisfiers, and motivators and hygienes are used to describe characteristics of job satisfaction. Blum (1961) states that security is one of the most important determinants in career selection. His position is that individuals concerned about job security, financial provision, and the opportunity for tenure, select jobs where these environmental or hygiene factors are present. People who are less interested in security select jobs that provide opportunities for advancement, achievement, recognition, and responsibility (motivators or satisfiers).

In Wernimont's (1966) study, achievement, responsibility, and the work itself were most often reported as satisfiers, whereas the absence of recognition and advancement were most often reported as dissatisfiers. Dunnette, Campbell, and Hakel (1967) found supervision, responsibility, achievement, and recognition to be both satisfiers and dissatisfiers.

Soliman (1970) found that if the environment is able to meet the needs of the worker, the motivators are a more important source of satisfaction than are hygiene factors. If the environment does not meet the needs of the worker, then the hygienes are a more important source of dissatisfaction than the motivators.

Andrisani (1978) states that, in relation to job satisfaction, subjects showed an increased interest in intrinsic aspects of the work (work itself, capacity to do work, responsibility or independence, and chance for advancement), along with a decrease in the extrinsic aspects (earnings and fringe benefits, job security, working conditions, supervision, interpersonal relations, hours of work, company policy and administration).

Warr, Cook, and Wall (1979) have examined various aspects of the job situation and divide job satisfaction items into two separate categories: (a) intrinsic (freedom to choose one's own method of working, recognition, amount of variety in the job) and (b) extrinsic (physical working conditions, fellow workers, immediate boss, pay, hours, relations between management and workers, and job security).

Attempts to relate wages to job satisfaction have resulted in contradictory and ambiguous findings. Lawler and Porter (1963) and Smith and Kendall (1963) report a positive correlation between income or wages and overall job satisfaction. However, Redeffer (1964) studied teachers' responses and found that "personnel policies and practices rather than salary levels are the key to high or low morale among teachers" (pp. 63-64).

Opsahl and Dunnette (1966) conclude that little is known about how pay interacts with other factors. They report that, in their study, higher salaries frequently went hand-in-hand with other factors, such as job level and experience, which might have influenced job satisfaction. On a list of job satisfiers, salary was often ranked low, but on a list of job dissatisfiers, salary was often ranked high. Lawler (1971) reports that job performance, age, sex, seniority, organizational level, education, skill, time-span, nonmonetary outcomes, and method of payment are all related to satisfaction with pay.

Supervision is another factor of job satisfaction that has been studied. Vroom (1964) notes that a high level of satisfaction occurs when a supervisor is considerate of his/her employees. It has been assumed that participative, democratic supervision would produce the greatest satisfaction, whereas authoritarian leadership would produce the least satisfaction. The data available from Vroom do not support the relationship.

Slocum and Missjauk (1970) found a positive relationship between job satisfaction and satisfaction with the supervisor, management, and the company. House, Filley, and Gujarati (1971) investigated the relationship between subordinates' expectations of supervisory behavior and job satisfaction. When sixteen measures of job satisfaction were utilized, leader consideration was related to satisfaction on eleven of the measures, and initiating structure was related to satisfaction in ten of the measures. According to Thompson (1971), the more supportive the supervisory style, the higher the degree of satisfaction.

Gruneberg (1976) reviewed journal articles on job satisfaction which examined Herzberg's two-factor theory, possible sources of job satisfaction and/or dissatisfaction, occupational differences, absenteeism, turnover, and productivity.

Thus, it seems that researchers investigating characteristics of job satisfaction are unable to agree upon specific factors as characteristics of job satisfaction. The lack of agreement exists because different researchers study different aspects of the work situation, and discrepancies among studies occur because factors included in some studies do not appear in other studies.

Sources of Research

Many studies of teacher job satisfaction are completed as the research for a dissertation. These studies typically deal with teachers' attitudes toward a subject of interest to the doctoral candidate or the faculty at the institution where the dissertation is being completed.

A number of studies of teacher job satisfaction grow out of evaluations of educational programs. Many of these evaluations are conducted by school districts; they include assessments of the operation and effects of special programs funded by the district, the state or the federal government and assessments of educational needs as an initial step in developing special programs to secure funding from state or federal sources.

Other evaluations are conducted by state departments of education.

Both large and small federally funded programs have generated multiple evaluations.

Research Methods

Researchers have used a variety of methods to study teacher job satisfaction. One approach has been to ask teachers to respond to questionnaire items. A number of different response modes are used to reflect teachers' attitudes toward the topic of interest within the study. Sometimes researchers use open-ended questions to allow the teachers to give their responses in whatever form they choose. Other times researchers use fill-in responses to allow the teachers the opportunity to generate responses rather than simply choose them. The most commonly used structured response mode is the scaled response that measures the degree of either frequency or agreement with each statement. At other times, researchers give teachers a series of statements and ask them to rank order them in terms of a specific criterion, thereby forcing the teachers to choose between alternatives.

Other studies use interviews of individual teachers as the basic method of data collection. Studies using interview data generally include a smaller sample of teachers than do studies based on questionnaires because of the time required to collect and analyze the interview data.

Another approach has been to conduct polls of large samples of teachers, often measuring attitudes toward a variety of topics. National organizations sometimes conduct polls of a national sample of teachers (e.g., the National Education Association polls). Sometimes state departments of education will poll a sample of teachers within the state on a topic of current interest within the state or the effects of new state legislation. More often, doctoral candidates conduct such polls as their dissertation research.

A final approach has been to conduct case studies of teachers' attitudes. Usually case studies focus on one or a few teachers with information compiled over an extended period of time, e.g., weeks, months or even a full school year. A case study may investigate one topic or may cover several related topics. Case studies often involve extended classroom observations, interviews, and analysis of documents.

3. OVERVIEW OF BIBLIOGRAPHIC TOPICS

The bibliography entries are divided into nine sections: (a) beginning teachers, (b) elementary school teachers, (c) secondary school teachers, (d) subject area teachers, (e) college teachers, (f) teacher motivation, (g) teacher administrator relationship, (h) teacher stress and burnout, and (i) teaching. Each section is discussed in turn. In addition, the bibliographic entries are listed in the author, title, and subject indexes.

I. Beginning Teachers

Studies of beginning teachers' job satisfaction can be grouped into several types of studies. Some focus on the student teaching experience (Mahan, 1981). Student teacher attitudes toward role perception, teaching skills, and the school bureaucracy are examined. Other studies analyze the data gathered in following studies of education graduates (de Voss, 1980). The surveys included graduates who are currently practicing teachers as well as those who chose another profession. Kepner and Nelson (1981) suggest that those responsible for providing preservice experiences for future teachers should assist them to become aware of the school climate and how to adjust to it. A number of studies describe preservice teacher education, inservice training programs, technical assistance, program improvement, and teacher education. A few studies identify and describe specific conditions, policies, and practices which cause problems for beginning teachers. For example, Cain (1984) investigates the relationship between inservice practices, rapport with the principal, interaction with peers, quality of resources and job satisfaction. Teacher induction and socialization have been studied. One study views teacher education along a continuum from a preservice level to a beginning level to an experienced level and then develops profiles for each level (Driscoll, 1983). The development of teacher perspectives during the first year can be explored in terms of curriculum, teacher's role, teacher-pupil relationships, and student diversity. Tabachnick (1983) conducts case studies of four teachers, beginning with the student teaching experience through the first year of teaching. First year teachers' experiences have been a continuing focus of descriptive studies (e.g., Ellis, 1982), while the satisfying/dissatisfying factors of mentor teachers constitute a relatively recent area of focus of descriptive studies (e.g., Barnard, 1986).

II. Elementary School Teachers

Studies that compare levels of job satisfaction among elementary school teachers occur relatively frequently. Elementary schools have been compared in terms of open classrooms and self-contained classrooms. For example, Murphy (1976) focuses on the personality traits of open-area team teachers and self-contained classroom teachers while Packard and others (1978) examine teacher work groups, including team functions, team management, unit characteristics, and systematic relationships among team functions. A few studies compare teacher job satisfaction between predominantly black and white schools (e.g., Deville, 1976), while other studies investigate the differences in the interests of male and female elementary teachers (Robinson, 1978). Many of the studies describe sources of satisfaction and dissatisfaction, such as job involvement (Wiener and Gechman, 1977), organizational structure (Williams, 1981), decision making (Henderson, 1976), and planned educational change, e.g., Coley's (1980) study of Individually Guided Education. Relatively infrequently,

Introduction: Teacher Job Satisfaction xvii

studies compare job satisfaction of elementary teachers in different countries. One study describes job satisfaction of rural and urban elementary school teachers in Thailand (Kirtdum, 1984). Other studies investigate job satisfaction among late career entry teachers (Parker, 1985), substitute teachers (Pascale and others, 1984), and outstanding elementary school teachers (Easterly, 1983).

A large number of studies examine the types of intrinsic rewards of teaching and their relation to teacher characteristics and variables in the work setting. Plihal's (1982) study identifies two types of rewards. Some studies explore the relationship between job satisfaction and teacher absenteeism (Bridges, 1979), between job satisfaction and teacher stress (Raschke and others, 1985), between teacher job satisfaction and principal leadership style (Guagulwong, 1981), and between teacher job satisfaction and student achievement (Frank, 1982).

III. Secondary School Teachers

Studies on secondary school teachers include junior high school, middle school, and senior high school teachers. A few studies examine the relationship between job satisfaction and the level of implementation of basic middle school characteristics. For example, Demps (1978) compares the perceptions of teachers and administrators in middle schools. Other studies identify sources of satisfaction and dissatisfaction among senior high school teachers using the research of Herzberg. Clarke's (1976) study analyzes internal and external job factors related to teaching.

A number of studies discuss the organizational incentives that are valued by secondary teachers and attempt to discover what organizational incentives are valued by secondary teachers at various stages of their careers (Metzdorf, 1984). Studies on career rewards sometimes focus on reasons for entry into the profession, daily worklife, changes in the reward structure, and stages of career and professional development. Kreis (1983) explores the relationship between security, affiliation, self esteem, autonomy, and self actualization, and levels of job satisfaction among urban high school teachers, while Ligon (1985) tests Holland's theory to determine if preferences for teaching methods were related to personality type, subject area, and years of teaching experience.

Surveys to assess sources of stress among high school teachers have been conducted. For example, Litt (1985) correlates teacher role, school climate, coping resources, and work problems with teacher stress. Interrelationships among organizational climate, job satisfaction, teacher absenteeism, and teacher turnover have been investigated by McElroy (1984). Some studies describe the professional preparation of junior and senior high school teachers (Young, 1983), the degree of participation in decision making (Rochelle, 1983), and unionism among secondary school teachers (Ghanavi, 1984). Studies that compare secondary teacher job satisfaction in foreign countries are included.

IV. Subject Area Teachers

Studies of subject area teachers' job satisfaction can be grouped into several types of studies. Some focus on special education teachers in general, while others focus on visually handicapped teachers, teachers of the deaf, emotionally handicapped teachers, severely or profoundly retarded teachers, learning disabled teachers, and resource specialists. Abelson (1986) compares job satisfaction among various groups of special education teachers, while other studies compare regular education teachers and special education teachers. Other studies focus on vocational education teachers in general, while others focus on home economics teachers (Stealey, 1982), industrial teachers (Bloemker, 1983), and vocational agriculture teachers (Grady, 1985). These studies assess professional identification, reasons for the decision to remain in the profession, and the most and least satisfying aspects of teaching. For example, Brod (1986) describes the most effective means to encourage good teaching, while also examining the causes of low staff morale.

A few studies examine teacher job satisfaction in terms of educational needs and educational oportunities. One illustration of this type of study is the work of Bowers (1986) that finds a significant correlation between increases in educational opportunities and increases in job satisfaction among English teachers. Some studies compare teacher role, role conflict, role ambiguity, and role perception with teacher job satisfaction. For example, Moller (1981) measures music teachers' general, intrinsic, and extrinsic job satisfaction. There are studies that investigate the relationship between organizational structure and teacher job satisfaction. One study involves preschools and day care centers (Rodriguez, 1982).

Some studies describe teacher job satisfaction in foreign countries, while other studies describe the differences between rural and urban school districts (Horn, 1985).

V. College Teachers

Many studies identify sources of satisfaction and dissatisfaction among faculty in higher education. For example, Wittenauer (1980) uses ten attitude factors which Herzberg labeled as either satisfiers or dissatisfiers. Problems affecting the profession of college teaching are also considered. Broesamie (1984) cites lack of rewards, recognition, status, and salaries, while Fuller (1985) discusses dwindling enrollments and funding, a changing student body, curricular adjustments, and teacher distrust. The problems of job-related stress among college faculty are increasing, and the issue of burnout must be addressed to not only cure but prevent burnout. Burnout among community college humanities teachers is looked at by Agte (1984) in terms of student-worker boredom, alienation, exhaustion, and indifference.

Studies assessing job satisfaction among community college faculty are numerous. In a study by Hutton and others (1985), relationships with supervisors and peers and teaching are considered sources of greatest satisfaction, while professional development opportunities, time allocation, and student preparation are considered sources of least satisfaction. Cowan (1982) surveys community college teachers to identify the rewards that contribute to job satisfaction. One study compares levels of satisfaction among full-time and part-time community college faculty at an urban institution (Neely, 1981). The poor fit between the person and the environment is considered as one source of job stress and job strain by Boberg (1982).

A few studies examine the relationship between faculty involvement in decision-making and job satisfaction. Klapachan (1983) compares faculty participation in decision-making in terms of academic rank, formal education, teaching experience at the university, total years of teaching experience, and types of school. Other studies investigate the relationship betwen supervisory intervention behaviors and faculty job satisfaction. For example, Skalak (1985) studies nursing faculty satisfaction in relation to eight specific supervisory interventions. Recruitment, retention, and retirement satisfaction among faculty members of public and private universities have been studied. Torbati (1979) compares satisfaction at work and retirement among active and retired faculty members. Several studies discuss job satisfaction among university faculty in foreign countries. Higgs (1985), for example, investigates the relationships among role conflict, role ambiguity, career stage, and the variables of intrinsic and extrinsic job satisfaction among Canadian physical education faculty.

VI. Teacher Motivation

Studies on teacher motivation can be divided into several groups. Many studies are based on Herzberg's Two-Factor Theory. Engelking (1985) uses a critical incident questionnaire adapted from Herzberg's Motivation-Hygiene Theory to identify sources of job satisfaction and dissatisfaction. In another study, Perko (1985) examines the factors that contribute to job satisfaction and dissatisfaction in order to test Herzberg's Theory. Other studies relate Herzberg's Hygiene-Motivation Theory to Maslow's Hierarchy of Needs Theory. For example, in a study by Frataccia and Hennington (1982), the needs that teachers have difficulty in satisfying are described in terms of the need for psychological growth and the need to avoid unpleasantness as well as the motivation component and the hygiene component. Some studies examine the relationship between teacher morale and perceived need deficiencies using Maslow's Hierarchy of Needs. Warren (1982) uses a Maslow Needs Hierarchy Instrument to assess the need levels of teachers. A few studies investigate the relationship of expectancy work motivation to teacher job satisfaction. For example, Binnie (1984) studies the relationship of expectancy work motivation, school size, teaching experience, locus of control, and absenteeism to teacher job satisfaction. Several studies are based on the Hackman-Oldham job enrichment theory. Charters and others (1984) revise the Job Diagnostic Survey for use with teachers.

Introduction: Teacher Job Satisfaction

A large number of studies measure levels of teacher motivation. Fox's (1986) study describes the development of an instrument to measure sources of teacher motivation and satisfaction with the principal's administration of the school. Some studies survey higher order needs (autonomy, variety) or low order needs (pay) and job satisfaction. For example, Pastor and Erlandson (1982) conclude that teacher job satisfaction is significantly related to higher order needs. Myths about teachers' attitudes toward merit pay are discussed by Dunwall (1986). One study compares secure and riffed reemployed teachers in terms of pay, co-worker and principal's supervision, and individual expectancy motivation (Kaminetzky, 1985).

VII. Teacher Administrator Relationship

Some studies have assessed the effects of administrative practices on teacher job satisfaction. For example, Andrew and others (1985) describe an action plan for administrators that takes into account the relationship between teacher morale and principal leadership, interpersonal relationships, rewards, workload, and professional development opportunities. Other studies have explored the influence of principal leadership on teacher satisfaction and motivation. An example is the study by Morris (1981) that analyzes teachers' perceptions of their work environment. Nelson (1980) applies the path-goal theory of leadership to school organizations and assesses the dimensions of principals' leader behaviors. Many studies investigate the relationship beween principal leader behaviors and the locus of control and role ambiguity of teachers (Rohman, 1985), teacher satisfaction with supervision (Winkler, 1983), situational control and school effectiveness (Stone, 1979), teacher stress (Roberts, 1983), and teachers' participation in decision making and student achievement (Marra, 1978).

Interpersonal relationships between elementary school principals and teachers are studied in order to determine possible correlations between the need for control by principals and teachers (Tice, 1981). In a study by Dansie (1986), teacher autonomy, contact with the principal, and teacher job satisfaction are examined. Grigsby (1981) investigates the relationship between the principals' perceived communication behavior and teacher job satisfaction.

Elementary and secondary school principals from urban, suburban, and rural school districts are included as well as administrators from foreign countries. Personal variables generally include age, gender, marital status, length of service, and salary.

VIII. Teacher Stress and Burnout

Studies on stress in teaching focus on staff problems, role conflict, role ambiguity, children's behavior and attitudes, working conditions, and middle and top management (Dunham, 1984). Sources of stress and the most frequent symptoms of stress are examined by different groups of teachers in a study by Broiler (1982). One study reports on the factors that cause physical and mental stress among Black, White, and Hispanic inner-city, elementary schools (Bruno, 1981), while another study compares levels of stress experienced by regular classroom teachers and by special education teachers (Moracco and others, 1981).

Questionnaires designed to measure teacher stress include the Teaching Events Stress Inventory (Cichon and Koff, 1978) and the Teacher Stress Inventory (Murphy, 1984). A cross validation study of the Maslach Burnout Inventory was conducted by Iwanicki and Schwab (1981) on classroom teachers, while Foxworth and others (1984) tested the factorial validity of the Teacher Occupational Stress Factor Questionnaire on elementary school teachers of the gifted.

Many studies examine the relationship between classroom teacher background variables and aspects of teacher burnout. For example, Schwab and Iwanicki (1982) find a significant relationship between sex, age, and grade level and emotional exhaustion, depersonalization, and personal accomplishment. Other studies discuss ways to identify and manage stress. One study presents specific techniques for managing stress and then reviews them (Sparks and Hammond, 1981). Another study recommends giving teachers realistic expectations about what can be done in today's classrooms and helping them to develop a strong, positive self-image (Riccio, 1983).

IX. Teaching

Some studies describe the choice of teaching as a profession. For example, Jantzen (1981) conducts a survey of college students preparing to become teachers to determine the reasons why they chose to become teachers. Service, interest in children, and leadership were cited. Moore (1986) discusses the differences between job satisfaction and career satisfaction by finding out how teachers view their work on a daily basis and as a lifelong commitment. One study examines why some education majors chose not to become teachers (Bogard, 1983). Other studies focus on identifying and describing the factors that influence the decisions of teachers to leave the teaching profession. In a study by McGrath (1986), personal, organizational, and environmental factors are analyzed to determine their relationship to and influence on career change decisions among secondary school teachers. The most frequently teacher-reported teaching likes and dislikes among elementary, junior high, and senior high school teachers are presented by Trotter (1984).

Questionnaires designed to measure job satisfaction include the Purdue Teacher Opinionaire, the Minnesota Satisfaction Questionnaire, and the Job Descriptive Index. Cobb (1986) studies rapport with the principal, satisfaction with teaching, rapport among teachers, teacher salaries, teacher workload, curriculum issues, teacher status, and community support using the Purdue Teacher Opinionaire. The Teacher Job Descriptive Index was developed by Conroy (1979). The original five areas of the JDI were retained and the Student Area was added. Rayder and Body (1975) field test the Educational Forces Inventory to describe the influence of thirteen factors on teacher morale and classroom effectiveness. The Teacher Job Satisfaction Questionnaire was developed by Lester (1984) to assess nine areas of teacher job satisfaction: supervision, colleagues, working conditions, pay, responsibility, work itself, advancement, security, and recognition.

4. FUTURE DIRECTIONS OF RESEARCH

Research on teacher job satisfaction will focus on teacher education programs. University involvement in the educational system will be expanded, and the entry policy for new teachers will be re-examined. Studies will be conducted to determine the effectiveness of teacher education programs in various states. Programs that counsel prospective teachers will provide coaching or directing experiences. The appropriateness of specific training programs in universities that offer undergraduate training to middle school teachers will be studied. Teacher training universities will provide student teachers with pre-service experiences in different educational settings.

More in-service training programs, professional activities and meaningful incentives will be needed. In-service programs to improve job skills will be investigated and introduced into the schools to prepare teachers for new teaching experiences. Research should be done to determine what kinds of programs will be most effective for teachers facing transfers and reassignments. Longitudinal studies will be conducted to determine the long-term effects of reduction in force on teacher job satisfaction. The search for personalities and behavior which characterize open and non-open teachers will continue. Pre-school orientation programs that include community involvement and school practices, policies, and procedures will be developed. In-service programs in team-teaching practices and group effectiveness should be provided by school administrators.

More research needs to be conducted regarding the relationship between organizational climate and teacher job satisfaction. The perceptions of urban teaching staffs, middle school teachers, and different secondary school departments will be examined. All levels of schooling will be investigated as well as several school districts of varying sizes. Teacher attrition should be studied in open and closed school climates. Teacher absenteeism in open and closed school climates should be studied. A study on teacher effectiveness in open and closed school climates should be conducted. An investigation of organizational behavior in the school setting that looks at the characteristics of the role and the person occupying it should be done.

Research is needed to determine the causes and effects of middle road management in community colleges. The relationships between job involvement, job satisfaction, and job performance should be studied. The factors that contribute to teaching effectiveness in various educational institutions should be investigated. Studies using different size institutions, state or private institutions, and different departments should be conducted to determine their effects on teacher job satisfaction. Tenure of full-time faculty members might be considered in future studies.

Meaningful work opportunities for teachers must be developed. Adding responsibility and planning opportunities for increased teacher involvement will be needed. Teacher rewards for outstanding accomplishments or classroom production will be enlarged. The relationship between teacher job satisfaction and differentiated staffing will be explored.

The jobs of principal and teacher will be re-conceptualized. Job satisfaction might be enhanced by assigning duties to teachers based on their needs. Teachers should be included in administrative decision making situations, such as student admissions, curriculum change, and class size. Training programs for supervisors should emphasize the value of human relations skills and technical skills. Further study should be undertaken to examine the causes of variance with respect to teacher job satisfaction and leadership behavior in terms of organizational climate, size of school districts, and ages of teachers and supervisors.

Investigations should focus on the positive aspects of teaching that improve teacher well-being. Studies may examine well-being factors that distinguish the older teachers from the younger teachers. Studies using different geographical areas should be conducted to determine if demographic and cultural differences affect teacher job satisfaction and job stress.

Further research is needed to determine the impact of personality and situational variables on teachers' perceptions of need-for-involvement in decision making. Replication studies should be conducted to determine whether teachers who have been involved in the collective bargaining process for varying periods of time differ in their levels of job satisfaction. More research studies should be replicated over a longer period of time, in different geographical areas, in all educational settings, and with larger populations.

The development of a more refined questionnaire to measure Herzberg's Theory should be undertaken. The Job Descriptive Index should be revised. The Minnesota Satisfaction Questionnaire should be reworded in teacher vocabulary to avoid problems of interpretation. Follow-up studies should be conducted to measure teacher job satisfaction.

It is hoped that this bibliography will form one base for future research on teacher job satisfaction.

REFERENCES

Abelson, A. Geoffrey. "A Factor-Analytic Study of Job Satisfaction Among Special Educators." *Educational and Psychological Measurement* 46, no. 1 (Spring 1986): 37-43.

Agte, Lloyd. *The Burned-Out Community College Humanities Instructor: Causes and Cures.* 1984. ERIC, ED 258 642.

Andrew, Lloyd D., and others. *Administrator's Handbook for Improving Faculty Morale.* 1985. ERIC, ED 268 663.

Andrisani, P. *Work Attitudes and Labor Market Experience.* New York: Praeger Publications, 1978.

Athanasiou, R., J. P. Robinson, and K. B. Head. "Measures of Occupational Attitudes and Occupational Characteristics." Ann Arbor: University of Michigan, Institute for Social Research, 1969. (Draft)

Barnard, Barbara. "Satisfying/Dissatisfying Factors of California Mentor Teachers." Ed.D. dissertation, University of Southern California, 1986.

Binnie, David George. "The Relationship of Expectancy Work Motivation, Selected Situational Variables and Locus of Control to Teacher Job Satisfaction." Ed.D. dissertation, University of South Florida, 1984.

Bloemker, Darvin Alan. "Factors Associated with the Retention of Industrial Educators." Ed.D. dissertation, University of Missouri-Columbia, 1983.

Blum, S.H. "The Desire for Security." *Journal of Educational Psychology* 52 (1961): 317-321.

Boberg, Alice Duxter. "Faculty Under Stress: Person-Environment Fit Theory." Ph.D. dissertation, The University of Michigan, 1982.

Bogad, Carolyn McWilliams. *The Process of Deciding "Not" to Become a Teacher.* 1983. ERIC, ED 230 515.

Bowers, Roberta June. "The Relationships Among Educational Needs, Educational Opportunities, and Job Satisfaction for Indiana Secondary English Teachers." Ed.D. dissertation, Indiana University, 1986.

Bridges, Edwin M. Job Satisfaction and Teacher Absenteeism. 1979. ERIC, ED 202 146.

Brod, Rodney L., and others. "Insights from Vocational Teachers of the Year." Vocational Education Journal 61, no. 2 (March 1986): 29-31.

Broesamie, John J. Academic Turbulence and the Crisis of Professional Satisfaction. 1984. ERIC, ED 253 155.

Broiles, Patricia Hope. "An Inquiry into Teacher Stress: Symptoms, Sources and Prevalence in Public Schools." Ph.D. dissertation, Claremont Graduate School, 1982.

Bruno, James E. "Morale-Affecting Stressors: An Analysis of Black, White, and Hispanic Elementary Schools." Urban Education 16, no. 2 (July 1981): 175-203.

Cain, Brenda Leigh. "The Relationship Between Selected School Context and Support Variables and the Perceived Success and Satisfaction of Beginning Elementary Teachers." Ph.D. dissertation, University of Minnesota, 1984.

Charters, W.W., Jr., and others. Feasibility Studies of Teacher Core Job Characteristics. Final Report. 1984. ERIC, ED 245 383.

Chung, K.H. "Incentive Theory and Research." Personnel Administration 35 (1972): 31-41.

Cichon, Donald J., and Robert H. Koff. The Teaching Events Stress Inventory. 1978. ERIC, ED 160 662.

Clarke, Robert Leo. "Sources of Teacher Job Satisfaction and Dissatisfaction for Senior High School Teachers." Ed.D. dissertation, University of Pennsylvania, 1976.

Cobb, Sara Frances Head. "Job Satisfaction of Teachers in a Selected County as Measured by the Purdue Teacher Opinionaire." Ed.D. dissertation, University of Southern Mississippi, 1986.

Coley, Thomas Gregory. "The Implementation of Planned Educational Change: A Multivariate Analysis of the Decision Source for Change, Organizational Commitment, and Job Satisfaction Among Elementary School Teachers." Ph.D. dissertation, The University of Wisconsin-Madison, 1980.

Conroy, Joseph Patrick. "The Effect on the Job Descriptive Index Used for Measuring Teacher Job Satisfaction When a Student Area Is Added." Ed.D. dissertation, University of Denver, 1979.

Coughlan, R.J. "Job Satisfaction in Relatively Closed and Open Schools." Educational Administration Quarterly 7, no. 2 (1971): 40-59.

Cowan, Carole Anne. "A Study of Faculty Perceptions of Selected Morale Variables." Ed.D. dissertation, University of Massachusetts, 1982.

Dansie, Lamonte J., Jr. "An Analysis of Relationships Among Teacher Autonomy, Contact with the Principal, and Teacher Job Satisfaction." Ed.D. dissertation, University of Northern Colorado, 1986.

Demps, Henry Willie. "A Study of the Relationship Between Teachers' Perceptions of Job Satisfaction and Their Perceptions of the Level of Implementation of Eighteen Basic Middle School Characteristics." Ph.D. dissertation, Michigan State University, 1978.

De Ville, Louie Michael. "A Comparison of Teacher Job Satisfaction Between Predominantly Black and White Schools." Ed.D. dissertation, University of the Pacific, 1976.

deVoss, Gary, and Donald Hawk. Follow-Up of 1978/79 Graduates at the Ohio State University's College of Education Teacher Certification Program. Technical Report no. 5. 1980. ERIC, ED 201 618.

Driscoll, Amy. The Socialization of Teachers: Career Rewards and Levels of Professional Concern. 1983. ERIC, ED 241 474.

Dunham, Jack. Stress in Teaching. 1984. ERIC, ED 252 505.

Dunwell, Robert R. Merit, Motivation, and Mythology. 1986. ERIC, ED 268 112.

Easterly, Jean L. Perceptions of Outstanding Elementary Teachers About Themselves and Their Profession. Research Studies in Education, Technical Report No. 1. 1983. ERIC, ED 238 854.

Ellis, Joseph R., and Deloris J. Ellis. Professional Role Performance Difficulties Reported by First Year Home Economics Teachers in Illinois Public Schools. 1982. ERIC, ED 228 217.

Engelking, Jeri Lee. "Identification of Satisfying and Dissatisfying Factors in Staffs of Elementary and Secondary Public School Teachers from Two States." Ph.D. dissertation, University of Idaho, 1985.

Fox, William M. Teacher Motivation. 1986. ERIC, ED 275 677.

Foxworth, Marilyn D., Frances A. Karnes, and Rex L. Leonard. "The Factorial Validity of the Teacher Occupational Stress Factor Questionnaire for the Teacher of the Gifted." Educational and Psychological Measurement 44, no. 2 (Summer 1984): 527-532.

Frank, Arnold. "The Relationship Between Teacher Job Satisfaction and Student Reading Achievement, Time Off-Task, and Teacher Planning Time." Ph.D. dissertation, The University of Wisconsin-Madison, 1982.

Frataccia, Enrico V., and Iris Hennington. Satisfaction of Hygiene and Motivation Needs of Teachers Who Resigned from Teaching. 1982. ERIC, ED 212 612.

Fuller, Jack. Morale Is Bad. 1985. ERIC, ED 266 815.

Ghanavi, Gholamreza. "Collective Action and Unionism Among Secondary School Teachers." Ph.D. dissertation, United States International University, 1984.

Grady, Thomas L. "Job Satisfaction of Vocational Agriculture Teachers in Louisiana." Journal of the American Association of Teacher Educators in Agriculture 26, no. 3 (Fall 1985): 70-78, 85.

Grigsby, Carl Jaco. "The Relationship of the Principal's Communication Behavior to the Teacher's Perceived Job Satisfction." Ed.D. dissertation, University of Missouri-Columbia, 1981.

Gruneberg, M., ed. Job Satisfaction--A Reader. New York: Wiley & Sons, 1976.

Guagulwong, Thawin. "Leadership Styles, Maturity Levels, and Job Satisfaction in Elementary Schools." Ph.D. dissertation, The University of Oklahoma, 1981.

Henderson, Lester F. "Elementary Teacher Satisfaction and Morale and Perceived Participation in Decision-Making." Ed.D. dissertation, University of Arkansas, 1976.

Herzberg, F., B. Mausner, R. Peterson, and D. Capwell. Job Attitudes: Research and Opinion. Pittsburgh: Psychological Service of Pittsburgh, 1951.

Higgs, Colin. "Job Satisfaction of Canadian University Physical Education Faculty: The Influence of Work Orientation, Career Stage, Role Conflict, and Role Ambiguity." Ph.D. dissertation, University of Oregon, 1985.

Hilgert, R.L. "Satisfaction and Dissatisfaction in a Plant Setting." Personnel Administration 34 (1971): 21-27.

Hoppock, R. Job Satisfaction. New York: Harper and Brothers, 1935.

Horn, Jerry G. Recruitment and Preparation of Quality Teachers for Rural Schools. 1985. ERIC, ED 258 785.

House, R.J., A.C. Filley, and D.N. Gujarati. "Leadership Style, Hierarchical Influence, and the Satisfaction of Subordinate Role Expectations: A Test of Likert's Influence Proposition." *Journal of Applied Psychology* 55 (1971): 422-432.

Hutton, Jerry B., and Max E. Jobe. "Job Satisfaction of Community College Faculty." *Community/Junior College Quarterly of Research and Practice* 9, no. 4 (1985): 317-324.

Iwanicki, Edward F., and Richard L. Schwab. "A Cross Validation Study of the Maslach Burnout Inventory." *Educational and Psychological Measurement* 41, no. 4 (Winter 1981): 1167-1174.

Jantzen, J. Marc. "Why College Students Choose to Teach: A Longitudinal Study." *Journal of Teacher Education* 32, no. 2 (March-April 1981): 45-49.

Kaminetzky, Beverlee S. "The Relationship of Reduction in Force to Motivation and Aspects of Job Satisfaction of Teachers." Ed.D. dissertation, Rutgers University, The State University of New Jersey (New Brunswick), 1985.

Katzell, R.A., and D. Yankelovich. *Work, Productivity and Job Satisfaction*. New York: The Psychological Corporation, 1975.

Kaufman, A.H., and J.J. Buffer, Jr. "An Assessment of Job Satisfaction of Industrial Arts Education Educators." *Journal of Industrial Teacher Educators* 16, no. 1 (1978): 45-56.

Kepner, Henry S., Jr., and Robert W. Nelson. *Creating Conditions for Professional Practice in Education*. 1981. ERIC, ED 212 555.

Kirtdum, Anant. "A Study of Job Satisfaction of Rural and Urban Elementary School Teachers in Thailand." Ed.D. dissertation, Oklahoma State University, 1984.

Klapachan, Prachaya. "A Study of the Relationships Between Participation in the Decision-Making Process and Job Satisfaction Among the Faculty of a Midwestern Regional State University." Ph.D. dissertation, University of Kansas, 1983.

Kreis, Kathleen. The Relationship Between Job Satisfaction and Needs Fulfillment Among Urban High School Teachers. 1983. ERIC, ED 230 656.

Lawler, E.E. "Compensating the New Life-Style Worker." Personnel 48 (1971): 19-25.

Lawler, E.E., and L.W. Porter. "Perceptions Regarding Management Compensation." Industrial Relations 3 (1963): 41-49.

Lester, Paula E. "Development of an Instrument to Measure Teacher Job Satisfaction." Ph.D. dissertation, New York University, 1984.

Ligon, Jerry Alan. "Personality, Subject Area, Time in Service, and Instructional Methods: A Test of Holland's Theory." Ph.D. dissertation, Arizona State University, 1985.

Litt, Mark D., and Dennis C. Turk. "Sources of Stress and Dissatisfaction in Experienced High School Teachers." Journal of Educational Research 78, no. 3 (January-February 1985): 178-185.

Mahan, James M. A Comparison of Concerns of Secondary and Elementary Student Teachers. 1981. ERIC, ED 201 631.

Marra, Peter Robert. "Principal's Leadership Behavior, Teacher's Decisional Participation, Teacher's Job Satisfaction and Student Achievement." Ed.D. dissertation, Fordham University, 1978.

McElroy, Lee August, Jr. "An Analysis of the Relationships Among Control Variables, Organizational Climate, Job Satisfaction, Teacher Absenteeism, and Teacher Turnover in the Secondary Public School." Ed.D. dissertation, University of Houston, 1984.

McGrath, Edmund Roy, Jr. "The Exodus Syndrome: Factors Affecting Teacher Career Change." Ed.D. dissertation, Boston University, 1986.

Metzdorf, Virginia Ann. "Secondary Teachers' Responses to Organizational Incentives." Ph.D. dissertation, The University of Wisconsin-Madison, 1984.

Moller, Lynn Elliott. "The Relationship of Role Perceptions of the Secondary School Music Educator and the Resultant Effect on Job Satisfaction." Ph.D. dissertation, University of Kansas, 1981.

Moore, Barbara McGregor. "Satisfaction with Teaching as a Job and as a Career." Ph.D. dissertation, Claremont Graduate School, 1986.

Moracco, John C., and others. Stress in Teaching: A Comaprison of Perceived Stress Between Special Education and Regular Teachers. 1981. ERIC, ED 202 828.

Morris, Monica B. The Public School as Workplace: The Principal as a Key Element in Teacher Satisfaction. A Study of Schooling in the United States. Technical Report Series, no. 32. 1981. ERIC, ED 214 899.

Murphy, Dorothy Louise Hollar. "The Effects of Demographic and Personality Factors on Job Satisfaction or Self-Contained Classroom Teachers and Open-Area Team Teachers." Ed.D. dissertation, University of Houston, 1976.

Murphy, Gwendolyn. "Teacher Stress: Measurement and Management." Ed.D. dissertation, Boston University, 1984.

Neely, Janet Henchie. "A Study of Socialization and Job Satisfaction of Faculty at an Urban Two-Year Community College." Ph.D. dissertation, The Ohio State University, 1981.

Nelson, Mary Ann Elizabeth. "Leader Behavior and Its Relationship to Subordinate Job Satisfaction as Moderated by Selected Contingency Factors in Minnesota Public Schools: A Path-Goal Theory Approach." Ph.D. dissertation, University of Minnesota, 1980.

Opsahl, R.L., and M.P. Dunnette. "The Role of Financial Compensation in Industrial Motivation." Psychological Bulletin 63 (1966): 94-118.

Packard, John S., and others. Management Implications of Team Teaching: Final Report. 178. ERIC, ED 161 153.

Parker, Phyllis J. Burnes. "An Investigation of Job Satisfaction Among Late Career Entry Teachers at the Elementary Level." Ed.D. dissertation, George Peabody College for Teachers of Vanderbilt University, 1985.

Pascale, Pietro J., James C. King, and Lou Mastrian. "The Development and Validation of an Elementary School Substitute Teacher Questionnaire." Educational and Psychological Measurement 44, no. 2 (Summer 1984): 507-511.

Pastor, Margaret C., and David A. Erlandson. "A Study of Higher Order Need Strength and Job Satisfaction in Secondary Public School Teachers." Journal of Educational Administration 20, no. 2 (Summer 1982): 172-183.

Perko, Laura Lee. "Job Satisfaction of Teachers in the Portland Metropolitan Area: An Examination of Differing Factors and Their Relationship to Herzberg and Lortie Theories." Ed.D. dissertation, Portland State University and University of Oregon, 1985.

Plihal, Jane. Types of Intrinsic Rewards of Teaching and Their Relation to Teacher Characteristics and Variables in the Work Setting. 1982. ERIC, ED 215 978.

Raschke, Donna B., and others. "Teacher Stress: The Elementary Teacher's Perspective." Elementary School Journal 85, no. 4 (March 1985): 559-564.

Rayder, Nicholas F., and Bart Body. The Educational Forces Inventory: A New Technique for Measuring Influences on the Classroom. 1975. ERIC, ED 179 580.

Redeffer, F.L. "Studies of Teacher Morale." School and Society 92 (1964): 63-64.

Riccio, Anthony C. "On Coping with the Stresses of Teaching." <u>Theory into Practice</u> 22, no. 1 (Winter 1983): 43-47.

Roberts, Kerry Lee. "An Analysis of the Relationship of Principals' Leadership Style to Teacher Stress and Job Related Outcome." Ph.D. dissertation, Washington State University, 1983.

Robinson, Daniel Clarence. "An Investigation of the Extent to Which Members of a Single Occupation (Elementary Teacher) Show Different or Identical Interests Depending upon Whether They Are Male or Female or Members of Black or Caucasian Racial Groups." Ph.D. dissertation, Iowa State University, 1978.

Rochelle, William Jerry. "Participation in Decision Making and Job Satisfaction: An Empirical Test of the Vroom and Yetton Model in Selected Secondary Schools." Ph.D. dissertation, Georgia State University--College of Education, 1983.

Rodriguez, Robert Alan. "Structural Coupling and Teacher Job Satisfaction in Preschools and Day Care Centers." Ed.D. dissertation, University of Kansas, 1982.

Rohman, Gary Bernard. "A Study of the Interaction of High School Principals' Leader Behaviors and the Locus of Control and Role Ambiguity of Teachers in Determining Their Job Satisfaction." Ed.D. dissertation, Rutgers University, The State University of New Jersey (New Brunswick), 1985.

Schwab, Richard L., and Edward F. Iwanicki. "Who Are Our Burned Out Teachers?" <u>Educational Research Quarterly</u> 7, no. 2 (Summer 1982): 5-16.

Sergiovanni, T.J. "Satisfaction and Dissatisfaction of Teachers." In <u>Organization and Human Behavior: Focus on Schools</u>. Edited by F.D. Carver and T.J. Sergiovanni. New York: McGraw-Hill, 1969.

Skalak, Constance Havird. "A Study of the Relationships Between Perceived and Reported Supervisory Intervention Behavior and Faculty Job Satisfaction." Ed.D. dissertation, University of Georgia, 1985.

Slocum, J.W., Jr., and M.J. Misshauk. "Job Satisfaction and Productivity." Personnel Administration 33 (1970): 52-58.

Smith, P.C., and L.M. Kendall. "Retranslation of Expectations: An Approach to the Construction of Unambiguous Anchors for Rating Scales." Journal of Applied Psychology 47 (1963): 149-155.

Soliman, H.M. "Motivation-Hygiene Theory of Job Attitudes: An Empirical Investigation and an Attempt to Reconcile Both the One- and-Two-Factor Theories of Job Attitudes." Journal of Applied Psychology 54 (1970): 452-461.

Sparks, Dennis, and Janice Hammond. Managing Teacher Stress and Burnout. 1981. ERIC, ED 200 522.

Stealey, Patricia Ann Terrill. "The Relation of Home Economics Teachers' Professional Identification and Personal Characteristics to Job Satisfaction." Ed.D. dissertation, Virginia Polytechnic Institute and State University, 1982.

Stone, E.F., and L.W. Porter. "Job Characteristics and Job Attitudes: A Multivariate Study." Journal of Applied Psychology 60, no. 1 (1975): 57-64.

Stone, Vera. "Principal's Leadership Style, Situational Control and School Effectiveness." Ph.D. dissertation, University of California, Berkeley, 1979.

Tabachnick, B. Robert, and others. The Development of Teacher Perspectives. 1983. ERIC, ED 240 112.

Thompson, D.E. "Favorable Self-Perception, Perceived Supervisory Style, and Job Satisfaction." Journal of Applied Psychology 55 (1971): 349-352.

Tice, Paul Gary. "Teacher Job Satisfaction and the Personal Need for Control by Principals and Teachers." Ph.D. dissertation, George Peabody College for Teachers of Vanderbilt University, 1981.

Torbati, Maryam Behzadpour Torbati, Masoud. "Job and Retirement Satisfaction Among Faculty Members of Public and Private Universities." Ph.D. dissertation, United States International University, 1979.

Trotter, John Rhodes. "What Teachers Like and Dislike About Teaching." Ed.D. dissertation, University of Georgia, 1984.

Vroom, V.H. Work and Motivation. New York: John Wiley & Sons, 1964.

Warr, P., J. Cook, and T. Wall. "Scales for the Measurement of Some Work Attitudes and Aspects of Psychological Well-Being." Journal of Occupational Psychology 52 (1979): 129-148.

Warren, Darrel Lee. "A Study of the Relationship Between Teacher Morale and Perceived Needs Deficiency of Maslow's Needs Hierarchy." Ed.D. dissertation, University of Missouri-Columbia, 1982.

Wernimont, P.F. "Intrinsic and Extrinsic Factors in Job Satisfaction." Journal of Applied Psychology 50, no. 1 (1966): 41-50.

Wiener, Yoash, and Arthur S. Gechman. "Commitment: A Behavioral Approach to Job Involvement." Journal of Vocational Behavior 10, no. 1 (February 1977): 47-52.

Williams, Jeanette Allen. "The Effect of Organizational Structure of Schools and Role Orientation of Teachers on Job Satisfaction of Teachers." Ed.D. dissertation, Rutgers University, The State University of New Jersey (New Brunswick), 1981.

Winkler, Abby Lynn. "The Relationships Between Elementary School Teacher Perceptions of Principal Leadership Style/Style Adaptability and Teacher Job Satisfaction/Satisfaction with Supervision." Ed.D. dissertation, The Catholic University of America, 1983.

Wittenauer, Martha Anne. "Job Satisfaction and Faculty Motivation." Ed.D. dissertation, Indiana University, 1980.

Young, Mable Goodwin. "A Study of the Comparison of Job Satisfaction and Professional Preparation of Selected Junior and Senior High School Teachers in Colorado." Ed.D. dissertation, University of Northern Colorado, 1983.

Teacher Job Satisfaction

I. BEGINNING TEACHERS

1. Bandy, Helen. <u>The Identification of Skills and Characteristics Needed by Country School Teachers.</u> Education Reports. 1980. ERIC, ED 234 942.

    Discusses the use of survey instruments to assess the advantages and disadvantages of teaching in rural schools.

2. Barnard, Barbara. "Satisfying/Dissatisfying Factors of California Mentor Teachers." Ed.D. dissertation, University of Southern California, 1986.

    Identifies three factors (Achievement, Recognition, and Responsibility) contributing to mentor teacher job satisfaction and three factors contributing to job dissatisfaction (Interpersonal Relations, Status, and Working Conditions).

3. Becvar, Raphael Jacob. "Job Satisfaction of First-Year Teachers: A Study of Discrepancies Between Expectations and Experiences." Ph.D. dissertation, University of Minnesota, 1969.

    Investigates the relationship between the actual experience of beginning teachers and the anticipated experience using the Minnesota Satisfaction Questionnaire.

4. Blair, A. K. Advisers to Rural Schools. A Survey of the Advisory Service Which Is Specially Provided for Small Rural Schools in New England. 1960. ERIC, ED 212 400.

   Describes sources of dissatisfaction among rural teachers and includes suggestions for inservice teacher education.

5. Brogdon, Richard; William Spencer; and Fachon Funk. "The Effects of Associate Teaching on Teacher Morale." High School Journal 69 (April-May 1986): 239-244.

   Examines the relationship between student teacher placement and morale using the Purdue Student-Teacher Opinionaire.

6. Burden, Paul R. Professional Development as a Stressor. 1982. ERIC, ED 218 263.

   Discerns three stages of professional development and outlines the changes in professional characteristics of each stage.

7. Cain, Brenda Leigh. "The Relationship Between Selected School Context and Support Variables and the Perceived Success and Satisfaction of Beginning Elementary Teachers." Ph.D. dissertation, University of Minnesota, 1984.

   Describes specific conditions, policies and practices that augment or decrease the satisfaction of first-year elementary school teachers using the Purdue Teacher Opinionaire.

8. Cortis, Gerald. "Twelve Years On--A Longitudinal Study of Teacher Behaviour Continued." Educational Review 31 (15 November 1979): 205.

   Studies beginning teachers for psychological, biographical, and educational variables and then examines trends to predict present levels of satisfaction and teaching success.

9. Dawson, Judith A. Support for Educational Change: Its Forms, Functions, and Sources. 1981. ERIC, ED 203 531.

   Describes four basic functions of external assistance in school change; one function is morale maintenance.

10. deVoss, Gary, and Donald Hawk. Follow-Up of 1978/79 Graduates at the Ohio State University's College of Education Teacher Certification Program. Technical Report 5. 1980. ERIC, ED 201 618.

    Reports the results of a follow-up survey on graduates who are beginning teachers using a Concerns/Problems questionnaire.

11. Driscoll, Amy. The Socialization of Teachers: Career Rewards and Levels of Professional Concern. 1983. ERIC, ED 241 474.

    Views teacher education along a continuum from a preservice level to a beginning level to an experience level and then develops profiles for each level using the results of questionnaires measuring job satisfaction, communication patterns, and professional concern.

12. Driscoll, Amy, and Diane Caine Shirey. "Job Satisfaction, Professional Concerns, and Communication Patterns of Teachers: Differences along the Professional Continuum." Teacher Educator 21 (Summer 1985): 2-14.

    Compares preservice elementary teachers, first-and-second year elementary teachers, and five-to-ten year elementary teachers to measure job satisfaction, communication patterns, and professional concern.

13. Drummond, Robert J. 1978 Follow-Up Study of University of Maine at Orono College of Education Graduates 1975 to 1977. 1978. ERIC, ED 175 869.

    Surveys education graduates to determine the competencies they lacked in their first year of teaching.

14. Edmonds, Edward L., and Frederic Bessai. <u>First Class, A Survey of Canadian Teachers in Their First Year of Service</u>. 1979. ERIC, ED 183 526.

    Profiles first-year Canadian teachers using a questionnaire based upon biographical information, teachers' qualifications, areas of specialization, teaching assignments, potential problems, sources of assistance, and overall job satisfaction and professional growth.

15. Ellis, Joseph R., and Deloris J. Ellis. <u>Professional Role Performance Difficulties Reported by First Year Home Economics Teachers in Illinois Public Schools</u>. 1982. ERIC, ED 228 217.

    Identifies professional roles and activities that beginning home economics teachers consider difficult.

16. Ellis, Joseph R., and Gwendolyn Mathews. "Beginning Teachers' Perception of Their Difficulties with Performance of Professional Roles." <u>Journal of the Association for the Study of Perception</u> 17, no. 2 (1982): 22-28.

    Indicates the difficulties encountered by first-year teachers by rank ordering each of the seven roles associated with teaching.

17. Fagen, M. Michael, and Glen Walter. "Mentoring among Teachers." <u>Journal of Educational Research</u> 76 (November-December 1982): 113-118.

    Describes experiences of mentors and beginning teachers that indicate a significant relationship between having a mentor and job satisfaction.

18. Goetsch, David L. <u>Vocational Instructor's Survival Guide</u>. 1981. ERIC, ED 199 406.

    Provides information on the non-teaching responsibilities of the vocational education teacher and offers suggestions for improving instruction through inservice teacher education.

19. Gorrell, John J., and others. "An Analysis of Perceived Stress in Elementary and Secondary Student Teachers and Full-Time Teachers." Journal of Experimental Education 54 (Fall 1985): 11-14.

    Analyzes elementary, secondary, and student teacher responses to an inventory of potentially stressful situations.

20. Haberman, Martin. "Toward More Realistic Teacher Education." Action in Teacher Education 1 (Summer 1978): 8-17.

    Discusses the need for more realistic teacher education regarding the school bureaucracy and the group dyanmics of the classroom teacher.

21. Hatoff, Blossom. Reading Specialists 1974-1979 Graduates of Kean College: A Follow-Up Study. 1980. ERIC, ED 185 520.

    Surveys reading specialist graduates and reports that 86 percent are enjoying their present positions as classroom teacher, reading specialist, or remedial reading teacher.

22. Herwood, Mary Carol. "Alternative Career Options of Unemployed and Underemployed Graduates of Teacher Preparation Programs and the Implications for Teacher Supply." Ph.D. dissertation, State University of New York at Buffalo, 1980.

    Compares self-reported job satisfaction of fulltime teachers to those in other fields with teachers being more satisfied.

23. Kepner, Henry S., Jr., and Robert W. Nelson. Creating Conditions for Professional Practice in Education. 1981. ERIC, ED 212 555.

    Discusses the importance of the school climate for stimulating professional growth and assisting beginning teachers to adjust to teaching.

24. King, Delva Jean. "The Effects of Mentoring and Support Training Groups upon Job Satisfaction, Attitudes, Needs, Performance, and Morale of Beginning Teachers." Ph.D. dissertation, Texas Woman's University, 1986.

    Describes three models of beginning teacher induction programs and the results on job satisfaction, morale, attitude, needs assessment, and teacher evaluation.

25. Klosterman, Kerry J. "Occupational Cognition, Experience, Satisfaction and Self: Teacher Trainees' Vocational Self Constructs." Ph.D. dissertation, University of Western Ontario (Canada), 1978.

    Postulates an occupational role experience variable and examines its effect on self/teacher congruence and occupational satisfaction of student teachers.

26. Krupp, Judy-Arin. "A Phenomenological Study of Teacher Perceptions of Life Developmental Changes as Related to Inservice Behaviors and Needs." Ph.D. dissertation, University of Connecticut, 1980.

    Interviews teachers of various age groups about their life-developmental changes and their perceived effects on their behavior and needs related to inservice education.

27. Lasley, Thomas J. State Agency Involvement in Teacher Induction. 1981. ERIC, ED 199 203.

    Describes the ways that a state department of education can assist beginning teachers including creating conditions conducive to teacher job satisfaction.

28. Lovett, Martha T. "Job Performance and Job Satisfaction of Beginning Teachers." Ph.D. dissertation, Bowling Green State University, 1982.

    Focuses on the relationship between first-year teachers' job satisfaction and job performance.

29. Mahan, James M. A Comparison of Concerns of Secondary and Elementary Student Teachers. 1981. ERIC, ED 201 631.

   Ranks three categories of concerns about teaching (methods, cultural, and personal) for elementary and secondary school student teachers.

30. McArthur, John T. The First Five Years of Teaching: Their Effect on Pupil Control Ideology and Commitment to Teaching. 1980. ERIC, ED 191 799.

   Reports the results of a longitudinal study focusing on socialization in terms of sex, teaching subjects, stability of tenure, original training institution, and commitment to teaching.

31. McArthur, John. "Teacher Socialization: The First Five Years." Alberta Journal of Educational Research 25 (December 1979): 264-274.

   Describes the socialization adjustment and then the plateau phase of beginning teachers as they internalize the values of teaching.

32. Miller, Larry E. "Relationship between First-Year Teachers' Morale and Behavior." Journal of the American Association of Teacher Educators in Agriculture 18 (November 1977): 11-18.

   Dispels the myth that vocational agriculture teachers have high morale as evidenced by a study of beginning agricultural education teachers in Virginia.

33. Morris, John E., and others. "Student Teacher Morale: A Comparison of Morale Among Four Groups of Student Teachers." College Student Journal 14 (Winter 1980): 347-355.

   Compares morale profiles of kindergarten/elementary, elementary, secondary, and secondary noneducation majors.

34. Mulligan, Kathleen. "An Investigation into the Relationship between Supervision of Student Teachers and Day Care Center Cooperating Teachers." Ph.D. dissertation, The Pennsylvania State University, 1984.

    Examines differences between day care center teachers who supervise student teachers and those who do not as to their attitudes about supervision and its relationship to self-concept, professionalism, job satisfaction and demographic variables.

35. Paibulnukulkij, Ampai. "The Relationships of Selected Variables to Job Satisfaction of Recent Graduates in College of Education at Mississippi State University." Ed.D. dissertation, Mississippi State University, 1977.

    Analyzes the relationships of selected variables to job satisfaction of first-year teachers using the Purdue Teacher Opinionaire.

36. Pierce, Atheal. "A Relationship between Intrinsic and Extrinsic Job Satisfaction and the Performance of Prospective Teachers." Ph.D. dissertation, The Ohio State University, 1969.

    Examines the relationship between intrinsic and extrinsic job satisfaction of student teachers.

37. Power, Paul G. "The Transition from Education Student to Beginning Teacher: Personality, Self-Perceptions, Vocational Characteristics, Commitment, and Work Satisfaction." Ph.D. dissertation, Johns Hopkins University, 1979.

    Performs a longitudinal study of student teacher characteristics and their relation to personality, self-perceptions, job satisfaction professional adjustment, commitment, and evaluation of teaching.

38. Shepherd, James M. "Personal Demographic, Cultural Adaptation and Job Satisfaction Variables as They Relate to Teacher Retention of First Year Import Teachers in Binational Schools of the Latin American and Caribbean Area." Ed.D. dissertation, Memphis State University, 1980.

    Uses a multivariate analysis to study the differences between two groups of beginning teachers: those who plan to return for a second year and those who do not.

39. Sparani, Ervin F. "Selected Self-Perceptions of Secondary Student Teachers as They Relate to Self-Initiated Experiences with Children and Youth." Ph.D. dissertation, University of Michigan, 1983.

    Identifies three auxiliary references (directing, teaching, and coaching) of student teachers that relate to affective measures: commitment to teaching, confidence, satisfaction with teaching, self-esteem, and satisfaction with life.

40. Stafford, Curtis Ronald. "Predicting Job Satisfaction of First Year Teachers." Ed.D. dissertation, University of Illinois at Urbana-Champaign, 1957.

    Examines the relationships among personality needs, placement factors, student teaching, and job satisfaction of beginning teachers.

41. Stewart, John Junious. "A Study of the Relationships among Job Satisfactoriness, Occupational Competency, Job Satisfaction, and Demographic Characteristics for Beginning Trade/Industrial and Technical Education Teachers in Georgia." Ed.D. dissertation, University of Georgia, 1984.

    Investigates the relationships among job satisfactoriness, occupational competency, job satisfaction and demographic characteristics of beginning trade/industrial and technical teachers.

42. Stillwell, Jim L. "Attitudes of Student Teachers toward Selected Areas of Teaching." *Teacher Educator* 16 (Summer 1980): 9-13.

    Shows the effects of student teaching on attitudes toward teaching.

43. Tabachnick, B. Robert, and others. *The Development of Teacher Perspectives.* 1983. ERIC, ED 240 112.

    Explores teachers' experiences beginning with the student teaching experience through the first year of training.

44. Tisher, R. P., and others. *The Induction of Teachers: A Bibliography and Description of Activities in Australia and the U.K.; Research Report on Stage I of the Teacher Induction Project. Beginning to Teach, Volume 1.* 1978. ERIC, ED 162 961.

    Studies the transition from student teacher to beginning teacher and provides an annotated bibliography on induction and socialization.

45. Tisher, Richard P., and others. *The Induction of Beginning Teachers in Australia.* 1978. ERIC, ED 151 325.

    Reports on the entry of first-year teachers into teaching and examines satisfaction with first-year activities.

46. Veenman, Simon. "Perceived Problems of Beginning Teachers." *Review of Educational Research* 54 (Summer 1984): 143-178.

    Reviews studies on problems of beginning teachers including job satisfaction, teacher education, principals' views, and inservice support.

47. Villeme, Melvin G. "The Relation of Teacher Attitude to Major, Employment Status, Teaching Level, and Satisfaction with Teaching for First-Year Teachers." <u>Humanist Educator</u> 19 (December 1980): 85-90.

    Studies the relationship between beginning teacher attitude and employment status, sex, satisfaction with teaching, and long-range teaching plans.

48. Waters, Randol Gilbert. "An Evaluation of the Beginning Teacher Supervision Program Conducted by the Department of Agricultural and Extension Education at the Pennsylvania State University." Ph.D. dissertation, the Pennsylvania State University, 1985.

    Evaluates the effectiveness of a first-year teacher supervision program using the Developmental Supervision Model and the Brayfield Rothe Index of Job Satisfaction.

49. Western Australian Education Department. <u>The Induction of Primary School Teachers. A Report</u>. 1977. ERIC, ED 163 608.

    Identifies ways to improve teacher induction and to give support to beginning teachers.

50. Womack, Sid T. <u>Suggestions from Student Teachers</u>. 1983. ERIC, ED 240 050.

    Cites discipline, stress, and relations with colleagues and supervisors as the three biggest problem areas of student teachers.

51. Wright, Gary R. <u>Generalizing Personnel Training Models Used in Business and Industry to School Settings</u>. 1981. ERIC, ED 218 230.

    Discusses the importance of inservice teacher programs to orient beginning teachers and to retrain or update teachers' skills.

II. ELEMENTARY SCHOOL TEACHERS

52. Allen, D. I., and others. "Need for Structure: Program Openness and Job Satisfaction among Teachers in Open Area and Self-Contained Classrooms." Alberta Journal of Educational Research 22 (June 1976): 149-153.

   Compares elementary teachers in open area classrooms and self-contained classrooms in terms of job satisfaction, need for structure, and program openness using the Job Satisfaction Index, O. J. Harvey's Conceptual Systems Test, and the Teacher Questionnaire.

53. "The American Elementary Teacher Today: Results of Instructor's First National Teacher Poll." Instructor 89, no. 6 (January 1980): 24, 26.

   Summarizes elementary teachers' likes and dislikes.

54. Bartek, Joseph Andrew. "A Study of Elementary Teacher Job Role as Perceived by Elementary Teachers and Their Principals." Ed.D. dissertation, University of San Francisco, 1984.

   Studies job satisfaction of elementary teachers using the Minnesota Job Description Questionnaire.

55. Bridges, Edwin M. <u>Job Satisfaction and Teacher Absenteeism</u>. 1979. ERIC, ED 202 146

    Examines the relationship between job satisfaction of elementary teachers and absenteeism.

56. Burden, Paul R. <u>Teachers' Perceptions of Their Personal and Professional Development</u>. 1981. ERIC, ED 210 258.

    Describes stages of elementary teacher career development and identifies characteristics of each stage.

57. Buxton, Mary Miller. "A Study of the Job Satisfaction of Elementary Teachers in Open-Space and Traditional Schools." Ed.D. dissertation, Ball State University, 1976.

    Compares job satisfaction of elementary teachers in open-space and self-contained settings using the Purdue Teacher Opinionaire.

58. Coley, Thomas Gregory. "The Implementation of Planned Educational Change: A Multivariate Analysis of the Decision Source for Change, Organizational Commitment, and Job Satisfaction Among Elementary School Teachers." Ph.D. dissertation, The University of Wisconsin-Madison, 1980.

    Investigates the relationship between factors which affect the change process and elementary teacher job satisfaction using the Organizational Commitment Questionnaire and the Job Descriptive Index.

59. Craycraft, Kenneth Roger. "Authoritarianism and Attitudes Toward Teaching in Teaming and Non-Teaming Situations." Ed.D. dissertation, Indiana University, 1977.

    Explores authoritarianism and elementary teacher attitudes in teaming and non-teaming situations using the Balanced F-Scale and the Purdue Teacher Opinionaire.

60. De Ville, Louis Michael. "A Comparison of Teacher Job Satisfaction Between Predominantly Black and White Schools." Ed.D. dissertation, University of the Pacific, 1976.

    Compares elementary teacher job satisfaction in predominantly black and white schools using the Purdue Teacher Opinionaire.

61. DiPasquale, Nicholas Anthony. "The Relation of Organizational Structure and Leadership Style to the Job Dissatisfaction and Job Satisfaction of Teachers in Suburban Elementary Schools." Ed.D. dissertation, New York University, 1978.

    Investigates organizational structure and the leadership style of the principal in relation to the extrinsic and intrinsic factors of elementary teachers' job dissatisfaction and satisfaction.

62. Easterly, Jean L. Perceptions of Outstanding Elementary Teachers About Themselves and Their Profession. 1983. ERIC, ED 238 854.

    Interviews outstanding elementary teachers about their attitudes, values, and work; lists characteristics of outstanding teachers and administrators.

63. Feagan, Sandra Yvonne. "Relationships of a Quality Circle Process on Job Satisfaction and Organizational Commitment in Elementary Schools." Ed.D. dissertation, University of Virginia, 1985.

    Studies the relationship between a quality circle process and elementary teacher job satisfaction and organizational commitment using the Job Satisfaction Survey and the Organizational Commitment Questionnaire.

64. Finger, Sophia Geller. "Leadership Style of the Quasi-Administrator and Teacher Job Satisfaction." Ed.D. dissertation, Yeshiva University, 1984.

    Explores the relationship between the perceived leadership behavior of the quasi-administrator and elementary special education teachers using the Leadership Behavior Description Questionnaire and the Job Satisfaction Index.

65. Fitzgerald, Sheila Mary. Career Needs and Satisfactions of Teachers: A Replication Study. 1978. ERIC, ED 167 497.

   Compares job satisfaction and job needs of elementary teachers in 1972 and 1977 using the Minnesota Satisfaction Questionnaire.

66. Fleming, Kenneth Paul. "An Analysis of the Relationship of Perceived Professionalism and Perceived Complexity of Organizational Environment to Job Satisfaction Among Elementary School Teachers." Ph.D. dissertation, University of South Florida, 1982.

   Examines the relationship between elementary teachers' professionalism and complexity of the work environment and job satisfaction using the Professional Orientation Scale, the School Environmental Complexity Scale, and the Job Descriptive Index.

67. Foxworth, Marilyn D., and Frances A. Karnes. "Occupational Stress and the Teacher of Gifted Elementary Students: A Preliminary Investigation." Roeper Review 6, no. 2 (1983): 105-107.

   Surveys elementary resource room teachers of gifted students about stress.

68. Frank, Arnold. "The Relationship Between Teacher Job Satisfaction and Student Reading Achievement, Time Off-Task, and Teacher Planning Time." Ph.D. dissertation, The University of Wisconsin-Madison, 1982.

   Investigates the relationship between elementary teacher satisfaction and student achievement, student use of time, and teacher planning time using the Purdue Teacher Opinionaire.

69. Frank, Thomas Gerard. "Teacher Absenteeism: A Study of the Association of Selected Teacher-Reported Job Attributes and Frequency of Absence." Ph.D. dissertation, State University of New York at Buffalo, 1975.

   Focuses on 13 elementary teacher-reported job attributes and short-term absence.

70. Freedman, Sara, and others. The Effects of the Institutional Structure of Schools on Teachers. Final Report. 1982. ERIC, ED 234 047.

Interviews female elementary teachers and analyzes the relationship between their self-esteem, job satisfaction, and sense of efficacy.

71. Galanter, Wynne Leslie. "Elementary School Staff Support System Effects on Program Implementation and Job Satisfaction." Ph.D. dissertation, Fordham University, 1978.

Studies the effects of five support system variables on open education and elementary teachers' job satisfaction.

72. Galloway, David, and others. "Sources of Satisfaction and Dissatisfaction for New Zealand Primary School Teachers." Educational Research 27, no. 1 (February 1985): 44-51.

Reports sources of satisfaction and dissatisfaction of primary and intermediate teachers and compares them to Herzberg's two-factor theory.

73. Gechman, Arthur S., and Yoash Wiener. "Job Involvement and Satisfaction as Related to Mental Health and Personal Time Devoted to Work." Journal of Applied Psychology 60, no. 4 (August 1975): 521-523.

Measures job involvement, satisfaction, and mental health of female elementary teachers using a daily log and self-reports.

74. Gist, Ronald Colonel. "Organizational Structure and Teacher Job Satisfaction." Ed.D. dissertation, University of Denver, 1979.

Examines organizational structure and sense of competence motivation in relation to elementary teachers' job satisfaction using the Inventory of School Openness, the Test of Imagination, and the Job Descriptive Index.

75. Gnecco, Donald R. "The Perceptions of Autonomy and Job Satisfaction Among Elementary Teachers in Southern Maine." Ed.D. dissertation, George Peabody College for Teachers of Vanderbilt University, 1983.

    Investigates the relationship between elementary teachers' autonomy and job satisfaction.

76. Gould, Patricia Ann. "An Investigation of Organizational Communication in Elementary Schools: A Field Study." Ed.D. dissertation, Virginia Polytechnic Institute and State University, 1982.

    Compares organizational communication patterns of two elementary schools with overall teacher job satisfaction.

77. Grant, Joseph Oswald Clarendon. "Open Space Elementary School: Effects on Teachers' Job Satisfaction, Participation in Curriculum Decision-Making, and Perceived School Effectiveness." Ph.D. dissertation, State University of New York at Buffalo, 1977.

    Assesses participative decision-making, elementary teachers' job satisfaction, and perceived school effectiveness using a modified Decisional Condition Instrument and a questionnaire developed by the researcher.

78. Guagulwong, Thawin. "Leadership Styles, Maturity Levels, and Job Satisfaction in Elementary Schools." Ph.D. dissertation, The University of Oklahoma, 1981.

    Explores the relationship between principals' leadership styles and the maturity levels of elementary teachers and their job satisfaction using the LEAD Other, the Maturity Scale, and the Job Descriptive Index.

79. Guerrieri, Sandra Irene. "Teacher Personality Characteristics in Selected Open and Non-Open Elementary Schools." Ed.D. dissertation, The University of Arizona, 1980.

    Develops a profile of personality characteristics using the California Psychological Inventory, the Sixteen Personality Factor, and the Teacher

Satisfaction/Compatibility Questionnaire to describe the open and non-open elementary teacher.

80. Haller, Emil J. Strategies for Change. 1969. ERIC, ED 040 501.

    Interviews elementary teachers to determine their attitudes toward educational change and job satisfaction.

81. Harrison, Rose. A Descriptive Study of the Perceived Influence of Institutional Interruptions on the Morale and Work of Teachers and Pupils in Elementary Schools. 1983. ERIC, ED 231 041.

    Describes the effects of interruptions on elementary teachers' morale and students' morale and work.

82. Hartley, Carolyn Williams. "The Development and Test of a Typology of Control." Ed.D. dissertation, Rutgers University, The State University of New Jersey, 1984.

    Develops a typology to classify elementary teachers based upon locus of control and pupil control ideology to determine if there are significant differences in job satisfaction among the four teacher types.

83. Harvey, Paulette Lemma. "The Development and Evaluation of a Collaborative and Goal-Focused Staff Development Intervention." Ed.D. dissertation, The Pennsylvania State University, 1983.

    Discusses the influence of a collaborative and goal-focused staff development intervention on elementary teachers' perceptions of colleague interaction, sense of efficacy, and job satisfaction.

84. Hauser, Paula. "The Self-Esteem of Regular and Special Education Elementary Teachers as Related to Job Satisfaction." Ed.D. dissertation, University of Kansas, 1981.

    Compares elementary teachers to elementary special education teachers in relation to self-esteem and job satisfaction using the Tennessee Self-Concept

Scale and the Minnesota Satisfaction Questionnaire-Short Form.

85. Henderson, Charles Henry, Jr. "The Relationship of Teacher Morale to the Racial Composition of the Student Bodies in Selected Elementary Schools in Metropolitan Atlanta." Ed.D. dissertation, Mississippi State University, 1977.

    Compares elementary teachers' job satisfaction to the racial composition of schools using the Purdue Teacher Opinionaire.

86. Henderson, Lester F. "Elementary Teacher Satisfaction and Morale and Perceived Participation in Decision-Making." Ed.D. dissertation, University of Arkansas, 1976.

    Studies the relationship between perceived participation in decision-making and elementary teacher satisfaction using the Psychological Participation Index, the Purdue Teacher Opinionaire, and the Minnesota Satisfaction Questionnaire.

87. Johnson, John Robert. "Elementary Teacher Perceptions of Certain Organizational Processes and Job Satisfaction in Schools with Self-Contained and Differentiated Staffing Classrooms." Ph.D. dissertation, Syracuse University, 1975.

    Studies differences between self-contained classroom structure and differentiated staff structure and elementary teacher job satisfaction using the Profile of a School (Form T) and the Minnesota Satisfaction Questionnaire.

88. Joo, Sam Hwan. "Relationships of School Bureaucratization, Elementary School Teachers' Professional and Bureaucratic Orientation, Conflict, and Job Satisfaction in a Selected School District." Ph.D. dissertation, University of Minnesota, 1981.

    Investigates the relationships of school bureaucratization, elementary teachers' professional and bureaucratic orientation, conflict, and job satisfaction using the Organizational Inventory, the Professional and Bureaucratic Orientation Scale, the Conflict Assessment Questionnaire, and the Minnesota Satisfaction Questionnaire.

89. Kasten, Katherine L. "The Efficacy of Institutionally Dispensed Rewards in Elementary School Teaching." Journal of Research and Development in Education 17, no. 4 (Summer 1984): 1-13.

   Interviews elementary teachers to identify the value and effectiveness of institutional rewards.

90. Kirtdum, Anant. "A Study of Job Satisfaction of Rural and Urban Elementary School Teachers in Thailand." Ed.D. dissertation, Oklahoma State University, 1984.

   Examines job satisfaction of elementary teachers in rural and urban areas using the Job Satisfaction Questionnaire developed by the researcher.

91. Knopp, Robert, and Robert R. O'Reilly. Job Satisfaction of Teachers and Organizational Effectiveness of Elementary Schools. 1978. ERIC, ED 177 719.

   Analyzes the relationship between elementary teachers' job satisfaction and perceived school effectiveness.

92. Kremeier, John Henry. "Perfectionism: An Investigation of Its Construct Validity and Its Relationship to Job Satisfaction." Ph.D. dissertation, University of Colorado at Boulder, 1985.

   Provides an inquiry into the possible relationship between perfectionism and elementary teachers' job satisfaction.

93. Lebowitz, Ruth. "Women Elementary-School Teachers and the Feminist Movement." Elementary School Journal 80, no. 5 (May 1980): 239-245.

   Examines female elementary teachers' attitudes toward their work and the Feminist Movement.

94. Lebowitz, Ruth. "The Relationship of the Views Women Elementary Teachers Have of Their Work and Their Attitudes Toward the Feminist Movement." Ed.D. dissertation, Columbia University, Teachers College, 1979.

   Investigates the relationship between female elementary teachers' attitudes about their work and the Feminist Movement using a Feminist Scale and questions about job satisfaction, aspirations, and expectations.

95. Lenz, O. Victor, Jr. "The Effects of Reduction in Force on the Morale of Elementary Classroom Teachers." Ph.D. dissertation, Saint Louis University, 1978.

   Studies the effects of reduction in force on elementary teachers' job satisfaction.

96. Lewis, Angel Lucille Fowler. "Job Satisfaction, Decisional Discrepancy, Academic Social Climate, and Academic Achievement in Selected Title I Elementary Schools." Ph.D. dissertation, Fordham University, 1981.

   Examines teacher job satisfaction with salary, student achievement, and interpersonal relationships in high and low achieving Title I elementary schools.

97. Mawter, Paul Thomas. "Teacher Professionalism and Decision-Making Modes in Selected Elementary Schools as Determinants of Job Satisfaction." Ph.D. dissertation, University of Oregon, 1975.

   Studies the relationships between elementary teacher professionalism, decision-making modes, and job satisfaction using the Professional Orientation Scale, the Decision Mode Index, and the Job Description Index.

98. Meek, Byron L. "An Exploratory Study of Male Primary Teachers: Their Perceptions of Professional Status and Potential for Increasing Their Number." Ed.D. dissertation, The University of North Dakota, 1977.

   Interviews male elementary teachers and describes their perceptions about teaching.

99. Milgram, Roberta M., and Nitzah O. Feldman. "Creativity as a Predictor of Teachers' Effectiveness." Psychological Reports 45, no. 3 (December 1979): 899-903.

    Investigates creative activity and creative thinking as predictors of elementary teachers' job satisfaction using the Wallach and Kogan Creativity Battery and the Tel-Aviv Educational Incidents Test.

100. Misko, Giuseppina. "Organizational Characteristics and Teacher Psychic Reward." Ph.D. dissertation, University of Oregon, 1982.

    Discusses the relationship between organizational characteristics (decision-making, resources, class size, autonomy, and support) and elementary teacher psychic reward (job satisfaction) using the Minnesota Satisfaction Questionnaire.

101. Morris, Betty Nowlin. "The Relationship of Teacher Perceptions of Organizational Climate to Job Satisfaction in the Elementary Schools of a Metropolitan School District." Ed.D. dissertation, University of Houston, 1975.

    Describes elementary teachers' perceptions of organizational climate and job satisfaction using the Job Description Index and the Organizational Climate Description Questionnaire.

102. Morton, David Sterling. "The Relationship Between Teacher Perception of Elementary School Organizational Climate and Student Achievement." Ph.D. dissertation, Michigan State University, 1977.

    Analyzes elementary teachers' perceptions of organizational climate and student achievement using the Leadership Behavior Description Questionnaire, the Organizational Climate Description Questionnaire, and an adaptation of the Short-Form Measure of Self-Actualization.

103. Murphy, Dorothy Louise Hollar. "The Effects of Demographic and Personality Factors on Job Satisfaction of Self-Contained Classroom Teachers and Open-Area Team Teachers." Ed.D. dissertation, University of Houston, 1976.

    Compares two groups of elementary teachers in terms of personality characteristics, open-area team teaching or self-contained teaching and job satisfaction using the Sixteen Personality Factor Questionnaire, the Dogmatism Scale, the Purdue Teacher Opinionaire, and the Teacher Orientation Study.

104. Obanya, Pai. "Aspects of the Social Self of Nigerian Primary School Teachers." Psychologia Africana 17, no. 3 (December 1978): 161-167.

    Investigates reasons why elementary teachers leave.

105. Packard, John S., and others. Management Implications of Team Teaching: Final Report. 1978. ERIC, ED 161 153.

    Summarizes the results of the Management Implications of Team Teaching Study for elementary schools investigating the effects of multi-unit organization on teaching and job satisfaction.

106. Packard, John S., and others. Governance and Task Interdependence in Schools: First Report of a Longitudinal Study. 1976. ERIC, ED 143 134.

    Reports on team teaching in elementary schools and its implications for decision making, social relations, and work fulfillment.

107. Parker, Phyllis J. Burnes. "An Investigation of Job Satisfaction Among Late Career Entry Teachers at the Elementary Level." Ed.D. dissertation, George Peabody College for Teachers of Vanderbilt University, 1985.

    Analyzes the job satisfaction of second career elementary teachers.

108. Pascale, Pietro J., James C. King, and Lou Mastrian. "The Development and Validation of an Elementary School Substitute Teacher Questionnaire." *Educational and Psychological Measurement* 44, no. 2 (Summer 1984): 507-511.

   Describes the development and validation of the Elementary School Substitute Questionnaire to measure their needs and concerns.

109. Plihal, Jane. *Types of Intrinsic Rewards of Teaching and Their Relation to Teacher Characteristics and Variables in the Work Setting.* 1982. ERIC, ED 215 978.

   Studies elementary teachers' perceptions of the intrinsic rewards of teaching and factors in the work setting.

110. Plihal, Jane. *Intrinsic Rewards of Teaching.* 1981. ERIC, ED 200 599.

   Interviews elementary teachers about sources of satisfaction, types of intrinsic rewards, enjoyment of teaching, and student achievement.

111. Price, Gary G., and others. *Procedures Used in Phase I of the IGE Evaluation to Scale the Variable Teacher Job Satisfaction. Report from the Project on Evaluation of Practices in Individualized Schooling.* 1978. ERIC, ED 182 237.

112. Randklev, Beth Stangeland. "The Relationships Among Performance Ratings, Job Satisfaction Perceptions, and Preferred Non-Monetary Rewards for Elementary School Teachers." Ph.D. dissertation, The University of North Dakota, 1984.

   Investigates the relationship among elementary teachers' job satisfaction, preferred rewards, teachers' performance, and demographic variables using the Teacher Performance Assessment Instrument, the Job Descriptive Index, and a preferred rewards instrument developed by the researcher.

113. Raschke, Donna B., and others. "Teacher Stress: The Elementary Teacher's Perspective." *Elementary School Journal* 85, no. 4 (March 1985): 559-564.

    Identifies factors that elementary teachers report contribute to job satisfaction and dissatisfaction.

114. Robinson, Daniel Clarence. "An Investigation of the Extent to Which Members of a Single Occupation (Elementary Teacher) Show Different or Identical Interests Depending upon Whether They Are Male or Female or Members of Black or Caucasian Racial Groups." Ph.D. dissertation, Iowa State University, 1978.

    Investigates the differences between elementary teachers' job satisfaction and interests based upon sex and racial background using the Kuder Occupational Interest Survey and a job satisfaction questionnaire.

115. Ross, Nina Preston. "An Assessment of the Effects of a Reading Workshop on Job Satisfaction of Elementary School Teachers." Ed.D. dissertation, Memphis State University, 1974.

    Assesses the effects of an intensive reading workshop on the job satisfaction of elementary teachers using the Minnesota Satisfaction Questionnaire.

116. Schackmuth, Thomas G. "Creating Job Satisfaction in a Static Teacher Market." *Clearing House* 52, no. 5 (January 1979): 229-232.

    Reviews job satisfaction factors in elementary schools.

117. Shackmuth, Thomas George. "The Relation of Organizational Structure and Personal Attributes to Work Satisfaction Among Public School Teachers." Ph.D. dissertation, Loyola University of Chicago, 1975.

    Inquires into the work satisfactions and self-images of elementary teachers.

118. Schaefer, Barbara Maxson. "Relationships Between the Number of Sources of Attachment to Work and Elementary Teachers' Total Satisfaction." Ed.D. dissertation, Northern Illinois University, 1982.

    Examines the relationships between teacher variables, sources of attachment, and elementary teachers' job satisfaction using a revised version of an instrument developed by Dubin to measure eight sources of attachment and the Minnesota Satisfaction Questionnaire.

119. Schmidt, William H., and Margret Buchmann. "Six Teachers' Beliefs and Attitudes and Their Curricular Time Allocations." *Elementary School Journal* 84, no. 2 (November 1983): 162-171.

    Studies the relationship between three elementary teacher variables and time allocations.

120. Shobe, Robert Earl. "Quality of Work Life as Perceived by Elementary School Principals and by Elementary School Teachers." Ph.D. dissertation, Indiana State University, 1983.

    Describes the quality of work life in education of elementary teachers by examining job satisfaction, job involvement, motivation, and other aspects of a person's life.

121. Smilansky, J. "External and Internal Correlates of Teachers' Satisfaction and Willingness to Report Stress." *British Journal of Educational Psychology* 54, no. 1 (February 1984): 84-92.

    Looks at elementary teachers' work satisfaction in terms of internal variables and job-related stress in terms of external variables.

122. Smith, Frederick D. *Factors Involved in Job Satisfaction Among Teachers in the Bureau of Indian Affairs System on the Navajo Reservation.* 1977. ERIC, ED 235 990.

    Interviews elementary teachers on a Navajo reservation to determine positive and negative aspects of their jobs.

123. Stone, Menia Gillian. "Team-Teaching Practices and Job Satisfaction in Open-Space Schools." Ed.D. dissertation, University of Miami, 1976.

    Surveys elementary teachers in open-space team-teaching schools to study the relationship between team-teaching and elementary job satisfaction using the Team Teaching Qustionnaire, the Purdue Teacher Opinionaire, and a Biographical Data Sheet.

124. Theodory, George C., and Mafakhir Hadbai. "Retesting Fiedler's Contingency Theory in Islamic Schools." Journal of Psychology 8, no. 1 (May 1982): 15-18.

    Tests Fiedler's Style/Situational Control Match Theory in Islamic elementary schools.

125. Thompson, Lauretta Naylor. "Perceived Job Satisfaction of Teachers in Individually Guided Education and Non-Individually Guided Education Schools." Ed.D. dissertation, George Peabody College for Teachers of Vanderbilt University, 1983.

    Compares elementary teachers' job satisfaction in Individually Guided Education and non-IGE schools using the Minnesota Satisfaction Questionnaire.

126. VandenBoogert, Carol Ann. "The Socioeconomic Status Relationship of Teacher and Student, and Teacher Behavior." Ph.D. dissertation, Michigan State University, 1983.

    Considers the relationship between teacher and student socioeconomic status and teacher satisfaction.

127. Wangberg, Elaine G., and others. "Working Conditions and Career Options Lead to Female Elementary Teacher Job Dissatisfaction." Journal of Teacher Education 33, no. 5 (September-October 1982): 37-40.

    Examines job dissatisfaction among female elementary teachers; working conditions is one reason for dissatisfaction.

128. Warner, Wanda Mary. "Decision Involvement and Job Satisfaction in Wisconsin Elementary Schools." Ph.D. dissertation, The University of Wisconsin-Madison, 1981.

   Studies the relationship between participation in decision making and elementary teachers' job satisfaction.

129. Wiener, Yoash, and Arthur S. Gechman. "Commitment: A Behavioral Approach to Job Involvement." *Journal of Vocational Behavior* 10, no. 1 (February 1977): 47-52.

   Develops a work commitment measure using female elementary teachers and correlates it with a job satisfaction measure.

130. Williams, Jeannette Allen. "The Effect of Organizational Structure of Schools and Role Orientation of Teachers on Job Satisfaction of Teachers." Ed.D. dissertation, Rutgers University, the State University of New Jersey, 1981.

   Shows the effect of organizational structure of schools and teachers' role orientation on elementary teacher job satisfaction using the Structural Properties Questionnaire Form 4, the Professional and Bureaucratic Orientation Scales, and the Purdue Teacher Opinionaire.

131. Wu, Jin-Shiang. "Predictors of Job Satisfaction Among Elementary School Teachers in Southern Taiwan, the Republic of China." Ed.D. dissertation, University of Northern Colorado, 1984.

   Investigates the relationships between personal and demographic variables of elementary teachers and principals' leadership style on teacher job satisfaction using the Leader Behavior Description Questionnaire and the Minnesota Satisfaction Questionnaire.

III. SECONDARY SCHOOL TEACHERS

132. Ahmed, Saad Hassan. "A Study of Personal and Job Facets as Determinants of Job Satisfaction for Public Senior High School Teachers in the Commonwealth of Pennsylvania." Ph.D. dissertation, The Pennsylvania State University, 1984.

    Studies job satisfaction of senior high school teachers in terms of personal feelings, location of the school, and six facet-specific dimensions using the Perceived Equity Scale.

133. Anand, S. P. "School Teachers: Job Satisfaction vs. Extraversion and Neuroticism." *Indian Educational Review* 12, no. 2 (April 1977): 68-78.

    Examines age, sex, years of teaching, extraversion, and neuroticism of high school teachers using a job satisfaction scale developed by the researcher and the Maudsley Personality Inventory.

134. Andrew, Harold O., Jr. "Intrinsic and Extrinsic Rewards: Teacher Satisfaction in Wyoming Public Secondary Schools." Ed.D. dissertation, University of Wyoming, 1983.

    Investigates the relationship between intrinsic and extrinsic rewards and secondary school teachers' job satisfaction and longevity using the Teacher Reward and Satisfaction Scales.

135. Antonecchia, Donald. "Classroom Conflict Management and Secondary Teachers' Job Satisfaction." Ed.D. dissertation, Yeshiva University, 1983.

    Explores the relationship between high school teachers' preference for a specific mode of conflict management, gender, and job satisfaction using the Thomas-Kilmann Management of Differences Exercise and the Brayfield-Rothe Job Satisfaction Index.

136. Arulefela, Olufunke Adebanji. "A Study of the Relationship of Self-Actualization and Job Satisfaction of Certain Categories of Secondary School Teachers in the Nigerian States of Ondo, Oyo and Ogun." Ph.D. dissertation, New York University, 1984.

    Compares self-actualization and job satisfaction for various groups of secondary teachers using the Personal Orientation Inventory and the Minnesota Satisfaction Questionnaire (Short Form).

137. Barahimi, Iraj. "The Relationship Between Organizational Climate and Teachers' Job Satisfaction in Iranian Middle Schools." Ph.D. dissertation, George Peabody College for Teachers of Vanderbilt University, 1986.

    Determines the relationship between organizational climate and job satisfaction (extrinsic and intrinsic) of middle school teachers using the Organizational Climate Description Questionnaire and the Minnesota Satisfaction Questionnaire.

138. Behrman, Edward Henry. "Teacher-Student Relations as a Predictor of Teachers' Job Satisfaction." Ed.D. dissertation, University of Pennsylvania, 1976.

    Tests the hypothesis that secondary school teachers' interpersonal relations with students contribute more to job satisfaction than interpersonal relations with colleagues or superiors.

139. Bledsoe, Joseph C., and Gerald D. Haywood. "Prediction of Job Satisfactoriness and Job Satisfaction of Secondary School Teachers." <u>Psychological Reports</u> 49, no. 2 (October 1981): 455-458.

   Develops a regression equation to predict the job satisfactoriness and job satisfaction of high school teachers.

140. Bloland, Paul A., and Thomas J. Selby. "Factors Associated with Career Change among Secondary School Teachers: A Review of the Literature." <u>Educational Research Quarterly</u> 5, no. 3 (Fall 1980): 13-24.

   Reviews the literature on secondary school teachers' attrition.

141. Brassard, Marla Ruth. "Reinforcement Density: A Theoretical Application to Job Satisfaction." Ph.D. dissertation, Columbia University, 1979.

   Presents a theoretical application of reinforcement theory to high school teachers' job satisfaction using the You and Your Job instrument developed by the researcher.

142. Clarke, Robert Leo. "Sources of Teacher Job Satisfaction and Dissatisfaction for Senior High School Teachers." Ed.D. dissertation, University of Pennsylvania, 1976.

   Discusses secondary teachers' job satisfaction and dissatisfaction in terms of internal and external (Herzberg) factors using the Minnesota Satisfaction Questionnaire and interviews.

143. Daly, Richard Edward. "A Causal Analysis of Satisfaction, Performance, Work Environment and Leadership in Selected Secondary Schools." Ph.D. dissertation, University of California, Berkeley, 1980.

   Examines Likert's approach to the study of organizational effectiveness focusing on leadership, climate, trust, peer work environment, job satisfaction, and job performance of high schools.

144. Davis, Florence Geraldyne Turner. "Secondary Teacher Satisfaction-Dissatisfaction: A Symbolic Interactionist Analysis." Ph.D. dissertation, United States International University, 1981.

   Interviews high school teachers to identify sources of satisfaction-dissatisfaction.

145. Demps, Henry Willie. "A Study of the Relationship Between Teachers' Perceptions of Job Satisfaction and Their Perceptions of the Level of Implementation of Eighteen Basic Middle School Characteristics." Ph.D. dissertation, Michigan State University, 1978.

   Determines what relationships exist between middle school teachers' job satisfaction and their perceptions of eighteen middle school characteristics using the Minnesota Satisfaction Questionnaire and the Riegle middle school questionnaire.

146. Dempsey, Mary Ann. "The Effect of Role Perception of Regular and Special Education Teachers on Job Satisfaction (Role Conflict, Ambiguity, Intolerance)." Ph.D. dissertation, The Ohio State University, 1985.

   Analyzes the differences between regular and special education teachers at the middle and senior high schools in relation to role conflict, role ambiguity, and job satisfaction using the Job Descriptive Index, the Role Conflict and Ambiguity Scale, and the Intolerance of Ambiguity Questionnaire.

147. Flannery, David Michael. "Teacher Decision Involvement and Job Satisfaction in Wisconsin High Schools." Ph.D. dissertation, the University of Wisconsin-Madison, 1980.

   Describes the relationships between perceived secondary teacher influence, job satisfaction, and decision condition using the Decision Involvement Analysis Questionnaire, the Job Satisfaction Survey, and a Personal Data Qustionnaire.

148. Franklin-Rier, Alice Lorrice. "A Study of the Organizational Climate in High Schools of the District of Columbia and the Effect It Has on Selected Variables of Students and Teachers." Ed.D. dissertation, the George Washington University, 1983.

   Compares open- versus closed-climate high schools on student test performance in reading and mathematics, student attitudes toward school, student self-concept, and secondary teacher job satisfaction using the Organizational Climate Description Questionnaire, the Student Opinion Inventory, the Tennessee Self-Concept Scale, and the Minnesota Satisfaction Questionnaire.

149. Gana, Bukar. "Work Values and Job Satisfaction of Principals and Teachers of Nigerian Secondary Schools." Ph.D. dissertation, University of Missouri-Columbia, 1984.

   Investigates the work values and job satisfaction of secondary teachers using the Minnesota Satisfaction Questionnaire and the Work Values Inventory.

150. Gardner, David C., and Grace Joely Beatty. "Motivating Teachers for Vocational Curriculum Development of the Handicapped." *Education* 100, no. 4 (Summer 1980): 360-366.

   Surveys secondary teachers using the Teacher Opinion Survey to determine incentives for participation in curriculum development.

151. Ghanavi, Gholamreza. "Collective Action and Unionism Among Secondary School Teachers." Ph.D. dissertation, United States International University, 1984.

   Compares union and non-union high school teachers in terms of job satisfaction, age, salary, professionalism, number of years in the profession, and occupational orientation using the Tendency to Act Collectively Scale, the Job Satisfaction Scale, the Professionalism Scale, and the Occupational Orientation Scale.

152. Gupta, Kiran, and Badarum Nisha. "A Study of Job Satisfaction Among Secondary School Teachers." <u>Asian Journal of Psychology and Education</u> 4, no. 1 (1979): 25-30.

    Studies personal factors that affect junior and senior high job satisfaction using the Questionnaire for Secondary Teachers.

153. Haywood, Gerald D. "The Relationship of Job Satisfaction, Job Satisfactoriness and Personal Characteristics of Secondary School Teachers in Georgia." Ed.D. dissertation, University of Georgia, 1980.

    Examines the relationship between job satisfaction, job satisfactoriness, and demographic (personal) variables of junior and senior high school teachers using the Minnesota Satisfaction Questionnaire.

154. Heather, David D. "Perceptions of Pay Satisfaction Among Vocational and Nonvocational Secondary Teachers in Wisconsin." Ph.D. dissertation, University of Wisconsin-Madison, 1984.

    Compares pay satisfaction between vocational and nonvocational junior and senior high school teachers using the Pay Satisfaction Questionnaire.

155. Henderson, Robbe Lynn. "Perceptions of Urban Teachers About Specific Characteristics in Their Work Environment that Relate to Need Deficiencies." Ph.D. dissertation, University of Illinois at Urbana, 1982.

    Examines ideal, actual, and deficiency levels of high school teachers' satisfaction of psychological needs.

156. Hough, Michael John. "Staff Development Curricula for Australian High School Teachers: Validation of a Theory Based Generation of Preferred Learning Profiles." Ed.D. dissertation, University of Georgia, 1981.

    Designs a process to produce differentiated inservice curricula for high school teacher "types" incorporating teacher career stage, motivational preference, needs, and interests.

157. Kreis, Kathleen. <u>The Relationship Between Job Satisfaction and Needs Fulfillment Among Urban High School Teachers</u>. 1983. ERIC, ED 230 656.

    Conducts a study of urban secondary school teachers to explore the relationship between perceived security, affiliation, self-esteem, autonomy, self-actualization and job satisfaction.

158. Kreis, Kathleen Mary. "The Relationship Between Job Satisfaction and Needs Fulfillment Among Urban High School Teachers." Ed.D. dissertation, State University of New York at Buffalo, 1982.

    Explores the relationship between needs fulfillment and job satisfaction of urban secondary teachers using the Job Satisfaction Index and Part D of the Need-Satisfaction in Work Survey.

159. Lee, Koon-Hyon. "A Study of Job Satisfaction of Selected Parochial High School Teachers in Kansas." Ph.D. dissertation, Kansas State University, 1983.

    Studies job satisfaction of parochial and secondary school teachers using the Purdue Teacher Opinionaire.

160. Ligon, Jerry Alan. "Personality, Subject Area, Time in Service, and Instructional Methods: A Test of Holland's Theory." Ph.D. dissertation, Arizona State University, 1985.

    Tests Holland's theory with high school teachers using the Vocational Preference Inventory, a researcher developed Teacher Job Satisfaction Scale, and a researcher developed preference for Instructional Methods Scale.

161. Lindsey, Richard H. "The Snows of Yesteryear." <u>Clearing House</u>, 49, no. 4 (December 1975): 186-187.

    Cautions against viewing each educational innovation as the best solution to educational problems.

162. Mack, Kevin Patrick. "Secondary Schools' Management Systems and Relationship to Teacher Absenteeism." Ed.D. dissertation, George Peabody College for Teachers of Vanderbilt University, 1983.

    Builds on Likert's management systems theory to identify the relationship between secondary school teachers' perceptions of their school's management system and their attitudes toward absenteeism using the Profile of a School--Form T.

163. Manning, Tyra Lynn. "The Implementation of Pilot Middle Schools in Unified School District 501 Topeka, Kansas, and a Comparison of Teacher Perceptions in Middle Schools and Junior High Schools." Ed.D. dissertation, University of Kansas, 1979.

    Compares organizational climate and job satisfaction of middle school and junior high school teachers using the Organizational Climate Description Questionnaire and the Job Satisfaction Index.

164. Marion, Russell Aubrey. "Job Satisfaction and Conflict Among Public High School Teachers." Ph.D. dissertation, The University of North Carolina at Chapel Hill, 1976.

    Studies the relationship between secondary school teachers' perceptions of various educational conditions, job satisfaction, and conflict among staff.

165. McElroy, Lee August, Jr. "An Analysis of the Relationships Among Control Variables, Organizational Climate, Job Satisfaction, Teacher Absenteeism, and Teacher Turnover in the Secondary Public School." Ed.D. dissertation, University of Houston, 1984.

    Discusses the relationships among organizational climate, job satisfaction, absenteeism, turnover, age, experience, and years in the high school and district.

166. Metzdorf, Virginia Ann. "Secondary Teachers' Responses to Organizational Incentives." Ph.D. dissertation, The University of Wisconsin-Madison, 1984.

Uses incentive theory and adult developmental psychology to identify incentives valued by high school teachers.

167. Mokry, Anoush-Irawan. "Job Satisfaction in the Education Industry: A Case Study of Teachers' Interaction with Work Conditions in High School." D.B.A. dissertation, United States International University, 1980.

Identifies the factors that contribute to high and low job satisfaction of secondary school teachers using the Purdue Teacher Opinionaire.

168. Morris, Elizabeth Anne. "Job Satisfaction and Dissatisfaction of Teachers in Urban and Suburban Secondary Schools in Birmingham, Alabama." Ed.D. dissertation, The University of Alabama, 1979.

Compares urban and suburban high school teachers' job satisfaction.

169. Obi-Akatchak, Edward Emmanuel Otu. "A Comparative Analysis of Perceived Job Satisfaction Among Graduate and NCE Post-Primary School Teachers in Ogoja, Nigeria." Ph.D. dissertation, University of Minnesota, 1983.

Analyzes levels of job satisfaction for various groups of teachers.

170. Oladebo, Samson Adebayo. "An Investigation of Job Satisfaction and Dissatisfaction Among the Teachers in Secondary Institutions in Kano State, Nigeria." Ph.D. dissertation, Northwestern University, 1979.

Measures job satisfaction among high school teachers in terms of recognition, achievement, work itself, advancement, responsibility, salary, administrative policies, supervision, interpersonal relations, and working conditions.

171. Parkay, Forrest Winston. "Inner-City High School Teachers: The Relationship of Personality Traits and Teaching Style to Environmental Stress." Ph.D. dissertation, The University of Chicago, 1978.

    Analyzes secondary school teachers' modes of coping with stress, personality traits, attitudes, and teaching styles; considers perceived levels of satisfaction and success versus dissatisfaction and failure.

172. Pastor, Margaret Catherine Bottenberg. "Higher Order Need Strength and Job Satisfaction in Secondary Public School Teachers." Ph.D. dissertation, Texas A&M University, 1980.

    Identifies teacher needs and their relationship to high school teachers' job satisfaction using the Higher Order Need Strength Measure B and telephone interviews.

173. Pauley, Thomas Ray. "Preservice Training and Job Satisfaction Among Middle Grade Teachers." Ed.D., Northern Illinois University, 1978.

    Investigates the relationship between type of training received by middle school teachers and job satisfaction using the Job Descriptive Index and personal and demographic variables.

174. Pauli, Jerry Lavern. "The Opinions of the Intermediate Level Teachers in Montana Concerning Grades Five Through Eight." Ed.D. dissertation, University of Montana, 1982.

    Questions intermediate school teachers about their teacher education program, job satisfaction, and ideas about middle schools.

175. Pook, Mary Ellen Patrick. "A Study of the Relationship of Teacher Job Satisfaction and the Level of Implementation of Recommended Middle School Practices." Ph.D. dissertation, University of Colorado at Boulder, 1980.

    Studies the relationship between the level of implementation of recommended middle school practices and job satisfaction using the Purdue Teacher Opinionaire and the Middle School Practices Index developed by the researcher.

176. Reid, Edward John. "A Study of the Relationship Between Job Security, Feelings of Security, Job Satisfaction and Role Involvement of Teachers in Selected Public Secondary Schools in New York State." Ed.D. dissertation, State University of New York at Albany, 1979.

   Examines high school teachers' job security, feelings of job security, job satisfaction, and role involvement using a Survey of Teacher Opinion and Behavior developed by the researcher.

177. Rochelle, William Jerry. "Participation in Decision Making and Job Satisfaction: An Empirical Test of the Vroom and Yetton Model in Selected Secondary Schools." Ph.D. dissertation, Georgia State University--College of Education, 1983.

   Explores the effects of participation in decision making on high school teachers' job satisfaction using the Index of Organization Reaction.

178. Schneider, Gail T. "Teacher Involvement in Decision Making: Zones of Acceptance, Decision Conditions, and Job Satisfaction." Journal of Research and Development in Education 18, no. 1 (Fall 1984): 25-32.

   Describes the relationship between decision-making involvement and high school teachers' job satisfaction using a decision involvement analysis questionnaire.

179. Schultheis, Robert A. "Improving Teacher Professionalism." Business Education Forum 34, no. 2 (November 1979): 11-14.

   Describes the characteristics of a professional and productive high school teacher; mentions environment influences, professional development, and professional recognition.

180. Scott-Miller, Susan J. "An Investigation of the Relationship Between Biographical Characteristics and Job Satisfaction Among Middle School Teachers in Four Suburban School Districts." Doctoral dissertation, Portland State University, 1985.

    Studies middle school teachers' job satisfaction using the Purdue Teacher Opinionaire and biographical data.

181. Speed, Noel Eric. "Decision Participation and Staff Satisfaction in Middle and Junior High Schools that Individualize Instruction." Ph.D. dissertation, The University of Wisconsin-Madison, 1979.

    Relates decision-making participation to secondary school teachers' job satisfaction using the Decision Participation Analysis Questionnaire and the Job Satisfaction Survey.

182. Srivastava, Surya K. "Job Satisfaction Amongst Private and Public Secondary School Teachers." Perspectives in Psychological Researches 5, no. 2 (October 1982): 29-30.

    Compares public and private junior high school and senior high school teachers' job satisfaction.

183. Steitz, Jean A., and Carol M. Kulpa. "Occupational Involvement and Alienation Among Adults: The Effects of Gender and Age." International Journal of Behavioral Development 7, no. 4 (December 1984): 479-499.

    Studies gender and age in work alienation of secondary school teachers.

184. Stern, William Alvin. "Teacher Absenteeism at the Secondary School Level: An Investigation of Work-Related Attitudes and Demographic Correlates." Ph.D. dissertation, Michigan State University, 1980.

    Investigates causes of high school teachers' absenteeism by examining job satisfaction and job motivation using a modified form of the Job Description Index.

185. Sweeney, Jim. "Teacher Dissatisfaction on the Rise: Higher Level Needs Unfulfilled." Education 102, no. 2 (Winter 1981): 203-207.

    Looks at senior high school job satisfaction and higher level needs.

186. Sweeney, Jim. "Professional Discretion and Teacher Satisfaction." High School Journal 65, no. 1 (October 1981): 1-6.

    Reports on high school teacher job satisfaction, needs (following Maslow's classification), professional discretion, participation in decision making and trust.

187. Taylor, Graham H., and Brian Sayer. "Attitudes of Teachers Toward the 9-13 Middle School." Educational Research 25, no. 1 (February 1983): 71-74.

    Examines attitudes of middle school teachers toward middle schools, career advancement, and job satisfaction.

188. Thierbach, Gail Linnea. "Decision Involvement and Job Satisfaction in Middle and Junior High Schools." Ph.D. dissertation, The University of Wisconsin-Madison, 1980.

    Relates personal and situational variables to involvement in decision-making and secondary school teachers' job satisfaction using the Decision Involvement Analysis Questionnaire and the Job Satisfaction Survey.

189. Thompson, Anthony Peter. "Subjective Expectations and Job Facet Predictability in Job Satisfaction." Ph.D. dissertation, The University of Western Ontario (Canada), 1975.

    Measures the effects of subjective expectations and job facet predictability on secondary school teachers' job satisfaction using a General Affective Tone Score and the Job Descriptive Index work scale.

190. Weber, William Fred. "Job Satisfaction of Transferred and Reassigned Teachers." Ph.D. dissertation, The University of Michigan, 1975.

   Compares job satisfaction among secondary school teachers who were transferred and/or reassigned and those who were not, using the Job Descriptive Index and a researcher-developed questionnaire.

191. Weiser, Harold E., Jr. "A Study of the Relationship Between Organizational Climate and Teacher Morale." Ed.D. dissertation, University of New Orleans, 1974.

   Examines the relationship between high school teachers' morale and organizational climate using the Purdue Teacher Opinionaire and the Organizational Climate Description Questionnaire.

192. Young, Mable Goodwin. "A Study of the Comparison of Job Satisfaction and Professional Preparation of Selected Junior and Senior High School Teachers in Colorado." Ed.D. dissertation, University of Northern Colorado, 1983.

   Explores the relationship between secondary school teachers' job satisfaction and their professional preparation using a general information survey and the Purdue Teacher Opinionaire.

IV. SUBJECT AREA TEACHERS

193. Abdul Malek, Abdul Patah Bin. "Job Satisfaction of Vocational Agriculture Teachers in the Southeastern United States." Ph.D. dissertation, The Louisiana State University and Agricultural and Mechanical College, 1984.

    Examines teacher job satisfaction of vocational agriculture teachers and their demographic characteristics using the Job Descriptive Index.

194. Abelson, A. Geoffrey. "A Factor-Analytic Study of Job Satisfaction Among Special Educators." Educational and Psychological Measurement 46, no. 1 (Spring 1986): 37-43.

    Develops a teacher job satisfaction questionnaire and analyzes the job satisfaction of special education teachers.

195. Amirtash, Ali-Mohammad. "Determinants of Job Satisfaction Among Selected Male High School Physical Educators in the City of Tehran, Iran." Ph.D. dissertation, University of Oregon, 1982.

    Investigates the relationship between teacher job satisfaction, demographic variables, leadership style, and organizational climate of male secondary physical education teachers using translations of the Leader Effectiveness and Adaptability Description-Others, the Organizational Climate Descriptive Questionnaire--Form IV, and the Job Description Index.

196. Askar, Ali G. "A Study of Teacher Job Satisfaction in Kuwait." Ph.D. dissertation, the University of Michigan, 1981.

    Relates elementary, intermediate, and secondary teacher job satisfaction to personal and professional needs and reasons for becoming a teacher.

197. Attuwaybi, Omar Bashir. "An Investigation of the Job Satisfaction of Elementary and Junior High School Teachers in the Libyan Arab Republic." Ph.D. dissertation, University of Kansas, 1975.

    Tests Herzberg's motivation-hygiene theory on elementary and junior high school teachers using a questionnaire developed by the researcher around eight of Herzberg's job satisfaction factors.

198. Barker, Jerry Delaplane. "Influence of Quality of Worklife Variables on the Retention and Career Satisfaction of Science and Mathematics Teachers." Ph.D. dissertation, the University of Tennessee, 1986.

    Utilizes a survey instrument and interviews around the Quality of Worklife model of workplace satisfaction with science and mathematics teachers.

199. Bembry, Sylvia Ann. "A Comparative Attitudinal Analysis of Selected Business Teachers in Iowa Public Secondary Schools Concerning Their Current Job Satisfaction." Ph.D. dissertation, the University of Iowa, 1975.

    Studies job satisfaction of business education teachers in terms of demographic variables, fourteen job factors, and plans to remain or leave teaching using a questionnaire developed by the researcher.

200. Bina, Michael J. "Morale of Teachers of the Visually Handicapped: Implications for Administrators." *Journal of Visual Impairment and Blindness* 76, no. 4 (April 1982): 121-128.

    Compares teacher job satisfaction of the visually handicapped to regular education teachers using the Purdue Teacher Opinionaire.

201. Bina, Michael James. "A Study of Morale of Teachers of the Visually Handicapped in the Rocky Mountain High Plains Region--Implications for Administrators Regarding Teacher Burn-Out and Attrition." Ed.D. dissertation, University of Northern Colorado, 1980.

   Examines job satisfaction, dissatisfaction, and the potential for attrition of visually handicapped teachers using the Purdue Teacher Opinionaire.

202. Bledsoe, Joseph C., and William C. Baber. "Factor Invariance in the Measurement of Job Satisfaction." Perceptual and Motor Skills 48, no. 3, pt. 1 (June 1979): 985-986.

   Identifies two factors, intrinsic and extrinsic satisfaction, that contribute to the job satisfaction of high school business education teachers using the Minnesota Satisfaction Questionnaire.

203. Bloemker, Darvin Alan. "Factors Associated with the Retention of Industrial Educators." Ed.D. dissertation, University of Missouri-Columbia, 1983.

   Develops the Retention Factor Questionnaire to identify reasons for industrial teachers remaining in the profession.

204. Boeck, Debora G. "The Relationship of Special Education Teacher Job Satisfaction and the Implementation of Public Law 94-142." Ed.D. dissertation, Seattle University, 1979.

   Examines the relationship between special education teacher job satisfaction and compliance with PL 94-142.

205. Bowers, Roberta June. "The Relationships Among Educational Needs, Educational Opportunities, and Job Satisfaction for Indiana Secondary English Teachers." Ed.D. dissertation, Indiana University, 1986.

   Studies the relationships among educational needs, educational opportunities, and job satisfaction of high school English teachers using the Job Descriptive Index.

206. Boyd, Catherine Robertson. "The Relationship of Teacher Facilitation of Self-Directed Learning to Job Satisfaction of Secondary Home Economics Teachers." Ph.D. dissertation, The University of Alabama, 1982.

    Examines the relationship between home economics teachers' job satisfaction and their perceptions of their facilitation of self-directed learning using the short form of the Minnesota Satisfaction Questionnaire and the Teacher Facilitation of Self-Direction Inventory.

207. Braswell, Ray Eldon, Jr. "Differences in Perceived Teacher-Coach Job Attitudes as Identified by Senior High School Principals and Teacher-Football Coaches (Role-Conflict)." Ph.D. dissertation, North Texas State University, 1986.

    Discusses the dual role of senior high school teacher and athletic coach in terms of job related tension, participation in decision making, job involvement, and job satisfaction.

208. Brod, Rodney L., and others. "Insights from Vocational Teachers of the Year." *Vocational Education Journal* 61, no. 2 (March 1986): 29-31.

    Asks vocational teachers to rank the most and the least satisfying aspects of teaching.

209. Brown, Herman D., and others. *Personnel Training-- Secondary Vocational Agriculture Teacher Education.* 1985. ERIC, ED 261 252.

    Describes problems of secondary vocational agriculture teachers and offers suggestions for helping them.

210. Bullock, Jack Arlen. "An Investigation of the Personality Traits, Job Satisfaction Attitudes, Training and Experience Histories of Superior Teachers of Junior High School Instrumental Music in New York State." Ph.D. dissertation, University of Miami, 1974.

   Compares personality traits, job satisfaction, training and experience of superior junior high school instrumental music teachers using the Sixteen Personality Factor Questionnaire, the Minnesota Satisfaction Questionnaire, the Training and Experience Questionnaire developed by the researcher and the Personal Interview Questionnaire, also developed by the researcher.

211. Burcham, Stanley Preston. "Job Attitudes of Teachers with Coaching and Non-Coaching Responsibilities in Selected School Districts in the State of Illinois." Ph.D. dissertation, Southern Illinois University at Carbondale, 1982.

   Compares teachers who coach and teachers who do not in terms of job related tension, job involvement, and job satisfaction.

212. Calhoun, Calfrey C. "Planning a Career in Business Teaching." Business Education Forum 36, no. 1 (October 1981): 28, 29, 32-34.

   Discusses the job, opportunities, and preparation of business education teachers.

213. Casey, Catherine Elizabeth. "A Descriptive Study of the Isolate Sister-Teacher and the Quality of Community Life Among Roman Catholic Teaching Sisters." Ph.D. dissertation, The University of Texas at Austin, 1976.

   Compares Roman Catholic teaching sisters in terms of job satisfaction, religious family satisfaction, personality characteristics, mental adjustment, and background information.

214. Chen, Chin-Zue. "Patterns of Job Satisfaction and Stress on High School Industrial Arts Teachers in the State of Iowa." Ph.D. dissertation, Iowa State University, 1985.

   Investigates sources of job satisfaction and stress on high school industrial arts teachers using a questionnaire designed by the researcher.

215. Clay, Thomas. <u>Music in Ohio Schools. Final Report</u>. 1982. ERIC, ED 229 301.

   Describes music teachers' attitudes toward their teaching positions in elementary, junior/middle high, and senior high schools.

216. Collins, James Ronald. "Identification of Selected Factors Which Influence Job Satisfaction of Vocational Agriculture Teachers in Area VIII of Texas." Ed.D. dissertation, Oklahoma State University, 1982.

   Identifies factors that contribute to the job satisfaction of vocational agriculture teachers using a questionnaire designed by the researcher.

217. D'Alonzo, Bruno, and Douglas E. Wiseman. "Actual and Desired Roles of the High School Learning Disability Resource Teacher." <u>Journal of Learning Disabilities</u> 11, no. 6 (June-July 1978): 390-397.

   Develops a behavior scale to measure role expectations of high school learning disability resource teachers.

218. Davis, Frederick William. "Predictors of Overall Job Satisfaction Among Public School Physical Educators." Ph.D. dissertation, University of Oregon, 1981.

   Examines the relationship between leader behavior, organizational climate, professional orientation, demographic variables, and overall job satisfaction of physical education teachers using the Overall

Job Satisfaction Measure, the Leader Behavior Description Questionnaire (partial), the Organizational Climate Description Questionnaire, and the Bartol Professionalism Scale.

219. Decker, James Dean. "Job Satisfaction Factors of Special Education Teachers Employed in Residential Institutions for the Mentally Handicapped in New Mexico." Ed.D. dissertation, The University of New Mexico, 1980.

Assesses job satisfaction and dissatisfaction of teachers employed in residential institutions for the mentally handicapped using the Educational Work Components Study, the Job Descriptive Index, and the Faces Measure.

220. Devore, Mary Ann. "Work Perceptions and Job Satisfaction of Vocational Home Economics Teachers in Missouri." Ph.D. dissertation, University of Missouri-Columbia, 1980.

Ascertains the meaning and value of work and job satisfaction of consumer homemaking teachers and occupational home economics teachers using the Meaning and Value of Work Scale and the Job Satisfaction Scale.

221. Dinkel, Sharon Kay. "Job Satisfaction and Perception of Teaching of High School Teacher/Coaches." Ed.D. dissertation, the University of Utah, 1982.

Investigates job satisfaction and perceptions of teaching in high school teacher/coaches using the Brayfield-Rothe Index of Job Satisfaction.

222. Duke, Peggy O'Neal. "Communication Satisfaction of Business Education Teachers in an Urban School System." Ed.D. dissertation, George Peabody College for Teachers of Vanderbilt University, 1981.

Analyzes the relationship between communication satisfaction and job satisfaction on business education teachers using the Communication Satisfaction Questionnaire.

223. Dupuis, Mary M., and others. *The Content Area Reading Project: An Inservice Education Program for Junior High School Teachers and Teachers of Adults. Appendix A, The Instruments and Their Development: Presentation and Analysis of the Findings. Final Report.* 1977. ERIC, ED 155 666.

    Uses the Purdue Teacher Opinionaire to describe morale levels among junior high school teachers.

224. Earls, Neal Franklin. "Distinctive Physical Education Teachers: Personal Qualities, Perceptions of Teacher Education and the Realities of Teaching." Ed.D. dissertation, The University of North Carolina at Greensboro, 1979.

    Describes satisfaction and dissatisfaction of teaching for distinctive junior high/middle school physical education teachers using an in-depth semi-structured interview.

225. Eriksson, Karl Henrik. *Qualitative Evaluation of Teaching Service, Subject Teacher Line, KULT-A.* 1974. ERIC, ED 100 848.

    Identifies factors influencing subject teachers' job satisfaction using a Teachers Today instrument covering factors related to job satisfaction.

226. Even, Mary Jane. *Adult Basic Education Teacher Survey, 1975.* 1975. ERIC, ED 132 257.

    Surveys adult basic-education teachers' occupational attitudes toward their jobs and feelings about ABE teaching on a career; includes a review of the literature related to employee attitudes and job satisfaction.

227. Fair, James William. "A Comparative Analysis of the Job Satisfaction Determinants of Two Groups of Secondary Vocational Education Teachers." Ed.D. dissertation, Indiana University, 1977.

    Compares job satisfaction of trade and industrial teachers of regular and special education programs using the Job Descriptive Index.

Subject Area Teachers 55

228. Farber, Joel H. "Effects of Role Agreement on Resource Specialist Job Satisfaction and Mainstreaming Learning Disabled Students." Ed.D. dissertation, University of San Francisco, 1983.

　　Studies the relationship between the resource specialist role and job satisfaction using the Minnesota Satisfaction Questionnaire and the Resource Specialist Role Agreement Questionnaire.

229. Felder, Juanita Baker. "The Influence of Students' Cultural Behaviors upon the Job Satisfaction of English as a Second Language (ESL) Teachers at the Defense Language Institute, Lackland Air Force Base, Texas." Ed.D. dissertation, Texas A&M University, 1986.

　　Examines the influence of students' cultural behaviors on the job satisfaction of English as a Second Language teachers; includes a review of the literature on teacher job satisfaction.

230. Grady, Thomas L. "Job Satisfaction of Vocational Agriculture Teachers in Louisiana." *Journal of the American Association of Teacher Educators in Agriculture* 26, no. 3 (Fall 1985): 70-78, 85.

　　Identifies factors that affect the job satisfaction of vocational agriculture teachers.

231. Grady, Thomas Lewis. "The Relationship Between Job Satisfaction and Teacher Performance of Vocational Agriculture Teachers in Louisiana." Ph.D. dissertation, The Louisiana State University and Agricultural and Mechanical College, 1984.

　　Investigates the relationship between job satisfaction and teacher performance of vocational agriculture teachers using the Minnesota Satisfaction Questionnaire.

232. Gregory, Michael David. "A Descriptive Analysis of Factors Which Contribute to Job Dissatisfaction Among Secondary School Band Directors." Ed.D. dissertation, Auburn University, 1986.

   Develops the Band Director Job Satisfaction Questionnaire to identify sources of dissatisfaction among secondary school band directors.

233. Hadaway, Farrand J. "Selected Personal Characteristics Related to Job Satisfaction of Public High School Business Teachers." Ed.D. dissertation, University of Georgia, 1978.

   Investigates the relationships between six personal characteristics of high school business teachers and job satisfaction using the Minnesota Satisfaction Questionnaire.

234. Handley, Herbert M., and James F. Shill. Work Values and Job Attitudes Held by New Teachers in Vocational Education in Mississippi. Research Series No. 6. 1973. ERIC, ED 096 451.

   Describes the work values and job attitudes of vocational education teachers toward teaching using the Work Value Inventory and a vocational teacher attitude scale developed by the researcher.

235. Haughey, Margaret L., and Peter J. Murphy. "Are Rural Teachers Satisfied with the Quality of Their Work Life." Education 104, no. 1 (Fall 1983): 56-66.

   Investigates job satisfaction of rural teachers; finds satisfaction is related to autonomy, colleagues, and students.

236. Heckman, Michael Gary. "Job Satisfaction of Substitute and Regular Classroom Teachers." Ed.D. dissertation, Northern Illinois University, 1980.

   Compares job satisfaction of regular and substitute teachers using the Purdue Teacher Opinionaire.

237. Holley, Claudette Snead. "An Analysis of Stress and Its Relationship to the Satisfaction of Secondary Home Economics Teachers in Alabama." Ed.D. dissertation, the University of Alabama, 1985.

 Analyzes the relationship between stress, job satisfaction, and demographic variables of secondary home economics teachers using the Minnesota Satisfaction Questionnaire (short form) and the New York State United Teachers Stress Survey.

238. Horn, Jerry G. Recruitment and Preparation of Quality Teachers for Rural Schools. 1985. ERIC, ED 258 785.

 Recommends actions to overcome perceived negative aspects of teaching in rural areas.

239. Hunter, Janice K., and Jean D. Kline. "Challenge to the Chargers: A Junior High School Self-Improvement Study." NASSP Bulletin 69, no. 483 (October 1985): 109-113.

 Describes a pilot program which improved teacher morale and student performance.

240. Hyder, Carroll Ray. "An Assessment of the Effectiveness of Summer Workshops for Training Teachers to Use the Materials of the Industrial Arts Curriculum Project." Ph.D. dissertation, The Ohio State University, 1971.

 Determines the job satisfaction of industrial arts construction teachers using the Minnesota Satisfaction Questionnaire.

241. Johnston, Rebecca Lea. "Perceptions of Special Education Teachers in Texas Regarding Selected Job Related Factors." Ph.D. dissertation, North Texas State University, 1984.

 Examines factors affecting the teaching environment of special education teachers and focuses on factors that contribute to the decision to remain in or leave teaching.

242. Jones, Jean Waits. "Analysis of Communication Satisfaction in Four Rural School Systems." Ph.D. dissertation, George Peabody College for Teachers of Vanderbilt University, 1981.

    Studies the relationships between communication satisfaction, job satisfaction, and demographic variables of rural secondary teachers using the Communication Satisfaction Questionnaire.

243. Jorde-Bloom, Paula. "Teacher Job Satisfaction: A Framework for Analysis." *Early Childhood Research Quarterly* 1, no. 2 (June 1986): 167-183.

    Presents an overview of definitions and measures of job satisfaction of early childhood teachers.

244. Kanu, Isaac Nnanna. "An Analysis of Job Satisfaction and Participation in Inservice Education Programs of Wisconsin Post-Secondary Business and Office Education Teachers." Ph.D. dissertation, The University of Wisconsin-Madison, 1983.

    Studies the relationship between job satisfaction of post-secondary business and office education teachers and inservice education programs using the Job Descriptive Index.

245. Kaufman, Allan H., and James J. Buffer, Jr. "An Assessment of Job Satisfaction of Industrial Arts Teacher Educators." *Journal of Industrial Teacher Education* 16, no. 1 (Fall 1978): 45-56.

    Develops the National Job Satisfaction Study Instrument to measure job satisfaction of industrial arts teachers.

246. Kazanas, H. C., and Thoms G. Gregor. "The Meaning and Value of Work, Job Satisfaction and Productivity of Vocational Teachers, Graduates, Seniors, and College Preparatory Seniors." *Journal of Vocational Education Research* 2, no. 1 (1977): 29-39.

    Considers the value of work, job satisfaction, and productivity in vocational education.

ables of industrial education teachers who voluntarily participate in in-service programs using Holland's Vocational Preference Inventory and the Minnesota Satisfaction Questionnaire.

252. Kohan, Alan Richard. "Vocational Teacher Perceptions of Their Locus of Control, Job Satisfaction, and Superintendent Leader Behavior in Central Ohio Joint Vocational Schools." Ph.D. dissertation, The Ohio State University, 1985.

    Explores the relationships between vocational superintendent leadership behavior and vocational teacher locus of control in vocational teacher job satisfaction using the Leadership Behavior Description Questionnaire-Form 12, the Rotter Internal-External Scale, and the Job Descriptive Index.

253. Kotrlik, Joe W., and A.P. Malek. "Job Satisfaction of Vocational Agriculture Teachers in the Southeastern United States." Journal of the American Association of Teacher Educators in Agriculture 27, no. 1 (Spring 1986): 33-38.

    Examines the relationship between demographic variables and job satisfaction of vocational agriculture teachers.

254. Kovacevich, Dorothy A. "A Comparative Study of the Morale of Regular and Special Education Teachers." Ph.D. dissertation, Kent State University, 1974.

    Compares job satisfaction of special education teachers and regular teachers using the Purdue Teacher Opinionaire.

255. Kutie, Rita C. "The Electronic Office--Educator's Input Outside the Classroom." Journal of Business Education 58, no. 2 (November 1982): 50-51.

    Discusses the role of business education teachers in designing satisfying office jobs.

247. Kells, Patricia P., and others. <u>Kansas Survey Regarding Attrition of Special Education Personnel. Kansas Regent Institutions Special Project. Summary Report.</u> 1982. ERIC, ED 232 331.

    Assesses competencies for special education teachers and the importance of each competency on job satisfaction.

248. Kelsay, Jeri Diane. "Personal Characteristics and Job Satisfaction Dimensions of Personnel Working with Severely or Profoundly Retarded Students." Ed.D. dissertation, Northern Illinois University, 1978.

    Investigates personality characteristics and job satisfaction of teachers working with severely or retarded children using the Personal Orientation Inventory and the Minnesota Satisfaction Questionnaire.

249. Kesselheim, Alan J. "A Look at the Life of an Outdoor Educator." <u>Journal of Experiential Education</u> 4, no. 1 (Spring 1981): 39-41.

    Describes favorable and unfavorable aspects of being an outdoor educator.

250. King, Wayne, and James P. Key. "A Survey of Salaries and Working Conditions of Vo-Ag Teachers in the U.S." <u>Agricultural Education Magazine</u> 48, no. 4 (1975): 92-93, 95.

    Discusses beginning salaries for agriculture teachers and the changes in working conditions that have occurred.

251. Knold, John Arthur. "The Relationship Between Industrial Education Teachers' Voluntary In-Service Participation and Their Personality Characteristics, Job Satisfaction, and Locus-of-Control." Ph.D. dissertation, University of Washington, 1981.

    Focuses on personality characteristics, job satisfaction, locus-of-control, and personal vari-

256. Lebovitz, George. "Satisfaction and Dissatisfaction Among Judaic Studies Teachers in Midwestern Jewish Day Schools." Ed.D. dissertation, University of Cincinnati, 1981.

   Identifies sources of satisfaction and dissatisfaction of Judaic studies teachers using a questionnaire developed by the researcher based on Herzberg's Motivation-Hygiene Theory.

257. Lee, Jasper S. <u>Agricultural Education: Review and Synthesis of the Research, Fourth Edition. Information Series No. 298.</u> 1985. ERIC, ED 260 300.

   Reviews agricultural education research in terms of professionalism, master teachers, morale, satisfaction, and teacher retention.

258. Lee, Kerbe Bruce. "Communication Satisfaction in Private, Church-Related Schools." Ed.D. dissertation, The University of Tulsa, 1983.

   Analyzes communication satisfaction and job satisfaction of teachers in private, church-related schools using the Communication Satisfaction Questionnaire.

259. Macqueen, Laurence William. "An Importance-Weighted Approach to Overall and Job-Facet Satisfaction of Teachers." Ph.D. dissertation, Michigan State University, 1986.

   Assesses overall and job-facet satisfaction of teachers on fifty-eight aspects; identifies seven factors.

260. Mark, Diane Helen. "Reading Teachers' Perceptions of Individual Efficacy in Relation to Organizational Structure." Ed.D. dissertation, Columbia University Teachers College, 1984.

   Describes job satisfaction of reading teachers based on organizational structure, administrator relationships, reward, social affect, competence, and conflict.

261. Marshall, Raymond Loren. "Factors Related to Teacher Morale in Selected Overseas and United States Schools." Ed.D. dissertation, The University of Alabama, 1984.

    Compares job satisfaction of overseas teachers and United States school teachers using a questionnaire developed by the researcher.

262. Matthes, William A., and Robert V. Carlson. Conditions for Practice: The Reasons Teachers Selected Rural Schools. 1986. ERIC, ED 273 409.

    Compares rural, urban, and suburban teachers in relation to reasons for accepting their present teaching position.

263. Meyers, Charles. "Teachers for the Social Studies." The Social Studies Teacher 3, no. 1 (September-October 1981): 1, 3.

    Examines teaching challenges and professionalism for social studies teachers.

264. Miller, Larry E. "Correlation of Selected Variables with the Morale of Virginia Teachers of Agricultural Education." Journal of the American Association of Teacher Educators in Agriculture 19, no. 1 (1978): 29-38.

    Investigates the relationship between demographic variables and the morale of agricultural education teachers.

265. Miller, Larry E. A Five-Year Follow-Up Study of the Non-Teaching Agricultural Education Graduates--1968-73. 1974. ERIC, ED 112 163.

    Determines reasons why agricultural education teachers leave teaching and provides information for teacher educators and preparation programs.

266. Milliken, William James. "Relationship of Work Values to Job Satisfaction in the Maryland Cooperative Extension Service." Ph.D. dissertation, University of Maryland, 1977.

   Studies demographic variables, work values, and job satisfaction of the Maryland Cooperative Extension Service faculty using the Values for Working and the Extension Workers Job Satisfaction Inventory.

267. Modiano, Rachel. "Mentoring Among Special Education Teachers." Psy.D. dissertation, Rutgers University, the State University of New Jersey, 1986.

   Interviews special education teachers who participated in a mentoring program in terms of professional development, stress management, job satisfaction, and future aspirations.

268. Moller, Lynn Elliott. "The Relationship of Role Perceptions of the Secondary School Music Educator and the Resultant Effect on Job Satisfaction." Ph.D. dissertation, University of Kansas, 1981.

   Examines the effects of role perception on job satisfaction of secondary school music teachers using Barnes' Instrumental Music Educator Describer (adaptation) and the Minnesota Satisfaction Questionnaire (short form).

269. Muncrief, Martha. "Work Adjustment of Vocational Education Teachers." Journal of Vocational Education Research 4, no. 4 (Fall 1979): 35-48.

   Investigates job satisfaction and work adjustment of high school vocational education teachers using the Minnesota Importance Questionnaire and the Minnesota Job Description Questionnaire.

270. Muncrief, Martha Crawford. "Work Adjustment of Vocational Education Teachers." Ph.D. dissertation, Ohio State University, 1973.

    Describes vocational needs, job satisfaction, and job success of secondary business, home economics, and industrial education teachers.

271. Nederveen, Paul. *Teacher Job Satisfaction and Modern Language Curricular Variables in Alberta.* 1982. ERIC, ED 216 514.

    Explores the relationship between curricular influences and the job satisfaction of foreign language teachers.

272. Neely, Jerry Richard. "The Impact of a Substantial Pay Raise on Teacher Performance and the Job Satisfaction in Region IX Service Center Area of Texas." Ed.D. dissertation, North Texas State University, 1975.

    Studies the effect of a salary increase on job satisfaction and job performance using the Job Descriptive Index and the Minnesota Satisfactoriness Scale.

273. Nicholson, Jean Hagewood. "Analysis of Communication Satisfaction in an Urban School System." Ph.D. dissertation, George Peabody College for Teachers of Vanderbilt University, 1980.

    Examines the relationships among communication satisfaction, job satisfaction, and demographic variables using the Communication Satisfaction Questionnaire and the Personal and School Information Questionnaire.

274. Nickel, Barbara Bruce. "Job Satisfaction as It Relates to Professional Support of Teachers of the Emotionally Handicapped." Ed.D. dissertation, University of South Carolina, 1985.

    Relates the importance of administrator and parental support in the job satisfaction of teachers of the emotionally handicapped using the Minnesota Satisfaction Questionnaire and the Supportive Activities Questionnaire developed by the researcher.

275. Norvell, Christine Ann. "Characteristics of Perceived Leadership, Job Satisfaction, and Central Life Interests in High-Achieving, Low-Achieving, and Improving Chapter I Schools." Ph.D. dissertation, University of California, Los Angeles, 1984.

   Compares leadership characteristics, teacher job satisfaction, and central life interests in Chapter I schools.

276. Oakes, Jeannie. *208 English Teachers. A Study of Schooling in the United States.* Technical Report Series, no. 11. 1980. ERIC, ED 214 881.

   Develops a profile of secondary school English teachers in comparison to other subject teachers.

277. Oberlin, Megan Haupt. "Effects of Leadership on Perceived Job Satisfaction and Influence Among Intermediate School District Special Education Personnel in Michigan." Ph.D. dissertation, Michigan State University, 1980.

   Examines the effects of leadership and demographic variables on job satisfaction and influence of intermediate school special education teachers using the Leadership Behavior Description Questionnaire, the Job Description Index, and the Control Graphs by Tannenbaum.

278. Olson, Richard R. "Vocational Stability and Job Satisfaction Characteristics of Postsecondary Technology Instructors." *Journal of Industrial Teacher Education* 11, no. 3 (1974): 5-14.

   Identifies predictive factors of vocational stability and job satisfaction for teachers of postsecondary technology subjects.

279. O'Such, Twila Gaye. "A Comparison of Components in the Employment Satisfaction of General and Special Class Teachers." Ed.D. dissertation, Columbia University, 1974.

   Compares job satisfaction of general and special education elementary school teachers using the Minnesota Satisfaction Questionnaire.

280. Peek, Thomas R. <u>K-12: What the Data Show About Public Education in Minnesota.</u> 1985. ERIC, ED 265 233.

   Identifies four major problems in the public education system including job dissatisfaction.

281. Phelps, Tom K. "A Survey of Factors Affecting Job Satisfaction and Dissatisfaction of Music Educators in High Schools and Junior High Schools in Idaho." Ph.D. dissertation, The University of Utah, 1982.

   Designs a questionnaire to determine the effect of various factors on secondary school music teacher job satisfaction.

282. Plessman, Connie Kay Staehr. "The Relationship Between Personality Characteristics and Job Satisfaction of Secondary Marketing Education Teachers." Ph.D. dissertation, The University of Nebraska-Lincoln, 1985.

   Examines the relationship between personality characteristics, demographic and attitudinal variables and job satisfaction of marketing teachers using the Myers-Briggs Personality Indicator and the Minnesota Satisfaction Questionnaire.

283. <u>Proceedings of the Annual National Agricultural Education Research Meeting (9th, St. Louis, Missouri, December 3, 1982).</u> 1982. ERIC, ED 229 519.

   Addresses issues of inservice education, job satisfaction, and morale of agricultural education teachers.

284. Ravin, Noach. "The Effects of Individual and Job Characteristics on Job Satisfaction of Supplementary and Hebrew Day Schools' Hebrew Teachers." Ph.D. dissertation, The American University, 1981.

   Surveys the current job satisfaction levels among Hebrew day school teachers using the Job Satisfaction Continuum Scale, Individual Characteristics, and the Job Characteristics and Job Satisfaction Questionnaires.

285. Richards, Charlotte Jean. "Role Conflict Concerning Teachers of the Mentally Retarded and Its Relationship to Confidence in Leadership, Effectiveness, and Satisfaction." Ph.D. dissertation, The University of Wisconsin-Madison, 1974.

   Focuses on the relationship between role conflict and job satisfaction, effectiveness, and confidence in the principal's leadership of special education teachers.

286. Rodriguez, Robert Alan. "Structural Coupling and Teacher Job Satisfaction in Preschools and Day Care Centers." Ed.D. dissertation, University of Kansas, 1982.

   Investigates the relationship between organizational structure and job satisfaction of preschool and day care center teachers using the Minnesota Satisfaction Questionnaire.

287. Romero, Det, and others. Interactions Between Family and Day Care Systems. Final Technical Report. 1975. ERIC, ED 182 006.

   Studies job satisfaction of day care center teachers and the relationship between families of children enrolled and the day care centers.

288. Saidian, Mehdi. "A Study of Job Satisfaction as Measured by the Minnesota Satisfaction Questionnaire as Applied to Selected Male and Female Vocational and Technical Teachers of Esfahan, Iran." Ph.D. dissertation, University of Kansas, 1980.

   Examines the relationship between the job satisfaction of vocational technical teachers and educational experience using the Minnesota Satisfaction Questionnaire.

289. Salit, Vivian L. "An Analysis of Role Perceptions of Title I Project Teachers." Ed.D. dissertation, Yeshiva University, 1981.

   Analyzes role conflict and job-related tension and job dissatisfaction of Title I teachers using

Project Teacher Activities, the Experienced Role Conflict Index, the Job-Related Tension Index, and the Job Satisfaction Index.

290. Savoie, Rodolphe J. "The Job Satisfaction Level of New Brunswick's French Business and Trade and Industrial Education Teachers in Relation to Attitudes and Other Demographic Variables." Ed.D. dissertation, The University of Tennessee, 1983.

   Studies the relationship between demographic variables and overall job satisfaction of business and trade and industrial education teachers using the Minnesota Teacher Attitude Inventory and the Minnesota Satisfaction Questionnaire.

291. Schwartz, Terry Ann, and others. <u>Teacher Dissatisfaction and Alienation as Related to Mainstreaming in Education</u>. 1980. ERIC, ED 191 194.

   Reports the results of a survey regarding teacher role in implementing PL 94-142 and job satisfaction.

292. Severe, Salvatore Francis. "The Relationship Between Organizational Climate and Mainstreaming." Ph.D. dissertation, Arizona State University, 1981.

   Discusses the relationship between mainstreaming and organizational climate using the Mainstreaming Planning Inventory and the Organizational Climate Description Questionnaire.

293. Sheely, Harlan Herbert. "A Study of Preferred Environment and Job Satisfaction of Special Intermediate School District 916 and Component District Faculty." Ed.D. dissertation, University of Minnesota, 1975.

   Explores differences in vocational high school faculty environmental preferences and job satisfaction using the Faculty Environmental Preference Scale and the Friedlander Instrument.

294. Shih, Yew-Sheng. "Determinants of Job Satisfaction Among Public Special School Teachers in Taiwan, the Republic of China." Ed.D. dissertation, University of Northern Colorado, 1984.

    Compares job satisfaction of special education teachers and regular teachers using the Minnesota Satisfaction Questionnaire (Short Form).

295. Silvester, Thomas Joseph. "A Comparison of Job Satisfaction of South Carolina Teachers Involved in Two Different Systems of Instructional Organization." Ph.D. dissertation, University of South Carolina, 1975.

    Compares job satisfaction of teachers in IGE multi-unit schools and traditionally organized schools using the Teacher Attitude Checklist.

296. Simmons, John. "When the Morale Really Slips." English Journal 75, no. 5 (September 1986): 56-58.

    Notes the importance of personal satisfaction and academic self-esteem in improving English teachers' morale.

297. Sonpon, Theophilus Nimley. "An Analysis of Teachers' Perceived Sources of Job Satisfaction at the Monrovia Consolidated School System: A Public School District in Liberia." Ph.D. dissertation, University of California, Los Angeles, 1983.

    Identifies sources of teacher satisfaction and dissatisfaction with respect to salary, workload, and the teaching job itself.

298. Spector, Barbara S. "Incentives to Increase the Number of Qualified Science Teachers in Precollege Institutions." Science Education 68, no. 2 (April 1984): 153-162.

    Describes incentives to encourage people to become science teachers.

299. Status of Vocational Agriculture and the Changing Roles of Teachers of Vocational Agriculture in North Carolina. Final Report. 1978. ERIC, ED 170 525.

   Conducts a structured interview of vocational agriculture teachers to examine their current and changing roles.

300. Stealey, Patricia Ann Terrill. "The Relation of Home Economics Teachers' Professional Identification and Personal Characteristics to Job Satisfaction." Ed.D. dissertation, Virginia Polytechnic Institute and State University, 1982.

   Measures professional identification and job satisfaction of home economics teachers using the Professionalism Scale and the Minnesota Satisfaction Questionnaire (short form).

301. Steinbach, Gary Milton. "Job Reinforcers and Job Satisfaction Among Public Secondary Industrial Arts Teachers in Minnesota." Ph.D. dissertation, University of Minnesota, 1979.

   Explores the relationships among job reinforcers, grade level assignments, job seniority variables, and intrinsic, extrinsic, and general job satisfaction using the Minnesota Job Description Questionnaire (Form E) and the Minnesota Satisfaction Questionnaire (short form).

302. Story, Marilyn Welshimer. "Some Attitudes That Indicate Job Satisfaction in Vocational Home Economics Teachers Graduated from Two Different Curriculums at Michigan State University." Ph.D. dissertation, Michigan State University, 1967.

   Compares job satisfaction of vocational home economics teachers from concept oriented and skill oriented curriculum using a questionnaire developed by the researcher.

303. Stunard, Sonja-Lou Linnea. "Job Satisfaction and Teacher Attitudes of Regular Classroom and Special Education Teachers." Ph.D. dissertation, University of Illinois at Chicago Circle, 1982.

   Analyzes the relationship between job satisfaction and type of class taught, regular or special education using the Minnesota Satisfaction Questionnaire and the Minnesota Teacher Attitude Inventory.

304. Treacy, Timothy James. "English Departmental Student Achievement, Organizational Climate and Job Satisfaction in Selected New York City High Schools." Ph.D. dissertation, Fordham University, 1982.

   Compares student achievement, organizational climate, and job satisfaction in high school English departments using the Sergiovanni-Trusty Job Satisfaction Questionnaire and the School Climate Profile (Part A).

305. Van Berkum, Clifford. "Living with Your Job." *Agricultural Education Magazine* 53, no. 3 (September 1980): 14.

   Discusses ways to improve the morale of vocational agriculture teachers.

306. Vandett, Nancy M. "One Point of View: So You Want to Be a Developmental Educator?" *Journal of Developmental and Remedial Education* 4, no. 3 (Spring 1981): 20-23.

   Lists the rewards of being a remedial teacher and discusses some of the drawbacks.

307. Weiner, Anne Marie. "Sex Role Preference and Job Satisfaction Among Secondary Home Economics Teachers." Ph.D. dissertation, The University of North Carolina at Greensboro, 1980.

   Studies the sex role preference, demographic variables, and job satisfaction of high school home economics teachers using the Measure of Sex Role Preference and the Job Description Index.

308. Wellington, Jerry. "The Flight from Physics Teaching." <u>Physics Education</u> 21, no. 2 (March 1986): 103-06.

    Presents case studies of physics teachers who left teaching; identifies factors contributing to low teacher morale.

309. Whaples, Gene C., and W. James Milliken. <u>An Exploratory Study of the Relationship of Job Satisfaction to Work Values in the Maryland Cooperative Extension Service</u>. 1977. ERIC, ED 154 133.

    Investigates the relationship between work values and job satisfaction using the Values for Working and the County Extension Agents' Job Satisfaction Inventory.

310. Wiggins, J.D. "The Relation of Job Satisfaction to Vocational Preferences Among Teachers of the Educable Mentally Retarded." <u>Journal of Vocational Behavior</u> 8, no. 1 (February 1976): 13-18.

    Administers the Hoppock Job Satisfaction Blank and the Vocational Preference Inventory to female teachers of the educable mentally retarded.

311. Wiggins, Jimmy Dale. "The Relationship Between Job Satisfaction and Vocational Preferences of Teachers of the Educable Mentally Retarded." Ed.D. dissertation, Indiana University, 1974.

    Uses the Holland Vocational Preference Inventory to predict job satisfaction of female teachers of the educable mentally retarded; uses the Hoppock Job Satisfaction Blank to measure satisfaction.

312. Wilson, Linda C. "A Profile of Female Agricultural Teachers in the Future Farmers of America Eastern Region and Their Job Satisfaction Level." Ed.D. dissertation, Virginia Polytechnic Institute and State University, 1980.

    Develops a profile of female agricultural teachers and discusses the relationship between demographic variables and job satisfaction using a Profile Questionnaire and the Minnesota Satisfaction Questionnaire.

313. Wright, Michael Duane. "Relationships Among Esteem, Autonomy, Job Satisfaction and the Intention to Quit Teaching of Downstate Illinois Industrial Education Teachers." Ed.D. dissertation, University of Illinois at Urbana-Champaign, 1985.

   Interviews industrial education teachers in terms of job satisfaction, esteem, autonomy, demographic variables, and the intention to quit teaching.

V. COLLEGE TEACHERS

314. Abreu, Jorge Rolando. "Job Satisfaction of the Faculty Members of the Schools of Education in Three Universities Granting Doctor of Philosophy Degrees in the State of Michigan." Ph.D. dissertation, The University of Michigan, 1980.

    Identifies and analyzes the importance of Herzberg's intrinsic factors to job satisfaction and Herzberg's extrinsic factors to job dissatisfaction of college teachers.

315. Ageel, Hamza Abdullah. "Job Satisfaction of Staff Members of Umm Al Qura University in Makkah, Saudi Arabia." Ph.D. dissertation, Michigan State University, 1982.

    Examines job satisfaction of college teachers using the Job Description Index and demographic variables; uses Herzberg's two factor theory for the conceptual basis.

316. Agte, Lloyd. *The Burned-Out Community College Humanities Instructor: Causes and Cures*. 1984. ERIC, ED 258 642.

    Discusses burnout among community college humanities teachers.

317. Alden, Steven Edward. "The Relationship Among Job Satisfaction, Attitudes Toward Collective Bargaining and Employment at Two- and Four-Year Institutions at the City University of New York and the State University of New York." Ph.D. dissertation, New York University, 1981.

    Explores the relationships among job satisfaction, type of institution, and attitudes toward collective bargaining of college teachers using the Herzberg and Maslow models.

318. Alder, Craig Eugene. "Relation of Structure to Satisfaction, Stress, and Performance Among Athletic Directors in Senior Colleges of the National Collegiate Athletic Association." Ed.D. dissertation, University of Northern Colorado, 1977.

    Presents information about the relationships between the organizational structure of university, and the job satisfaction, job-related stress, and job performance of athletic directors.

319. Alexander, Linda Louise. "A Causal Model of Turnover of Postsecondary Vocational Instructors Incorporating Demographic Factors, Work-Related Variables, and Job Satisfaction." Ph.D. dissertation, The University of Nebraska-Lincoln, 1986.

    Describes postsecondary vocational teachers at community colleges in terms of demographic variables, work-related factors, and job satisfaction using the Job Descriptive Index.

320. Allen, Robert E., and Timothy J. Keaveny. "Correlates of University Faculty Interest in Unionization: A Replication and Extension." Journal of Applied Psychology 66, no. 5 (October 1981): 582-588.

    Examines the relationships between perceived need for a union and age, salary level, and job satisfaction of college teachers.

321. Araghi, Manijeh Aghaseyed Khalil. "The Relationship Between University Faculty Job Satisfaction, Role Conflict, Task Clarity and Productivity." Ed.D. dissertation, University of Houston, 1981.

    Examines the relationship between role conflict, task clarity, productivity, and college teachers' job satisfaction using the Faculty Satisfaction with Rewards Instrument (adaptation), the Task Clarity and Role Conflict Instrument, and the Productivity Index developed by the researcher.

322. Asmussen, Christopher Burke. "College Faculty Satisfaction and Institutional Identification." Ph.D. dissertation, The Ohio State University, 1983.

    Explores the relationships of twenty-one variables on college teachers' job satisfaction and identification with their universities.

323. Assad, Soraya Wali El-Deen. "Women and Work in Saudi Arabia: A Study of Job Satisfaction in Higher Education." Ph.D. dissertation, Colorado State University, 1983.

    Explains key factors that contribute to female college teachers' job satisfaction.

324. Baird, Leonard L., and others. <u>Understanding Student and Faculty Life. Using Campus Surveys to Improve Academic Decision Making</u>. 1980. ERIC, ED 183 128.

    Provides a guide for assessing students and college faculty and describes how to interpret the results to improve the climate; includes a directory of instruments for assessing university environments.

325. Balazadeh, Gabriel. "A Comparative Study of Motivation to Work and Job Satisfaction Between Male and Female Faculty Members at a Midwestern Regional University." Ph.D. dissertation, University of Kansas, 1981.

    Tests the degree of differences that exist in motivation to work and job satisfaction between male and female college teachers using the Educational Work Component Study and the Job Descriptive Index.

326. Barlar, Douglas Garland. "Sources of Motivation Among College Music Faculty." Ph.D. dissertation, George Peabody College for Teachers of Vanderbilt University, 1983.

   Examines sources of satisfaction and dissatisfaction of college music teachers using Herzberg's Motivation-Hygiene Theory.

327. Barnes, Edwin Lewis. "Effects of Personality and Person-Environment Congruence on Job Satisfaction of Community College Faculty and Professional Staff." Ed.D. dissertation, Virginia Polytechnic Institute and State University, 1976.

   Investigates the effects of personality and person-environment congruence on job satisfaction of community college teachers using the Job Descriptive Index, Holland's Vocational Preference Inventory, and Holland's Environmental Assessment Technique.

328. Bednar, Anita Sparks. "The Relationship Between Job Satisfaction and Life Satisfaction Among Faculty in Selected Oklahoma Junior Colleges." Ph.D. dissertation, The University of Oklahoma, 1980.

   Tests the relationship between job satisfaction and life satisfaction among junior college teachers in terms of work itself, pay, supervision, co-workers, promotion, health, marriage, family, friends, and standard of living.

329. Boberg, Alice Duxter. "Faculty Under Stress: Person-Environment Fit Theory." Ph.D. dissertation, The University of Michigan, 1982.

   Studies the relationships between role stress and psychological strains of job and workload dissatisfaction among college teachers.

330. Bolding, James T., and James J. Van Patten. Creating a Healthy Organizational Climate. 1982. ERIC, ED 219 039.

   Reviews four areas of university management responsibility including individual stress and organizational health.

331. Bowen, Blannie Evans. "Job Satisfaction of Teacher Educators in Agriculture." Ph.D. dissertation, The Ohio State University, 1980.

   Describes the job satisfaction of agriculture college teachers using a modified version of an instrument developed by Wood to measure the 10 Herzberg motivator-hygiene factors and 14 items from the Brayfield-Rothe Job Satisfaction Index.

332. Boyenga, Kirk Warner. "Job Stress and Coping Behavior of Married Male and Female University Faculty Members." Ph.D. dissertation, Purdue University, 1978.

   Looks at gender, perceived job stress, marital satisfaction, job satisfaction, stress coping strategies, and other work output and demographic variables among assistant professors.

333. Briscoe, Mary Louise. "Reflections on Academic Burnout." ADE Bulletin 79 (Winter 1984): 1-7.

   Examines causes of college teachers' burnout.

334. Broesamie, John J. Academic Turbulence and the Crisis of Professional Satisfaction. 1984. ERIC, ED 253 155.

   Considers problems affecting college teachers and reasons for staying in the profession.

335. Brookes, Michael Clifford Todd. Generativity, Stuckness, and Insulation: Community College Faculty in Massachusetts. 1980. ERIC, ED 210 053.

   Examines the psychosocial conditions of generativity and stagnation and personal characteristics related to these conditions among community college teachers; designs a job satisfaction scale.

336. Buhmeyer, Kenneth J., and Hurshell H. Hunt. "Job Satisfaction and Level of Aspiration in Academic Employees." <u>Perceptual and Motor Skills</u> 54, no. 1 (February 1982): 290.

    Assesses job satisfaction, level of aspiration, years employed, age, and sex; finds support for Kalleberg's work on different sources of job satisfaction for different occupations.

337. Bulls, Bobby Stieh. "Values as a Predictor of Job Satisfaction of Business Technology Faculty Among Selected Community Colleges." Ed.D. dissertation, Virginia Polytechnic Institute and State University, 1980.

    Explores the relationship between values and job satisfaction of college business teachers using the Job Descriptive Index and the Rokeach Value Survey.

338. Campbell, Janis Maria Graham. "A Job Satisfaction Survey Study for Nursing Educators in Baccalaureate Nursing Programs." Ph.D. dissertation, The Ohio State University, 1978.

    Identifies sources of job satisfaction and dissatisfaction among college nursing teachers using a questionnaire adapted from Wood's study reflecting Herzberg's intrinsic and extrinsic factors.

339. Cares, Robert C., and Robert T. Blackburn. "Faculty Self-Actualization: Factors Affecting Career Success." <u>Research in Higher Education</u> 9, no. 2 (October 1978): 123-136.

    Measures the relationship between four personal variables related to college teacher growth and development, two environmental indices, and career success and job satisfaction.

340. Cares, Robert Calvin. "Self-Actualization Attitudes of Faculty and Their Perceptions of Their Career Success." Ph.D. dissertation, The University of Michigan, 1975.

    Studies the relationship of college teachers' career success and satisfaction perceptions with trust, support, tolerance, democratization and environmental control.

341. Cassara, Shirley. "Increasing Job Satisfaction for Community College Faculty and Professional Staff Through a Stress Management Model." Ed.D. dissertation, University of Massachusetts, 1983.

    Examines mature professional developmental level, locus of control, stress management, and job satisfaction of community college teachers.

342. Chan, Roy Chin-Ming. "A Profile of Job Satisfaction for Graduate Physical Education Faculty Members." Ph.D. dissertation, North Texas State University, 1986.

    Profiles graduate physical education college teachers in terms of job satisfaction using the Job Descriptive Index.

343. Chapey, Geraldine M. "The Development of a Structure for Interpreting Human Relations Constructs in Higher Education." Doctoral dissertation, Rutgers University, The State University of New Jersey, New Brunswick, 1983.

    Investigates perceived need importance and job satisfaction among union leaders employed as college teachers using the Maslow Needs Hierarchy Questionnaire.

344. Christian, Patricia L. "The Relationship Between Faculty Expectations and Perceptions of the Department Chairperson's Role and Job Satisfaction of the Faculty." Ph.D. dissertation, The University of North Carolina at Chapel Hill, 1983.

    Focuses on the relationship between the discrepancy and job satisfaction of college teachers using the Job Descriptive Index.

345. Coltrin, Sally, and William F. Glueck. "The Effect of Leadership Roles on the Satisfaction and Productivity of University Research Professors." *Academy of Management Journal* 20, no. 1 (March 1977): 101-116.

    Discusses the influence of administrators' style, role model, and reward efforts on the job satisfaction of research professors.

346. Corcoran, Mary, and Shirley M. Clark. *Professional Socialization and Contemporary Career Attitudes of Three Faculty Generations*. AIR 1983 Annual Forum Paper. 1983. ERIC, ED 232 597.

    Compares the career socialization and present career attitudes of three groups of college teachers as one indicator of faculty vitality.

347. Corcoran, Mary, and Shirley M. Clark. *Development of Guidelines for Policy-Relevant Studies of Faculty Vitality Through an Institutional Case Study*. 1983. ERIC, ED 245 655.

    Describes faculty vitality in terms of organizational change, boundary maintenance, internal environments, control systems, reward systems, and job satisfaction and morale.

348. Cote, Margaret M. "Pride and Prejudice in the Teaching Profession." *Teaching English in the Two-Year College*, 8, no. 2 (Winter 1982): 87-90.

    Discusses opportunities for financial and nonfinancial satisfaction for college English teachers.

349. Cowan, Carole Anne. "A Study of Faculty Perceptions of Selected Morale Variables." Ed.D. dissertation, University of Massachusetts, 1982.

    Surveys community college teachers to identify the rewards that contribute to job satisfaction using a list of job satisfiers to be rank ordered.

350. Cupo, Anthony Francis. "New Jersey Public Community College Professors: A Study of the Relationships Between Compensatory and Spillover Leisure Activities and Level of Job Satisfaction." Ed.D. dissertation, Rutgers University, the State University of New Jersey, 1983.

   Studies the relationship between leisure activities and job satisfaction among community college teachers using the Minnesota Satisfaction Questionnaire (Short Form) and the Leisure Activities Questionnaire.

351. Davis, Larry, Ramon Cartwright, Phyllis Freeman, and Louis Carter. "A Qualitative Look at Black Female Social Work Educators." <u>Journal of Sociology and Social Welfare</u> 9, no. 1 (March 1982): 146-153.

   Assesses the job satisfaction of Black female college teachers.

352. De Frain, Jo Ann H. "College Teachers' Work Motivation, Central Life Interests, and Voluntarism as Predictors of Job Satisfaction and Job Performance." Ed.D. dissertation, University of Kansas, 1979.

   Investigates the ability to work motivation, central life interests, and voluntarism to predict college teachers' job satisfaction and job performance.

353. DeHart, A. Robert. "Thank God It's Monday." <u>Community and Junior College Journal</u> 52, no. 6 (March 1982): 12-15.

   Identifies factors that erode organizational vitality among college teachers and factors that influence personal vitality development.

354. Desroches, Jocelyn Jean-Yves. "The Concept and Determinants of Job Satisfaction: An Exploratory Study in the Colleges of Applied Arts and Technology in Ontario." Ph.D. dissertation, University of Toronto (Canada), 1976.

    Explores the determinants of college teachers' job satisfaction and generates a typology of four sub-components.

355. Diener, Thomas. "Job Satisfaction and College Faculty in Two Predominantly Black Institutions." <u>Journal of Negro Education</u> 54, no. 4 (Fall 1985): 558-565.

    Presents sources of satisfaction and dissatisfaction at two predominantly black colleges.

356. Dill, Gary A. <u>Do You Hear What I Hear? A Response to Faculty Perceptions</u>. 1985. ERIC, ED 279 263.

    Discusses causes of morale problems among college teachers.

357. Dobson, Cynthia, and Paula C. Morrow. "Effects of Career Orientation on Retirement Attitudes and Retirement Planning." <u>Journal of Vocational Behavior</u> 24, no. 1 (February 1984): 73-83.

    Examines career orientation, work commitment, job satisfaction, demographic variables, and retirement attitudes of college teachers.

358. Donahue, James Marie. "A Comparison of Factors Influencing Job Satisfaction and Dissatisfaction of Nursing Faculty with Faculty in Other Departments of Selected Private Liberal Arts Colleges in the Midwest." Ph.D. dissertation, The University of Iowa, 1978.

    Compares the job satisfaction of nursing faculty to liberal arts faculty using the Modified Friedlander Scale.

359. Dougherty, Thomas W., Allen C. Bluedorn, and Thomas L. Keon. "Precursors of Employee Turnover: A Multiple-Sample Causal Analysis." <u>Journal of Occupational Behaviour</u> 6, no. 4 (October 1985): 259-271.

    Measures job satisfaction, organizational commitment, intention to resign, and turnover rate of college teachers.

360. Douglas, Joel M., ed. <u>Collective Bargaining and the Quality of Work Life, Faculty Election Results Still Undecided, the Decennium Conference, a Modest Attitudinal Survey on Ten Years of Collective Bargaining</u>. 1982. ERIC, ED 219 003.

    Addresses the issues of collective bargaining and the quality of work life; defines quality of work life as changes in one's work environment in order to improve morale and stimulate motivation.

361. Driscoll, James W. "Trust and Participation in Organizational Decision Making as Predictors of Satisfaction." <u>Academy of Management Journal</u> 21, no. 1 (March 1978): 44-56.

    Assesses the importance of trust and participation in decision making as predictors of college teachers' job satisfaction.

362. Earp, William Arthur, Sr. "The Effect of Participation in Collaborative Supervision on Cooperating Teachers' Job Satisfaction and on Their Evaluation of Fellow Teachers, Student Teachers, and Supervisors as Sources of New Instructional Ideas." Ed.D. dissertation, The University of Tennessee, 1975.

    Investigates the effects of participation in collaborative supervision on cooperating teachers' job satisfaction using the Purdue Teacher Opinionaire.

363. Ejiogu, Aloy M. "Participative Management in a Developing Economy: Poison or Placebo?" *Journal of Applied Behavioral Science* 19, no. 3 (1983): 239-247.

    Examines the importance of 15 work-value variables from the Work Values Inventory among college teachers.

364. Fearnow, Charles D. "A Comparative Analysis of a Four- and Five-Day Workweek Among Community College Faculty with Respect to Job Satisfaction." Doctoral dissertation, University of Maryland, 1985.

    Compares job satisfaction and dissatisfaction of community college teachers with different work schedules using a modification of the Job Satisfaction/Dissatisfaction Scale.

365. Feild, Hubert S., and William F. Giles. "Dimensions of Faculty Members' Sensitivity to Job Satisfaction Items." *Research in Higher Education* 6, no. 3 (May 1977): 193-199.

    Discusses the results from the Faculty Job Attitude Survey administered to college teachers at a large university.

366. Findley, Benjamin Flavious, Jr. "The Relationship Among Selected Personal Variables and Job Satisfaction of College Business Teachers in Colorado." Ed.D. dissertation, University of Northern Colorado, 1975.

    Identifies factors in the work environment that contribute to job satisfaction among college business teachers using the Minnesota Satisfaction Questionnaire; examines the relationship between personal variables and job satisfaction.

367. Fink, L. Dee. "First Year on the Faculty: Being There." *Journal of Geography in Higher Education* 8, no. 1 (1984): 11-25.

    Studies the transition from graduate student to full-time college geography teacher; presents information about factors that affect performance and satisfaction.

368. Fink, L. Dee. "The Situational Factors Affecting Teaching." New Directions for Teaching and Learning (The First Year of College Teaching), no. 17 (March 1984): 37-60.

Examines situational factors affecting the teaching of college geography teachers.

369. Fink, L. Dee. First Year on the Faculty: A Study of 100 Beginning College Teachers. 1982. ERIC, ED 222 109.

Explores the relationship among type of contract, work load, degree of identification with the institution and ability to find intellectual companionship with peers and job satisfaction of new college geography teachers.

370. Flaningam, Rita Rice, and Shannon V. Taylor. "Part-Time Faculty: Gender Differences in Job Duties, Support, and Satisfaction." Journal of the National Association of Women Deans, Administrators, and Counselors 47, no. 3 (Spring 1984): 8-13.

Surveys part-time, full-time, and nontenure track college teachers.

371. Fordham, Walter Malval, Jr. "An Investigation of the Effects of Perceived Teacher Stress and Perceived Work Environment Complexity on Job Satisfaction of the Physical Education Faculty in Division I-AA Colleges and Universities." Ph.D. dissertation, The Florida State University, 1986.

Investigates the effects of perceived teacher stress and work environment complexity on job satisfaction of college physical education teachers using the Perceived Work Environment Measure, the Teacher Occupational Stress Factor Questionnaire, and the Job Descriptive Index.

372. Fowler, Deborah Lynn. "An Analysis of Sex and Departmental Differences in the Perceptions of Assistant Professors Regarding Work Environments, Mentoring, and Academic Employment." Ph.D. dissertation, University of Illinois at Urbana-Champaign, 1980.

    Analyzes sex and departmental differences in the perceptions of assistant professors regarding satisfaction with their departmental work environment, the quality of mentoring relationships, and academic employment.

373. Fox, Gary C. "Factors that Motivate Part-Time Faculty." Community Services Catalyst 14, no. 1 (Winter 1984): 17-21.

    Describes the Nominal Group Technique and its application in identifying conditions that help or hinder college teachers' effectiveness.

374. Freeman, Nancy S. Role Orientation of Community College Occupational Faculty. 1981. ERIC, ED 211 142.

    Compares vocational education teachers in terms of part-time and full-time employment, cosmopolitan/local theory, and role orientation.

375. Friedlander, Jack. "The Relationship Between General Job Satisfaction and Specific Work-Activity Satisfaction of Community College Faculty." Community/Junior College Research Quarterly 2, no. 3 (April-June 1978): 227-239.

    Examines general and specific work-activity satisfaction measures of community college teachers.

376. Fuller, Jack. Morale Is Bad. 1985. ERIC, ED 266 815.

    Describes the problem of declining morale among community college teachers.

377. Gaite, A. J. H., and others. The TAFE Project: The Teaching Functions and Activities of Technical College Teachers in Western Australia. Co-operative Research Series Report No. 4. 1980. ERIC, ED 209 199.

   Develops a profile of Technical and Further Education college teachers.

378. Giles, William F., and Hubert S. Feild. "Effects of Amount, Format, and Location of Demographic Information on Questionnaire Return Rate and Response Bias of Sensitive and Nonsensitive Items." Personnel Psychology 31, no. 3 (Fall 1978): 549-559.

   Administers a job satisfaction survey to college teachers and analyzes responses including demographic variables, format, and placement of items.

379. Giles, William F., and Hubert S. Feild. "The Relationship of Satisfaction Level and Content of Job Satisfaction Questionnaire Items to Item Sensitivity." Academy of Management Journal 21, no. 2 (June 1978): 295-301.

   Investigates the relationship between item satisfaction and item sensitivity among college teachers using a job satisfaction questionnaire.

380. Gomez-Meijia, Luis R., and David B. Balkin. "Faculty Satisfaction with Pay and Other Job Dimensions Under Union and Nonunion Conditions." Academy of Management Journal 27, no. 3 (September 1984): 591-602.

   Compares union and nonunion college teachers' job satisfaction using five measures of job satisfaction and a pay satisfaction scale.

381. Gonnet, Katherine Ann McDonald. "An Investigation of Eleven Job Satisfaction Variables as They Pertain to Full-Time Community College Faculty." Ed.D. dissertation, North Texas State University, 1983.

   Investigates eleven factors of job satisfaction among full-time community college teachers using Herzberg's theory as a foundation for selecting items for the HEMI Faculty Attitude Survey.

382. Goodwin, Dennis Harold. "A Comparative Study of the Perceptions of Faculty and Administrators Regarding the Importance of Selected Factors in Determining Faculty Job Satisfaction in the Alabama Public Junior Colleges." Ph.D. dissertation, University of Southern Mississippi, 1978.

    Compares the perceptions of college teachers and administrators in junior colleges who have influence over many of the factors affecting the job satisfaction of college teachers.

383. Grandjean, Burke D., Linda H. Aiken, and Charles M. Bonjean. "Professional Autonomy and the Work Satisfaction of Nursing Educators." Nursing Research 25, no. 3 (May-June 1976): 216-221.

    Examines the job satisfaction of nursing teachers with twenty-one job characteristics.

384. Haji-Hashim, Abu Bakar. "An Analysis of Job Satisfaction Among Academic Staff of Universities in Malaysia." Ph.D. dissertation, Ohio University, 1985.

    Studies college teachers' job satisfaction using the facet and overall approaches; uses the Brayfield-Rothe Index and develops a facet questionnaire.

385. Hammer, Tove H., and Michael Berman. "The Role of Noneconomic Factors in Faculty Union Voting." Journal of Applied Psychology 66, no. 4 (August 1981): 415-421.

    Discusses satisfaction with the content of the work and satisfaction with economic issues on pro-union voting among full-time college faculty at a private college.

386. Hanser, Lawrence M., and Paul M. Muchinsky. "Work as an Information Environment." Organizational Behavior and Human Performance 21, no. 1 (February 1978): 47-60.

    Indicates that college teachers are able to distinguish between job satisfactions and the work information environment as constructs using the

Job Descriptive Index and factor analysis of sources of information in a work environment items.

387. Hanser, Lawrence Morley. "Employee Information Environments and Job Satisfaction: A Closer Look." Ph.D. dissertation, Iowa State University, 1977.

    Investigates the relationship of the work environment to job satisfaction among college teachers using the Job Descriptive Index.

388. Harrison, Murelle Guidry. "Job Satisfaction Among Faculty Members in a Large Black Southern University." Ph.D. dissertation, Louisiana State University and Agricultural and Mechanical College, 1979.

    Explores the effects of sex, rank, and age on the overall job satisfaction of black college teachers.

389. Harshberger, Richard Francis. "Job Satisfaction/ Dissatisfaction and the Motivation to Work of Full-time University Teaching Faculty: An Analysis." Ed.D. dissertation, North Carolina State University at Raleigh, 1975.

    Tests Herzberg's Motivator-Hygiene Theory among college teachers using an instrument designed by the researcher.

390. Hashemi, Alireza Shapur. "An Investigation of Job Satisfaction Among Faculty Members of a Large Multi-Purpose University in the Dallas-Fort Worth Metroplex." Ph.D. dissertation, North Texas State University, 1985.

    Investigates job satisfaction of full-time college teachers in relation to gender, rank, and types of activity using the Job Descriptive Index.

391. Higgs, Colin. "Job Satisfaction of Canadian University Physical Education Faculty: The Influence of Work Orientation, Career Stage, Role Conflict, and Role Ambiguity." Ph.D. dissertation, University of Oregon, 1985.

   Explores the relationships among role conflict, role ambiguity, career stage, local work orientation, and cosmopolitan work orientation and intrinsic and extrinsic job satisfaction among college teachers.

392. Hill, Earl A. <u>A Study of Commitment to the Work Organization Among Community College Teachers of Developmental/Remedial Courses</u>. 1984. ERIC, ED 245 764.

   Conducts a study to examine the relationships among community college teachers' self-role congruence, length of service, total job satisfaction, organizational commitment, and the propensity to leave the university.

393. Hill, Earl Augustus. "The Impact of Self-Role Congruence, Length of Service, Job Satisfaction and Organizational Commitment on Propensity to Leave: A Study of Community College Instructors of Developmental/Remedial Courses." Ph.D. dissertation, New York University, 1983.

   Ascertains whether, and to what degree, five facets of total job satisfaction are related to organizational and value commitment and to the propensity to leave among community college teachers.

394. Hill, Malcolm D. "Faculty Sex Composition and Job Satisfaction of Academic Women." <u>International Journal of Women's Studies</u> 7, no. 2 (March-April 1984): 179-188.

   Compares job satisfaction of women in more highly male-dominated universities and less highly male-dominated universities.

395. Hollon, C. J., and G. R. Gemmill. "Interpersonal Trust and Personal Effectiveness in the Work Environment." *Psychological Reports* 40, no. 2 (April 1977): 454.

    Shows that orientation toward interpersonal trust was positively related to participation in decision making and college teachers' job satisfaction using the Interpersonal Trust Scale and the Job-Related Tension Index.

396. Holt, Frances Goodwin. "The Relationship of Need Fulfillment to Job Attitudes of Faculty in Higher Education." Ed.D. dissertation, The College of William and Mary in Virginia, 1981.

    Examines the need-satisfaction and job-satisfaction linkage in the need-satisfaction model among college teachers using a shortened form of the Maslow Satisfaction Items, the Job Descriptive Index and Rotter's Internal-External Scale.

397. Hopkins, Charles E., and Margaret M. Sullivan. *Organizational Change: Implications for Institutional Research.* 1981. ERIC, ED 210 997.

    Designs a survey instrument to measure political, sociological, and communication dimensions among college teachers.

398. Hoth, Evelyn Knott. "Factors of Faculty Job Satisfaction as Related to Communication Satisfaction." Ph.D. dissertation, Wayne State University, 1979.

    Tests Hoy-Miskel's three-factory theory of job satisfaction among college teachers using the Job Descriptive Index and the Communication Satisfaction Questionnaire.

399. Hudson, Larry Robert. "The Relationship Between Job Satisfaction and Selected Factors of Teaching Workload." Ph.D. dissertation, The University of Iowa, 1981.

    Defines teaching workload items and identifies their relationships with overall job satisfaction among college teachers.

400. Hunter, Mary, and others. "Morale Maladies in American and Foreign Higher Education: The Faculty Flameout Diagnosis." Texas Tech Journal of Education 10, no. 2 (Spring 1983): 101-113.

 Reports that morale is low among college teachers; offers suggestions for improving morale.

401. Hutton, Jerry B., and Max E. Jobe. "Job Satisfaction of Community College Faculty." Community/Junior College Quarterly of Research and Practice 9, no. 4 (1985): 317-324.

 Studies community college teachers' job satisfaction using the Job Satisfaction Inventory.

402. Ibrahim, Jamil Mahmud. "Job Satisfaction of Faculty Members at Selected Southern Universities." Ph.D. dissertation, University of Southern Mississippi, 1985.

 Explores the relationships among demographic variables and job satisfaction among college teachers using a modified version of the Minnesota Satisfaction Questionnaire.

403. Indiresan, Jayalakshmi. "Bureaucratic Orientation and Job Satisfaction: A Cross Cultural Study of British and Indian Engineering Teachers." Indian Journal of Applied Psychology 19, no. 1 (January 1982): 43-50.

 Studies job satisfaction, bureaucratic orientation, and job involvement among engineering teachers using the Job Satisfaction Index and the Work Environment Preference Schedule.

404. Indiresan, Jayalakshmi. "Job Satisfaction of Engineering Teachers: A Cross-Cultural Study." Indian Journal of Applied Psychology 18, no. 1 (January 1981): 16-26.

 Compares English and Indian college teachers in relation to job satisfaction, career plans, job saliency, job involvement, financial position, and bureaucratic organization using the Job Satisfaction

Inventory, the Work Environment Preference Schedule, and a job involvement inventory.

405. Indiresan, Jayalakshmi. "Multivariate Analysis of Factors Affecting the Job Satisfaction of Engineering Teachers." *Indian Journal of Psychometry and Education* 6, nos. 1-2 (1975): 16-27.

    Identifies individual and situational factors that discriminate between highly satisfied and highly dissatisfied engineering teachers.

406. Jackson, Nancy Ann. "Satisfaction of Job Related Needs of Nursing Faculty." Ph.D. dissertation, University of Pittsburgh, 1981.

    Uses a modification of Alderfer's interview guide to determine if perceptions of existence, relatedness, and growth needs satisfaction differed among college nursing teachers.

407. Jackson, William K., and Judith B. Chandler, eds. *National Conference on Professional and Personal Renewal for Faculty. Proceedings (Atlanta, Georgia, April 10-12, 1986).* 1986. ERIC, ED 276 393.

    Discusses strategies for promoting faculty renewal in the proceedings of the 1986 National Conference on Professional and Personal Renewal for Faculty.

408. Kaplan, Leah Eileen. "Academic Health Educators: Demographic and Professional Descriptors, Levels of Job Satisfaction and Professional Attitudes." Ph.D. dissertation, Southern Illinois University at Carbondale, 1984.

    Examines professional and demographic variables, job satisfaction, and professionalism of health educators using the Hafan Job Satisfaction Index and the Bartol Professionalism Scale.

409. Karoonlanjakorn, Suthep. "Job Satisfaction Among Faculty Members at Non-Metropolitan Teachers Colleges in Central Thailand." Ph.D. dissertation, North Texas State University, 1986.

   Determines facet job satisfaction and overall job satisfaction among college teachers using the Faculty Job Satisfaction/Dissatisfaction Scale.

410. Kaufman, Allan Harvey. "A National Job Satisfaction Study of Industrial Arts Teacher Educators." Ph.D. dissertation, The Ohio State University, 1976.

   Develops the National Job Satisfaction Study Instrument to evaluate the primary job satisfactions of college industrial arts teachers.

411. Kim, Jai Bun. "Relationship of the Leadership Behavior of Nursing Educational Administrators and Job Satisfaction of Nursing Faculty Members in Korea." Ph.D. dissertation, George Peabody College for Teachers of Vanderbilt University, 1983.

   Investigates the relationship between leadership styles of nursing administrators and job satisfaction of college nursing teachers using the Leader Behavior Description Questionnaire and the Job Description Index.

412. Klapachan, Prachaya. "A Study of the Relationships Between Participation in the Decision-Making Process and Job Satisfaction Among the Faculty of a Midwestern Regional State University." Ph.D. dissertation, University of Kansas, 1983.

   Examines the relationships between demographic variables, participation in the decision-making process, and job satisfaction among college teachers using a modified form of the Job Descriptive Index.

413. Knoop, Robert. "A Test of Path-Goal Theory: Work Values as Moderators of Relations of Leaders and Subordinates." <u>Psychological Reports</u> 51, no. 1 (August 1982): 39-43.

    Investigates the influence of work values on the relationship between leaders' behavior and college teachers' job satisfaction.

414. Lacewell, William Edwin. "Job Satisfaction of Full-Time Faculty in the Community Colleges and Area Post-Secondary Vocational-Technical Schools of Arkansas: An Analysis Based on Herzberg's Motivator-Hygiene Theory." Ed.D. dissertation, University of Arkansas, 1983.

    Measures job satisfaction of community college teachers using Herzberg's Motivator-Hygiene Theory.

415. Ladd, Everett Carll, Jr. <u>The Work Experience of American College Professors: Some Data and an Argument.</u> 1979. ERIC, ED 184 406.

    Surveys professional activities, concerns, and commitments of college teachers.

416. Losik, Robert Conrad. "A Study of the Effects of Participation in Decision Making by Adjunct Faculty in Continuing Education." Ed.D. dissertation, George Peabody College for Teachers of Vanderbilt University, 1984.

    Explores the effects of participation in decision making by adjunct college teachers on job satisfaction.

417. May, Barry Robert. "A Study of Herzberg's Motivation-Hygiene Theory of Job Satisfaction as It Relates to Academic Personnel in Selected Small Liberal Arts Colleges." Ph.D. dissertation, University of Illinois at Urbana-Champaign, 1976.

    Investigates Herzberg's Motivation-Hygiene Theory in relation to the job satisfaction and dissatisfaction of college teachers.

418. McNair, Betty S. "The Relationships Between Selected Faculty Characteristics and Teaching Effectiveness." Ph.D. dissertation, Georgia State University--College of Education, 1980.

    Focuses on the relationship between effectiveness and job satisfaction among college teachers.

419. Melendez, Winifred Albizu, and Rafael M. de Guzman. <u>Burnout: The New Academic Disease. ASHE-ERIC Higher Education Research Report No. 9.</u> 1983. ERIC, ED 242 255.

    Reviews the literature on burnout and offers ways to minimize or eliminate burnout in colleges.

420. Mellinger, George Paul. "An Investigation of Academic Job Satisfaction/Dissatisfaction in a Small Struggling Liberal Arts College." Ph.D. dissertation, University of Pittsburgh, 1982.

    Compares job satisfaction/dissatisfaction of college teachers and administrators using the Faculty Job Satisfaction Survey.

421. Miller, Gary Arthur. "Organizational Climate and Job Satisfaction of Independent College Faculty." Ph.D. dissertation, The University of Nebraska-Lincoln, 1986.

    Measures the job satisfaction and perceived organizational climate of college teachers using the Job Descriptive Index and Likert scales.

422. Mitcham, Maralynne Denise. "Job Satisfaction and the Impact of Individualized Contract Plans as a Method of Performance Evaluation for Allied Health Faculty." Ph.D. dissertation, University of Georgia, 1983.

    Studies individualized contract plans and the job satisfaction of allied health faculty using the Job Satisfaction Among Allied Health Faculty Scale.

423. Morgan, Thomas David. "An Investigation of the Factors Influencing Job Satisfaction-Dissatisfaction of Physical Education and Athletic Personnel in Selected Small Liberal Arts Colleges." Ph.D. dissertation, University of Illinois at Urbana-Champaign, 1974.

   Evaluates the applicability of Herzberg's Motivator-Hygiene Theory and ascertains the factors that physical education college teachers perceive as contributing to job satisfaction and dissatisfaction.

424. Morioka, Haruko Nagatani. "Herzberg's Theory Applied to Graduate Faculty in Departments of Physical Education Offering Doctoral Degrees." Ph.D. dissertation, The University of Iowa, 1983.

   Determines job factors that influence job satisfaction and dissatisfaction among physical education college teachers using Herzberg's satisfiers and dissatisfiers.

425. Murray, Malinda Lou. "Job Satisfaction and Job Dissatisfaction Experienced by Nurse-Faculty in Baccalaureate Nursing Programs." Ed.D. dissertation, Columbia University Teachers College, 1983.

   Identifies sources of job satisfaction and dissatisfaction among nursing teachers using a modified version of a Job Satisfaction/Dissatisfaction questionnaire based on Herzberg's Motivation-Hygiene Theory.

426. Myers, Lilian Bautista. "Cognitive Style Compatibility and Job Satisfaction of University Personnel: An Exploratory Study." Ed.D. dissertation, Oklahoma State University, 1980.

   Explores the relationship between cognitive style compatibility and job satisfaction among college teachers using the Embedded Figures Test and the Minnesota Satisfaction Questionnaire.

427. Neely, Janet Henchie. "A Study of Socialization and Job Satisfaction of Faculty at an Urban Two-Year Community College." Ph.D. dissertation, The Ohio State University, 1981.

    Measures intrinsic, extrinsic, and general job satisfaction among community college teachers and relates them to outside employment and socialization programs.

428. Neumann, Yoram, and Lily Neumann. "Faculty Work Orientations as Predictors of Work Attitudes in the Physical and Social Sciences." Journal of Vocational Behavior 21, no. 3 (December 1982): 359-365.

    Examines the relationship between specific and global work orientations to extrinsic and intrinsic attitudes toward career attraction, work satisfaction, and commitment among physical and social science college teachers.

429. Newton, Thomas Allen. "An Investigation of the Relationship Between Job Satisfaction and Social Interaction for Professors of Educational Administration." Ed.D. dissertation, Oklahoma State University, 1979.

    Investigates the relationship between perceived job satisfaction and social interaction among educational administration faculty using the Job Descriptive Index.

430. Nolan, Charles J., Jr. "The Joys of Teaching." Journal of General Education 36, no. 1 (1984): 46-49.

    Emphasizes the personal and emotional factors that attract and retain college teachers.

431. Olasiji, Thompson Dele. "Application of the Motivator-Hygiene Theory of Job Satisfaction and Job Dissatisfaction Among Administrators and Academic Staff of a Selected University in Nigeria." Ph.D. dissertation, The University of Oklahoma, 1983.

    Discusses factors that lead to job satisfaction and dissatisfaction among college teachers using Herzberg's theory.

432. Openshaw, Howard. "Job Satisfaction Determinants Among Faculty and Administrators: An Application of Herzberg's Motivation-Hygiene Model in Higher Education." Ph.D. dissertation, Georgia State University--College of Education, 1980.

    Conducts a study to test Herzberg's Motivation-Hygiene Theory of job satisfaction and dissatisfaction among college faculty.

433. Pacheco, Aimee. "A Study of Sex-Role Attitudes, Job-Involvement and Job-Satisfaction of Women Faculty at the University of Puerto Rico, Rio Piedras." Ph.D. dissertation, New York University, 1981.

    Identifies personal and professional characteristics of women faculty and examines their attitudes toward female roles and work using the Attitudes Toward Women Scale, the Job Involvement Scale, and the Minnesota Satisfaction Questionnaire.

434. Panrat-Isra, Suporn. "A Study of Educators' Perceptions Concerning Teacher Education in Selected Institutes in Thailand." Ed.D. dissertation, Oklahoma State University, 1982.

    Investigates the perceptions of vocational-technical college teachers toward teacher education training needs and job satisfaction.

435. Pearson, Della A., and Robert E. Seiler. "Environmental Satisfiers in Academe." *Higher Education* 12, no. 1 (January 1983): 35-47.

    Explores job satisfaction among college teachers.

436. Peters, Antoinette S., and Ross Markello. "Job Satisfaction Among Academic Physicians: Attitudes Toward Job Components." Journal of Medical Education 57, no. 12 (December 1982): 937-939.

   Analyzes the degree of congruence between what college physician teachers like to do and what they feel is necessary using a rank order of five job components.

437. Peters, Dianne S., and J. Robert Mayfield. "Are There Any Rewards for Teaching?" Improving College and University Teaching 30, no. 3 (Summer 1982): 105-110.

   Surveys college faculty about the reward system for teaching and research.

438. Phillips, Herbert. The Care and Feeding of Part-Time Teachers. 1984. ERIC, ED 251 144.

   Discusses the role of part-time community college teachers and highlights elements for improving morale.

439. Poindexter, Jeanette O'Neal. "The Relationship of Role Conflict and Role Ambiguity to Job Satisfaction Among College-Level Nursing Faculty." Ph.D. dissertation, The University of Michigan, 1982.

   Examines the relationship between perceptions of role conflict and role ambiguity with job satisfaction among college nursing teachers using the Role Conflict and Role Ambiguity Questionnaire and the Job Descriptive Index.

440. Polejewski, Shirley Ann Super. "Accounting Educators: Characteristics, Attitudes, Job Satisfaction and Commitment of Faculties Housed in Degree Granting Programs in a Select Area of the State of Minnesota." Ph.D. dissertation, University of Minnesota, 1983.

   Measures, analyzes, and compares job satisfaction and commitment among college accounting teachers.

441. Powell, J. P. "The Impact of the Steady State on the Professional Lives of Academics." *Vestes* 24, no. 1 (1981): 27-31.

    Studies the effects of enrollment and economic changes on faculty morale.

442. Prachadetsuwat, Narong. "An Investigation into the Sources of Job Satisfaction and Dissatisfaction as Perceived by Faculty Members and Administrators in Selected Private Higher Education Institutions in Thailand." Ed.D. dissertation, Northern Illinois University, 1985.

    Explains sources of job satisfaction and dissatisfaction among college teachers using Herzberg's Motivation-Hygiene Theory.

443. Prescott, William. "Job Preparation and Turnover Among University Music Department Chairs and Band Directors." Ed.D. dissertation, The University of Arizona, 1983.

    Investigates preparatory, compensatory, psychological (degree of job satisfaction), and demographic variables in relation to turnover among college music teachers.

444. Ramsden, Patricia Ann. "The Relationship Between Part-Time Faculty Job Satisfaction and Perceptions of Division Chairpersons' Leadership Behavior in Community Colleges." Ed.D. dissertation, George Peabody College for Teachers of Vanderbilt University, 1983.

    Explores the relationship between the job satisfaction of part-time community college teachers and their perceptions of the leadership behavior of their supervisors using the Minnesota Satisfaction Questionnaire (Short Form) and the Leadership Behavior Description Questionnaire (Form 12).

445. Ramsey, June K. <u>Faculty Perceptions of Institutional Quality and Vitality</u>. 1982. ERIC, ED 229 084.

    Surveys community college teachers in 1980 and 1982 to determine their present level of job satisfaction.

446. Ramsey, June Killinger. "A Survey of Attitudes, Perspectives, and Job Satisfaction Among Selected Community College Academic Faculty." Ph.D. dissertation, The Florida State University, 1981.

    Studies traditional/progressive perspectives and job satisfaction among community college teachers using a modification of Kerlinger's ESVII and a job satisfaction scale.

447. Rees, Mary A. "University Music Faculty: Work Attitudes, Recognition, and Satisfaction." Doctoral dissertation, University of Oregon, 1985.

    Examines differences among three types of music faculty in terms of job-related activities, status, rewards, and job satisfaction.

448. Reiss, Michele Ann. "The Role Strain, Job Satisfaction, and Career Experiences of Working Mothers in Academia at Various Stages of the Family Life Cycle." Ph.D. dissertation, University of Pittsburgh, 1983.

    Analyzes role strain, job satisfaction, career patterns and problems among college women teachers using a Career Survey Form, Hoppock's Job Satisfaction Blank Number Five, and a Role Strain Interview Schedule.

449. Riday, George E., and others. "Satisfaction of Community College Faculty: Exploding a Myth." <u>Community College Review</u> 12, no. 3 (Winter 1985): 46-50.

    Compares job satisfaction/dissatisfaction among secondary school, community college, and four-year college teachers.

450. Riday, George Eric. "Job Satisfaction: A Comparative Study of Community College Faculty to Secondary School and Four-Year College Faculty." Ed.D. dissertation, Brigham Young University, 1981.

   Compares job satisfaction of teachers from three different educational settings in terms of Achievement, Interpersonal Relations, Salary, Work Itself, and Working Conditions.

451. Ridnour, Rick E. "An Investigation of the Relationship Between Characteristics of Self-Actualization and of Job Satisfaction of Selected Faculty in Higher Education." Ph.D. dissertation, Iowa State University, 1985.

   Examines the relationship between self-actualization and the job satisfaction of college business teachers using the Personal Orientation Inventory and the Minnesota Satisfaction Questionnaire.

452. Rinehart, Richard L., ed. Collegial Environment Vitality. 1982. ERIC, ED 215 741.

   Presents papers on exemplary practices that improve the morale of community college teachers.

453. Rosenfeld, Dina J. "An Examination of Field Instructor Turnover in Relation to Agency and University Support, Job Satisfaction, and Intrinsic Satisfaction." Doctoral dissertation, Yeshiva University, 1985.

   Studies the intrinsic and extrinsic rewards of field instructors as they relate to their decision to continue field instruction.

454. Rotheram, Mary J., and Nan Weiner. "Androgyny, Stress, and Satisfaction: Dual-Career and Traditional Relationships." Sex Roles 9, no. 2 (February 1983): 151-158.

   Assesses androgyny, satisfaction, and stress among assistant professors.

455. Schoorman, Frederick David. "The Impact of Leadership Role Behavior on the Performance of Professionals as Subordinates: A Study of University Department Heads." Ph.D. dissertation, Carnegie-Mellon University, 1983.

   Describes the leadership roles of department heads and the impact on time allocation, commitment, satisfaction, and productivity among college teachers.

456. Schuster, Jack H. "The Faculty Dilemma: A Short Course." *Phi Delta Kappan* 68, no. 4 (December 1986): 275-282.

   Discusses low morale among college teachers.

457. Seibert, Mary Lee. "Formal Teacher Preparation, Job Performance, and Job Satisfaction of Allied Health Educators in Indiana." Ed.D. dissertation, Indiana University, 1979.

   Ascertains the relationships between job performance and job satisfaction of allied health teachers using the Job Descriptive Index and twenty-seven task statements.

458. Seidman, Earl. "Merging Access and Excellence: The Work of Community College Faculty." *Community, Junior and Technical College Journal* 57, no. 4 (February-March 1987): 43-45.

   Highlights difficulties encountered by community college teachers.

459. Seidman, Earl, and others. *The Work of Community College Faculty: A Study Through In-Depth Interviews. Final Report.* 1983. ERIC, ED 243 499.

   Reports the results of a study on community college teachers including social, political, and economic issues.

460. Seiler, Robert E., and Della A. Pearson. "Stress Among Accounting Educators in the United States." Research in Higher Education 21, no. 3 (1984): 301-316.

   Investigates the relationships between stress and work satisfaction, personality and stress-coping techniques among college accounting teachers.

461. Sherwin, Bruce John. "Development of a Rating Scale for Measurement of the Concept of Modal Organizational Orientation and the Prediction of Work Satisfaction on the Basis of Personal/Organizational Congruence." Ed.D. dissertation, The University of Tennessee, 1981.

   Uses organizational climate to classify and distinguish various types of organizations; develops the Modal Organizational Orientation Rating Scale Type III to measure the climates of four organizations.

462. Sistrunk, Patricia Dornbusch. "The Relationship Between Mississippi Public Junior College Instructors' Perceptions of Supervisory Behavior and Their Perceived Levels of Job Satisfaction." Ed.D. dissertation, Mississippi State University, 1982.

   Investigates the relationship between junior college teachers' perceptions of supervisory behaviors and job satisfaction using the Supervisory Behavior Description Questionnaire, Form 1, and the Purdue Teacher Opinionaire.

463. Skalak, Constance Havird. "A Study of the Relationships Between Perceived and Reported Supervisory Intervention Behavior and Faculty Job Satisfaction." Ed.D. dissertation, University of Georgia, 1985.

   Studies nursing teachers' job satisfaction in relation to supervisory intervention using the Faculty Job Satisfaction Instrument and the Supervisory Intervention Behavior Instrument.

464. Smith, Dianne B., and Walter T. Plant. "Sex Differences in the Job Satisfaction of University Professors." Journal of Applied Psychology 67, no. 2 (April 1982): 249-251.

    Compares male and female college teachers' job satisfaction using the Job Descriptive Index.

465. Smolen, Bernard W. "Effect of Faculty Participation in the Decision Making Process upon Perceptions of Organizational Climate and Job Satisfaction." Doctoral dissertation, University of Maryland, 1985.

    Examines the effects of participation in decision making on the organizational climate and job satisfaction of community college teachers using the Conway adaptation of the Alutto-Belasco Decisional Participation Scale, the Institutional Functioning Inventory, and the Job Descriptive Index.

466. Stecklein, John E., and Reynold Willie. "Minnesota Community College Faculty Activities and Attitudes, 1956-1980." Community/Junior College Quarterly of Research and Practice 6, no. 3 (April-June 1982): 217-237.

    Focuses on professional activities, satisfaction and dissatisfaction, collective bargaining, and demographic variables among community college teachers.

467. Stembridge, Allen Frederick. "A Study of Teacher Motivation in Five Selected Seventh-Day Adventist Colleges in the United States." Ed.D. dissertation, Andrews University, 1984.

    Describes positive and negative incidents related to teaching among college teachers and indicates levels of satisfaction and dissatisfaction based on Herzberg's theory.

468. Stitt, Wanda Lou. "Relationship of Selected Personal Attributes of Business Teacher Educators to Job Satisfaction." Ed.D. dissertation, University of Georgia, 1980.

   Examines the relation between personal characteristics and job satisfaction among college business teachers using the Minnesota Satisfaction Questionnaire.

469. Stumpf, Stephen A. "Career Roles, Psychological Success, and Job Attitudes." Journal of Vocational Behavior 19, no. 1 (August 1981): 98-112.

   Investigates Hall's psychological success-based model of career development using college business teachers.

470. Stumpf, Stephen A., and Samuel Rabinowitz. "Career Stage as a Moderator of Performance Relationships with Facets of Job Satisfaction and Role Perceptions." Journal of Vocational Behavior 18, no. 2 (April 1981): 202-218.

   Measures performance, job satisfaction, role ambiguity, and role conflict among college teachers.

471. Sudsawasd, Sophon. "A Study of Factors Measuring Faculty Job Satisfaction at Selected Universities in Thailand." Ph.D. dissertation, Iowa State University, 1980.

   Identifies factors measuring job satisfaction and dissatisfaction among college teachers using Herzberg's Two-Factor Theory.

472. Thornton, Dannetta Kennon. "A Study to Determine Relationships Between Job Satisfaction of Lawson State Community College Instructors and Their Teaching Effectiveness as Perceived by Students." Ph.D. dissertation, The University of Alabama, 1977.

   Examines the job satisfaction of community college teachers and their teaching effectiveness using the Purdue Teacher Opinionaire and the Lawson State Community College Faculty Evaluation Scale.

473. Torbati, Maryam Behzadpour Torbati Masoud. "Job and Retirement Satisfaction Among Faculty Members of Public and Private Universities." Ph.D. dissertation, United States International University, 1979.

   Investigates job satisfaction, retirement satisfaction, and personal characteristics among college teachers using the Job Descriptive Index and the Retirement Descriptive Index.

474. Trinca, Carl Ernest. "Pharmacy Faculty Job Satisfaction: Its Relationship to Environment, Rewards and Performance." Ph.D. dissertation, The University of Arizona, 1980.

   Studies the effects of work environment, personal characteristics, rewards, and performance on job satisfaction among pharmacy college teachers using the Minnesota Satisfaction Questionnaire (modified), eleven items from the 1972-1973 Quality of Employment Survey, and the University of Southern California Faculty Professional Interests Survey.

475. Uncapher, Barbara W. "Communication Patterns, Commitments, and Satisfactions of Faculty in a Geographically-Divided Multicampus University." Ph.D. dissertation, University of Pittsburgh, 1983.

   Explores the relationships among communication patterns, commitments, and job satisfaction of college teachers in a geographically-divided multicampus institution.

476. Van Wijk, Alfons. "Organizing Management to Maximize Community College Impact." New Directions for Community Colleges 10, no. 2 (June 1982): 79-91.

   Describes incentives that motivate community college teachers and probes factors related to job satisfaction.

477. Vatthaisong, Arkom. "A Study of Job Satisfaction and Dissatisfaction Among Faculty Members in Teacher Training Institutions in Thailand." Ph.D. dissertation, George Peabody College for Teachers of Vanderbilt University, 1982.

   Analyzes job satisfaction/dissatisfaction among college teachers using the Faculty Job Satisfaction/Dissatisfaction Scale.

478. Walsh, Edward J. "Prestige, Work Satisfaction, and Alienation. Comparisons Among Garbagemen, Professors, and Other Work Groups." Work and Occupations: An International Sociological Journal 9, no. 4 (November 1982): 475-496.

   Compares work dissatisfaction and alienation among college teachers and nonfactory/nonoffice occupations.

479. Wangphanich, Paisal. "Job Satisfaction of Faculty Members at Srinakharinwirot University, Thailand." Doctoral dissertation, University of Kansas, 1985.

   Surveys job satisfaction of college teachers and compares job satisfaction in terms of demographic variables; attempts to predict job satisfaction from demographic information and job-component satisfaction.

480. Washington, Earl Melvin. "The Relationship Between College Department Chairperson's Leadership Style as Perceived by Teaching Faculty and That Faculty's Feelings of Job Satisfaction." Ed.D. dissertation, Western Michigan University, 1975.

   Discusses college teachers' job satisfaction and the chairperson's leadership style using the Brayfield-Rothe index, an instrument developed by the researcher to measure job satisfaction, and the Leader Behavior Description Questionnaire.

481. Weber, Scott Jonathan Mark. "A National Study of University Faculty Work Satisfaction and Organizational Climate in Health Information Management Departments." Ed.D. dissertation, Boston University, 1986.

   Examines the relationship between organizational climate, personal variables, organizational variables, and job satisfaction among college health information management departments using the Organizational Climate Description Questionnaire and the Job Descriptive Index.

482. Wille, James Harold. "An Analysis of Career Motivations and Job Satisfactions Among Public Community College Faculty in Selected States." Ed.D. dissertation, Northern Illinois University, 1981.

   Surveys community college teachers' present level of job satisfaction.

483. Williams, Don, and others. "A Matter of Degree: Faculty Morale as a Function of Involvement in Decisions During Times of Financial Distress." Review of Higher Education 9, no. 3 (1986): 287-301.

   Examines college teachers' morale and participation in decision making during a time of retrenchment.

484. Williams, Frank Phillip. "A Study of Differential Perceptions of Leadership Behaviors of Community College Deans of Instruction and Their Relationship to the Job Satisfaction of Division/Department Chairpersons in Texas." Ed.D. dissertation, University of Houston, 1978.

   Compares the results of a study by Sumrall (1976) of Texas teachers' job satisfaction with the job satisfaction results of this study on community college department chairpersons.

485. Winkler, Larry Dean. "Job Satisfaction of University Faculty in the United States." Ph.D. dissertation, The University of Nebraska-Lincoln, 1982.

   Identifies factors that contribute the most and the least to college teachers' job satisfaction using the Job Descriptive Index and the Minnesota Satisfaction Questionnaire (Short Form).

486. Wissman, Janice Wanklyn. "The Effect of Faculty Gender on Job Satisfaction in Selected Sex-Typed Units Within Institutions of Higher Education." Ed.D. dissertation, University of Kansas, 1981.

   Investigates the effect of gender on the job satisfaction of college teachers using the Job Descriptive Index and an interview.

487. Wittenauer, Martha Anne. "Job Satisfaction and Faculty Motivation." Ed.D. dissertation, Indiana University, 1980.

   Describes satisfying or dissatisfying factors that may contribute to job satisfaction and motivation among college teachers using Herzberg's Two-Factor Theory of Motivation.

488. Zabel, Robert H., and others. "Relationships Between Selected Personal Characteristics of Special Education Teacher Educators and Their Job Satisfaction." Teacher Education and Special Education 7, no. 3 (Summer 1984): 132-141.

   Identifies five job satisfaction factors among college special education teachers.

489. Zimmerman, Woodford W. Faculty Morale Study (1981). The Ohio State University at Lima Self-Study Report No. 1. Institutional Research Series 1981. 1981. ERIC, ED 225 619.

   Identifies the factors that contribute the most and the least to college teachers' morale.

VI. TEACHER MOTIVATION

490. Azinger, Albert Truman. "An Investigation of Job Satisfaction Among Teacher Negotiation Team Chairpersons." Ph.D. dissertation, The University of Iowa, 1982.

    Examines teacher organizations to determine if they select people who get job satisfaction from hygiene factors (Herzberg's hygiene seekers) as chairpersons of teacher negotiation teams; develops an instrument using hygienic and motivational factors based upon Herzberg's theory.

491. Binnie, David George. "The Relationship of Expectancy Work Motivation, Selected Situational Variables and Locus of Control to Teacher Job Satisfaction." Ed.D. dissertation, University of South Florida, 1984.

    Studies the relationships among expectancy work motivation, school size, teaching experience, locus of control, absenteeism and teacher job satisfaction using the School Structure and Climate Study and the Hall-Smitley Personal Reaction Survey.

492. Bloom, Susan Ellen. "Expectancy Motivation Theory and School Outcomes." Ph.D. dissertation, University of Kansas, 1982.

    Investigates teacher expectancy theory in relation to teacher job satisfaction, student achievement, student attitudes, and organizational effectiveness.

493. Bowman, Daniel Carson. "Elements of Job Dissatisfaction Associated with Performance Evaluation." Ed.D. dissertation, University of Missouri-Columbia, 1977.

    Analyzes teacher performance evaluation in relation to Herzberg's motivation-hygiene theory and identifies those practices that contribute to teacher job dissatisfaction.

494. Brodinsky, Ben, and Shirley Boes Neill, eds. Building Morale. Motivating Staff: Problems and Solutions. AASA Critical Issues Report, 1983. ERIC, ED 227 549.

    Provides twelve chapters on teacher morale and motivation including case studies and an instrument to measure organizational health.

495. Cammarata, Jerome John. "Teacher Motivation: A Study to Determine the Motivating Potential of the Elementary and Secondary Teaching Job in Chester County." Ed.D. dissertation, University of Pennsylvania, 1983.

    Conducts a study using the Job Diagnostic Survey to examine aspects of teaching that are related to increased or decreased motivation among elementary and secondary school teachers.

496. Carey, Diane. Motivating and Dissatisfying Factors Among Professional Educators. 1980. ERIC, ED 185 661.

    Identifies positive and negative motivating factors among elementary and secondary school teachers.

497. Charters, W. W., Jr., and others. Feasibility Studies of Teacher Core Job Characteristics. Final Report. 1984. ERIC, ED 245 383.

    Tests the applicability of Hackman-Oldham's job enrichment theory on teaching; revises the Hackman-Oldham instruments for use with teachers.

498. Clark, Neil Irving. "Organizational Development in Schools and Its Effects on Absenteism, Job Satisfactions and Work Motivation." Ed.D. dissertation, University of South Dakota, 1981.

   Investigates the effects of Adventures in Attitudes (an organizational development strategy) on job satisfaction, work motivation, and absenteeism in elementary school teachers using the Job Diagnostic Survey.

499. Cruz-Rodriguez, Aristides. "The Application of Herzberg's Theory of Motivation to Work to Public Elementary School Teachers in Puerto Rico." Ph.D. dissertation, New York University, 1980.

   Assesses satisfaction and dissatisfaction of elementary school teachers using the Herzberg Questionnaire and develops two instruments for this study: the Teachers' Job Satisfaction and Dissatisfaction Inventory, and the Teachers' Characteristics Questionnaire.

500. Deschamp, P.A., and T.M. Beck. _Teacher Transfers: A Survey of Teachers' Opinions on Factors Influencing Their Period of Stay in Schools with a Low Staff-Retention Rate_. Studies in Rural Education No. 2. 1979. ERIC, ED 186 159.

   Compares retention rates for different types of schools, characteristics of teachers, and factors that encourage teachers to stay.

501. Dunwell, Robert R. _Merit, Motivation, and Mythology_. 1986. ERIC, ED 268 112.

   Discusses five myths about teachers' attitudes toward merit pay and motivation.

502. Ellis, Thomas I. _Motivating Teachers for Excellence_. ERIC Clearinghouse on Educational Management: ERIC Digest, Number 6. 1984. ERIC, ED 259 449.

   Emphasizes intrinsic rewards as sources of teacher motivation.

503. Engelking, Jeri L. "Teacher Job Satisfaction and Dissatisfaction." Spectrum 4, no. 1 (Winter 1986): 33-38.

   Uses the critical incidents methods to identify sources of teacher satisfaction and dissatisfaction.

504. Engelking, Jeri Lee. "Identification of Satisfying and Dissatisfying Factors in Staffs of Elementary and Secondary Public School Teachers from Two States." Ph.D. dissertation, University of Idaho, 1985.

   Identifies factors that contribute to job satisfaction and dissatisfaction using a critical incident questionnaire adapted from Herzberg's Motivation-Hygiene theory.

505. Erlandson, David A., and Margaret C. Pastor. "Teacher Motivation, Job Satisfaction, and Alternatives--Directions for Principals." NASSP Bulletin 64, no. 442 (February 1981): 5-9.

   Discusses the needs of teachers using the Higher Order Need Strength Measure B.

506. Fareri, Camille. "A Study of the Factors Contributing to Job Satisfaction of Female Teachers." Ed.D. dissertation, State University of New York at Albany, 1985.

   Describes positive, negative, and compensating aspects of teaching among female teachers who are neither satisfied nor dissatisfied with their present position using an identification questionnaire based on Herzberg's theory.

507. Fox, William M. Teacher Motivation. 1986. ERIC, ED 275 677.

   Describes the development and validation of an instrument to measure teacher motivation and satisfaction with the principal's administration of the school.

508. Frataccia, Enrico V., and Iris Hennington. <u>Satisfaction of Hygiene and Motivation Needs of Teachers Who Resigned from Teaching.</u> 1982. ERIC, ED 212 612.

   Examines the needs that teachers have difficulty in satisfying using Herzberg's Motivation-Hygiene Theory and Marlow's Hierarchy of Needs.

509. Garskof, Melvyn S. "Motivating Teachers with Nonfinancial Incentives: The Relationships of Compensatory-Time Jobs and the Need to Achieve to the Job Satisfaction of High School Teachers in New York City." Doctoral dissertation, New York University, 1985.

   Examines the relationship between high school teachers' job satisfaction and nonfinancial incentives (status pay, privilege pay, and power pay) using the Job Description Index and the Self Descriptive Questionnaire; uses Marlow's Need Hierarchy Theory and Herzberg's Motivation-Hygiene Theory.

510. Gordon, Peter Alan. "A Validation Study of the Theory of Work Adjustment: The Prediction of Teacher Satisfaction." Ph.D. dissertation, University of Minnesota, 1981.

   Identifies the vocational needs and present level of job satisfaction among tenured junior high school teachers; tests Proposition III of the Theory of Work Adjustment and establishes the occupational reinforcer pattern of these teachers.

511. Hafford, Helen Mary. "The Measurement of Factors of Satisfaction and Dissatisfaction Which Affect Tennessee Teachers in Their Work." Ed.D. dissertation, The University of Tennessee, 1976.

   Measures and evaluates the factors leading to satisfaction and dissatisfaction among elementary and secondary school teachers using the Minnesota Satisfaction Questionnaire and Herzberg's theory.

512. Harder, Wayne William. "Teacher Job Satisfaction: An Application and Expansion of the Job Characteristics Model of Work Motivation." Ph.D. dissertation, Marquette University, 1985.

   Applies the Job Characteristics Model of Work Motivation to elementary and secondary school teachers.

513. Hatry, Harry P., and John M. Greiner. Issues in Teacher Incentive Plans. 1984. ERIC, ED 244 340.

   Analyzes the effectiveness and problems of two kinds of teacher motivation plans: merit pay and nonmonetary performance-by-objectives plans.

514. Hebert, Elizabeth Ann. "A Study of Effective and Ineffective Supervisory Behavior in Special Education." Ph.D. dissertation, Loyola University of Chicago, 1983.

   Investigates the effectiveness of supervisory behavior in special education using Flanagan's critical incident techniques and Herzberg's Motivation-Hygiene Theory.

515. Helm, Darrell Gene. "Relationships Among Teachers' Satisfaction/Dissatisfaction Levels, Teacher Motivation, and Student Achievement." Ed.D. dissertation, University of Illinois at Urbana-Champaign, 1984.

   Explores job satisfaction and dissatisfaction, motivation, and student achievement using the Job Episodes Questionnaire and the Teacher Effort Index; uses Herzberg's Motivation-Hygiene Theory.

516. Holcomb, John. "When Faculty Zeal Sputters, Here's How to Rekindle Enthusiasm Among Teachers." American School Board Journal 170, no. 3 (1983): 38-39.

   Explains five ways to motivate teachers who feel trapped in their present positions.

517. Jeffs, Alvin. "Motivation as a Consideration in Organisational Change and Staff Development Within a Peripatetic Support Group." *Educational Management and Administration* 14, no. 1 (Spring 1986): 39-48.

   Explores motivational factors and training preferences of itinerant teachers.

518. Kaminetzky, Beverlee S. "The Relationship of Reduction in Force to Motivation and Aspects of Job Satisfaction of Teachers." Ed.D. dissertation, Rutgers University, The State University of New Jersey (New Brunswick), 1985.

   Investigates the relationship between reduction in force and job satisfaction and motivation by comparing riffed reemployed teachers and secure teachers.

519. Karugu, Geoffrey Kamau. "An Investigation of Job Satisfaction-Dissatisfaction Among Elementary School Teachers and Headteachers in Nairobi, Kenya, and a Comparison of Their Perceptions on Fourteen Selected Job Factors from Herzberg's Two-Factor Theory." Ed.D. dissertation, Northern Illinois University, 1980.

   Compares job satisfaction of elementary school teachers and headteachers using fourteen job factors from Herzberg's two-factor theory.

520. Kaufman, Johanna Wahl. "The Relationship Between Motivation of Wisconsin Elementary and Secondary School Teachers and Their Commitment to the Teaching Profession." Ph.D. dissertation, The University of Wisconsin-Madison, 1982.

   Develops a questionnaire to distinguish between teachers who are motivation "seekers" and "nonmotivation seekers" and explores the relationship between motivation and commitment to teaching.

521. Khillah, Khillah (Latif) Rady. "Motivation of Secondary-School Teachers in the Lake Union Conference of Seventh-Day Adventists Based on Herzberg's Dual-Factor Theory of Job Satisfaction and Motivation." Ph.D. dissertation, Andrews University, 1986.

    Modifies Herzberg's instrument to measure motivation among secondary school teachers.

522. Knoop, Robert. Job Involvement of Teachers. 1980. ERIC, ED 208 508.

    Examines the relationship between job involvement and personal variables, structural variables, and eight job factors among elementary and secondary teachers.

523. Kreis, Kathleen, and Mike Milstein. "Satisfying Teachers' Needs: It's Time to Get Out of the Hierarchical Needs Satisfaction Trap." Clearing House 59, no. 2 (October 1985): 75-77.

    Presents an approach to respond to teachers' job-related needs.

524. Ladipo, Betty. "Motivational Factors and Attitude Changes in Teachers." Ph.D. dissertation, Northwestern University, 1984.

    States that teacher attitudes, incentives, and motivational factors change in relation to the number of years of teaching experience.

525. MacPhail-Wilcox, Bettye, and Linda R. Hyler. "Improving the Quality of Worklife for Teachers: A Contingency Approach." Journal of Research and Development in Education 18, no. 3 (Spring 1985): 16-24.

    Reviews motivation literature and offers a contingency approach to improve the worklife of teachers.

526. Marozas, Donald S., and Deborah C. May. "Factors Which Motivate Job Acceptance and Profoundly Mentally Retarded Children." <u>Education and Training of the Mentally Retarded</u> 15, no. 4 (December 1980): 293-297.

   Identifies factors that motivate job acceptance among teachers of severely and profoundly mentally retarded students.

527. Matthews, Kenneth M., and C. Thomas Holmes. "A Method for Assessing Teacher Motivation." <u>NASSP Bulletin</u> 66, no. 458 (December 1982): 22-28.

   Measures factors affecting teacher motivation using the Student Achievement Diagnostic Questionnaire for Administrators.

528. McGowan, James Michael. "The Application of Herzberg Theory of Job Satisfaction to Iowa Public School Teachers." Ph.D. dissertation, The University of Iowa, 1981.

   Compares job satisfaction between teachers from districts with locally negotiated settlements and those from districts without locally negotiated settlements using Herzberg's job satisfaction factors.

529. Mehta, Manju. "A Study of the Relationship Between Job Satisfaction, Job Values and Need-Achievement." <u>Manas</u> 22, no. 2 (December 1975): 219-226.

   Examines the relationships between job factors, job satisfaction, and the need to achieve using Murray's test of achievement and the Brayfield-Rothe Index of Job Satisfaction.

530. <u>Merit Pay for Teachers</u>. The Best of ERIC on Educational Management, Number 74. 1984. ERIC, ED 243 171.

   Presents an annotated bibliography on merit pay for teachers and concludes with a review of research on teacher motivation.

531. Miskel, Cecil, and others. "A Test of Expectancy Work Motivation Theory in Educational Organizations." *Educational Administration Quarterly* 16, no. 1 (Winter 1980): 70-92.

    Relates expectancy work motivation, central life interests, voluntarism, and personal characteristics to teacher job satisfaction.

532. Miskel, Cecil, and Leonard E. Heller. *The Stability and Reliability of a Modified Work Components Study Questionnaire in the Educational Organization.* 1972. ERIC, ED 060 543.

    Revises the Work Components Study Questionnaire based on Herzberg's theory of work motivation to the educational work situation.

533. Newcombe, Ellen. *Rewarding Teachers: Issues and Incentives.* 1983. ERIC, ED 236 143.

    Provides a review of the literature on merit pay for teachers.

534. Ornstein, Allan C. "Motivations for Teaching." *High School Journal* 66, no. 2 (December-January 1983): 110-116.

    Discusses reasons for becoming a teacher and advantages and disadvantages of teaching.

535. Ornstein, Allan C. "Motivations for Teaching." *Illinois Schools Journal* 61, nos. 1-4 (1981): 3-14.

    Reviews advantages and disadvantages of teaching and discusses job satisfaction, stress, and burnout.

536. Pastor, Margaret C., and David A. Erlandson. "A Study of Higher Order Need Strength and Job Satisfaction in Secondary Public School Teachers." *Journal of Educational Administration* 20, no. 2 (Summer 1982): 172-183.

    Surveys higher order needs, lower order needs, and job satisfaction among secondary school teachers using the Higher Order Need Strength Measure B.

537. Perko, Laura Lee. "Job Satisfaction of Teachers in the Portland Metropolitan Area: An Examination of Differing Factors and Their Relationship to Herzberg and Lortie Theories." Ed.D. dissertation, Portland State University and University of Oregon, 1985.

Explores job satisfaction and dissatisfaction in relation to Herzberg and Lortie theories; discusses the influence of demographic variables on job satisfaction.

538. Rogers, Robert Edward. "An Investigation of Factors Related to Job Satisfaction and Dissatisfaction of Teachers in School Districts with Differing Labor Climates." Ph.D. dissertation, Saint Louis University, 1976.

Uses the sixteen factors of Herzberg's Motivation-Hygiene Theory to examine job satisfaction and dissatisfaction of teachers within school districts with labor harmony and with labor strife using a questionnaire designed by the researcher.

539. Schmidt, Gene L. "An Organizational Model for Employee Job Satisfaction." NASSP Bulletin 64, no. 436 (May 1980): 80-88.

Diagrams an organizational model to improve teacher job satisfaction.

540. Silver, Paula F. "Synthesis of Research on Teacher Motivation." Educational Leadership 39, no. 7 (April 1982): 551-554.

Suggests ways administrators can influence teacher motivation.

541. Smith, Catherine Begnoche. "Occupational and Organizational Determinants of Behavior at Work." Ph.D. dissertation, Michigan State University, 1976.

Reviews the literature on work motivation, work settings, and organizational structures in order to examine the effect of organizational and occupational factors on work involvement and dedication to work among teachers.

542. Spaedy, Marjorie Ann Schuster. "Merit Pay, Teacher Evaluation and Motivation." Ed.D. dissertation, University of Missouri-Columbia, 1985.

   Compares teachers who favor and teachers who oppose merit pay in terms of demographic, perceptual, attitudinal, and motivational variables using the Motivation Feedback Opinionnaire, the Minnesota Satisfaction Questionnaire, and the Life Interests Section of the Educational Work Components Study.

543. Sparks, Dennis. "The Human Factor in Business--And in Schools." Journal of Staff Development 5, no. 1 (May 1984): 6-13.

   Describes the role of a school staff developer in terms of job satisfaction, organizational health, and teacher motivation.

544. Sylvia, Ronald D., and Tony Hutchison. "What Makes Ms. Johnson Teach? A Study of Teacher Motivation." Human Relations 38, no. 9 (September 1985): 841-856.

   Investigates the motivations of teachers including work autonomy, intrinsic factors, and satisfaction of higher-order needs.

545. Szura, John P., and Mary E. Vermillion. "Effects of Defensiveness and Self-Actualization of a Herzberg Replication." Journal of Vocational Behavior 7, no. 2 (October 1975): 181-187.

   Describes self-actualization, internal versus external locus of control, repression versus sensitization, need for approval, and job satisfaction/dissatisfaction among male teachers using Herzberg's Motivation-Hygiene Theory.

546. Taylor, George Andrew, III. "A Study of Job Satisfaction as Perceived by the Certified Staff in Florida Public Elementary Schools." Ed.D. dissertation, University of Central Florida, 1986.

   Tests Herzberg's Motivation-Hygiene Theory in elementary schools using an instrument based upon the sixteen job factors in Herzberg's theory; discusses teacher job satisfaction and dissatisfaction.

547. Tucci, Albert William. "A Study of the Relationship Between Motivator and Hygiene Variables and the State of Satisfaction/Dissatisfaction of Teachers in the Howard County School System." Ed.D. dissertation, University of Maryland, 1984.

    Explores the relationship between Herzberg's motivator and hygiene factors and teacher job satisfaction/dissatisfaction using the Educational Work Components Study.

548. Warren, Darrel Lee. "A Study of the Relationship Between Teacher Morale and Perceived Needs Deficiency of Maslow's Needs Hierarchy." Ed.D. dissertation, University of Missouri-Columbia, 1982.

    Examines teacher morale and need deficiencies based on Maslow's Hierarchy of Needs using the Purdue Teacher Opinionaire and A Maslow Needs Hierarchy Instrument.

549. Watts, Heidi. "The Rewards of Teaching." Journal of Staff Development 5, no. 2 (December 1984): 78-88.

    Identifies money, status, affiliation, autonomy, responsibility, creativity, and psychic rewards as motivators.

550. Weinroth, Elissa Dosik. "Motivation, Job Satisfaction, and Career Aspirations of Married, Women Teachers at Different Career Stages." Ph.D. dissertation, The American University, 1977.

    Compares motivation, job satisfaction, and career aspirations of married female teachers at four stages of their careers using the Educational Work Components Study.

551. White, James D. <u>Identification and Comparison of Factors Influencing Oklahoma Vocational Agriculture Instructors to Remain in the Profession.</u> 1979. ERIC, ED 198 255.

   Identifies factors that influence vocational education teachers to remain in teaching.

552. Wilcox, Kay Ellen. "Motivation, Central Life Interests, Voluntarism, and Demographic Variables as Predictors of Job Satisfaction and Perceived Performance of Teachers." Ed.D. dissertation, University of Kansas, 1979.

   Develops and tests an instrument to predict teacher effectiveness which includes motivation, central life interests, voluntarism, and personal variables.

553. Wilson, Susie Russell. "An Investigation of the Relationship Between the Satisfaction with School Communication System and Teachers' Work Motivation." Ed.D. dissertation, Virginia Polytechnic Institute and State University, 1981.

   Investigates the relationship between school communication and teachers' work motivation using Downs' and Hazen's Communication Satisfaction Questionnaire and the Teachers' Work Motivation Questionnaire based on Vroom's expectancy work motivation model.

554. Zaremba, John Philip. "Relationship of Teacher Motivation to Innovativeness and Job Satisfaction." Ph.D. dissertation, The University of Wisconsin-Madison, 1978.

   Examines the relationship between teacher motivation, teacher innovativeness, and job satisfaction using the Herrick Motivation and Reward Scale, the Kirton Adaptation-Innovation Inventory, and the Mendenhall Job Satisfaction Questionnaire.

VII. TEACHER ADMINISTRATOR RELATIONSHIP

555. Andrew, Loyd D., and others. <u>Administrator's Handbook for Improving Faculty Morale</u>. 1985. ERIC, ED 268 663.

    Describes a study conducted by Phi Delta Kappa on administrative practices and teacher morale; presents a review of the literature, case studies, and assessment tools.

556. Baker, Calvin Philip. "The Relationship of the Principal's Leadership Style and Job Satisfaction of Teachers." Ed.D. dissertation, Mississippi State University, 1979.

    Examines the relationship between the principal's leadership style and teacher job satisfaction using the Management Appraisal Survey and the Minnesota Satisfaction Questionnaire.

557. Barnard, Janet Sue. "A Study of the Relationship Between Leadership Behavior of Principals in the Public Schools in East Tennessee and Job Satisfaction of the Teachers." Ed.D. dissertation, The University of Tennessee, 1983.

    Studies the leadership behaviors of principals and the job satisfaction of teachers using the Leadership Behavior Description Questionnaire and Brayfield's Index of Job Satisfaction.

558. Barth, Roland S. "The Principal and the Profession of Teaching." Elementary School Journal 86, no. 4 (March 1986): 471-492.

   Examines the role of principals in the professionalization of teaching and in the creation of an environment that helps teachers discover their talents and skills.

559. Benson, John. "The Bureaucratic Nature of Schools and Teacher Job Satisfaction." Journal of Educational Administration 21, no. 2 (Summer 1983): 137-148.

   Describes the relationship between a school's bureaucratization and teacher job satisfaction.

560. Bhella, Surjit K. "Principal's Leadership Style: Does It Affect Teacher Morale?" Education 102, no. 4 (Summer 1982): 369-376.

   Correlates principals' attitudes toward people and productivity.

561. Blackbourn, Joe M., and Sam T. Wilkes. The Relationship of Teacher Morale and Zones of Indifference. 1985. ERIC, ED 265 220.

   Examines the relationship between teachers' morale and teachers' acceptance of the principals' authority using the Purdue Teacher Opinionaire and the Zones of Indifference Instrument.

562. Blase, Joseph, and others. "Leadership Behavior of School Principals in Relation to Teacher Stress, Satisfaction, and Performance." Journal of Humanistic Education and Development 24, no. 4 (June 1986): 159-171.

   Studies the relationship between principals' leadership and teacher job satisfaction, stress, and performance.

563. Block, Ilene Gail. "Teacher Need-Satisfaction, Importance, and Control: A Comparative Analysis Between Principals' and Teachers' Perceptions." Ed.D. dissertation, University of Colorado at Boulder, 1986.

   Investigates principals' perceptions of teachers' needs and need-satisfaction using instruments designed by the researcher based on Herzberg's Motivation-Hygiene Theory, Vroom's Expectancy Theory, Levinson's stages of adult development, and Christensen, Burke, and Fessler's career stages.

564. Boynton, Phil, and others. "A Basic Survival Guide for New Teachers." *Clearing House* 59, no. 3 (November 1985): 101-103.

   Lists suggestions that administrators might share with first-year teachers.

565. Brewer, Fredrick Gary. "Secondary School Principals' Leadership Behavior and the Atmosphere of the School as Perceived by Teachers, Principals, and Superintendents." Ed.D. dissertation, Northwestern State University of Louisiana, 1980.

   Determines the relationship between organizational climate and principals' leadership styles using the Leader Behavior Description Questionnaire and the Oganizational Climate Description Questionnaire.

566. Brodinsky, Ben. "Teacher Morale: What Builds It, What Kills It." *Instructor* 93, no. 8 (April 1984): 36-38, 40, 44.

   Indicates the importance of autonomy, recognition, and participation in decision making for building teacher morale.

567. Burford, Charles Thomas. "The Relationship of Principals' Sense of Humor and Job Robustness to School Environment." Ph.D. dissertation, The Pennsylvania State University, 1985.

   Describes principals' sense of humor, job robustness, teachers' job satisfaction, loyalty, and school effectiveness using Feingold's Perceptiveness Test, the Robustness Semantic Differential, and the Miskel Indices of Loyalty, Job Satisfaction, and School Effectiveness.

568. Burke, John Stephen. "Leadership Styles of School Principals as Predictors of Organizational Climate and Teacher Job Satisfaction." Ed.D. dissertation, University of Kansas, 1982.

   Analyzes the relationships between principal's leadership style and organizational climate and teacher job satisfaction using Fiedler's Least Preferred Co-Worker Scale, the Organizational Climate Description Questionnaire, and the Job Descriptive Index.

569. Carlile, Candice. "Reading Teacher Burnout: The Supervisor Can Help." Journal of Reading 28, no. 7 (April 1985): 590-593.

   Lists ways that administrators can help teachers deal with stress.

570. Clark, Kenneth James. "Work-Related Value Systems and Teacher Morale." Ed.D. dissertation, University of La Verne, 1981.

   Explores work-related value system of teachers, principals' leadership behavior, and teacher morale using the Work Values Questionnaire, the Leader Behavior Description Questionnaire, and the Purdue Teacher Opinionaire.

571. Cooper, Lloyd, and Kathleen Forrer. "Those Forgotten Motivators." Clearing House 59, no. 7 (March 1986): 297.

   Presents a checklist for administrators to use in assessing their interpersonal relations with their faculty.

572. Craig, Larry Vernon. "The Effects of Organizational Climate and Leadership Behavior on Teacher Job Satisfaction in Selected Schools." Ph.D. dissertation, North Texas State University, 1979.

   Studies the relationships of organizational climate, leader behavior, and teacher job satisfaction using the Organizational Climate Description Questionnaire, the Leader Behavior Description Questionnaire, and the Minnesota Satisfaction Questionnaire.

573. Croft, John C., and others. Some Relationships Between Administrators' Opinions and Teachers' Quitting Behavior in an Urban Public School System. 1983. ERIC, ED 231 020.

   Constructs a model to examine the influence of administrators on teacher resignation.

574. Daniels, Sherwood Colvin. "Principals' Leadership in Inner-City Schools: A Comparative Study of Leadership Behavior, Job Satisfaction and Student Achievement." Ph.D. dissertation, Northwestern University, 1981.

   Compares perceptions and expectations of elementary school principals and teachers in terms of principals' leadership behavior, teacher job satisfaction, and student achievement using the Leader Behavior Description Questionnaire, Form XII, the Teacher Satisfaction Scale, and the Iowa Tests of Basic Skills.

575. Dansie, Lamonte J., Jr. "An Analysis of Relationships Among Teacher Autonomy, Contact with the Principal, and Teacher Job Satisfaction." Ed.D. dissertation, University of Northern Colorado, 1986.

   Analyzes the relationships among teacher autonomy, contact with the principal, and teacher job satisfaction using Johnson's Job Satisfaction Scale and an instrument designed by the researcher.

576. Deverin, Dennis Grant. "A Test of the Path-Goal Theory of Leadership in Educational Organizations." Ed.D. dissertation, Rutgers University, The State University of New Jersey (New Brunswick), 1977.

    Tests the path-goal theory of leadership in secondary schools using instruments developed to assess leadership styles, task structure, role clarity, job satisfaction, and teacher expectations.

577. Dodds, Larry Keith. "Relationships Between Teacher Perception of Job Satisfaction and Specific Factors of Teacher Effectiveness as Perceived by the Principal and the Teacher." Ed.D. dissertation, University of Missouri-Columbia, 1980.

    Studies teacher effectiveness and job satisfaction in relation to the teacher's perception and the principal's perception using the Purdue Teacher Evaluation Scale and the Purdue Teacher Opinionaire.

578. Dryden, Beverly J. "They Don't Have to Be Futile." Principal 63, no. 3 (January 1984): 36-39.

    Presents one principal's solution to low teacher morale-shared leadership.

579. Duffour, Richard P. "Must Principals Choose Between Teacher Morale and an Effective School?" NASSP Bulletin 70, no. 490 (May 1986): 33-37.

    Discusses the importance of agreed-upon values and teacher autonomy in promoting high teacher morale.

580. Duke, William H. "An Examination of Administrative Leadership Style in the Public High School." Ed.D. dissertation, Indiana University, 1984.

    Examines teachers' perceptions on the effectiveness of administrators, administrative teams, and teacher job satisfaction using Fiedler's Least Preferred Co-Worker Scale, Gross and Herriott's Executive Professional Leadership instrument, and the Minnesota Satisfaction Questionnaire Short Form.

581. Dvorak, Jack. <u>Secondary School Newspaper Advisor's Job Satisfaction: A Factor in Press Freedom</u>. 1977. ERIC, ED 163 510.

   Compares job satisfaction scores of school newspaper advisers to principals' score of symbaditic communication and leadership styles.

582. Ecker, Marc Avery. "The Relationship Between Leadership Style and Teacher Job Satisfaction." Ph.D. dissertation, United States International University, 1979.

   Discusses the relationship between leadership style and teacher job satisfaction using the Leader Behavior Description Questionnaire and the Purdue Teacher Opinionaire.

583. Elliott, Robert Charles. "Selected Middle School Teachers' Perceptions of Their Principals' Leadership as Related to the Years of Experience of Both." Ed.D. dissertation, University of Georgia, 1986.

   Compares teachers' satisfaction with their principals' leadership in relation to years of experience using Muller's Diagnostic Survey for Leadership Improvement.

584. Engel, Ross A. "Creating and Maintaining Staff Morale: The Personnel Administrator's Role in a Time of Ferment in Education." <u>Clearing House</u> 60, no. 3 (November 1986): 104-106.

   Defines teacher morale and discusses how leadership can build morale.

585. Espy, Annette McDonald. "The Principal's Leadership Style and the Job Satisfaction of Teachers in a Selected Urban School District." Ed.D. dissertation, The University of Florida, 1975.

   Determines the relationship of the principal's leadership style and teacher job satisfaction using the Principal Behavior Check List and the Teacher Human Relations Questionnaire.

586. Fox, James H., Jr. Middle School Reorganization--
Conversion to Excellence. Revised. 1984. ERIC,
ED 251 955.

   Describes middle school organization and its
effect on improving teacher morale.

587. Fraser, Ken P. "Supervisory Behavior and Teacher
Satisfaction." Journal of Educational Administration
18, no. 2 (October 1980): 224-231.

   Reports on actual and preferred supervisory
behavior and teacher job satisfaction during the
1978-1979 school year.

588. Glickman, Carl D. "The Supervisor's Challenge:
Changing the Teacher's Work Environment." Educational Leadership 42, no. 4 (December-January 1985):
38-40.

   Discusses ways for supervisors to bring teachers
together to work on instruction in a professional
atmosphere.

589. Grigsby, Carl Jaco. "The Relationship of the Principal's Communication Behavior to the Teacher's
Perceived Job Satisfaction." Ed.D. dissertation,
University of Missouri-Columbia, 1981.

   Investigates principals' perceived communication
behavior and teachers' job satisfaction using the
Audit of Administrator Communication and the Teacher
Job Satisfaction Inventory.

590. Habashi, Manouchehr. "A Study of Teachers' Job Satisfaction in Iran and the Relationships Between the
Dimensions of Teachers' Job Satisfaction and the
Patterns of Principal's Managerial Behavior as Perceived by the Teachers." Ph.D. dissertation, George
Peabody College for Teachers of Vanderbilt University,
1980.

   Uses Halpin's model to gain insight into patterns of principal leadership behavior that may
influence teachers' job satisfaction using the Leader
Behavior Description Questionnaire and the Job
Descriptive Index.

591. Hagensee, Theodore Edward. "A Comparison of the Leadership Styles of Principals and Factors of Organizational Climates of Selected Open Space Suburban Elementary Schools." Ed.D. dissertation, Loyola University of Chicago, 1980.

    Compares principals' leadership styles with teacher job satisfaction and organizational characteristics using the Reddin Management Style Diagnosis Test and the Organizational Climate Description Questionnaire.

592. Hammond, Dale Wayne. "The Teachers' Perceptions of the Principal's Power Sources and Their Relationship to Selected Organizational Variables." Ed.D. dissertation, Southern Illinois University at Edwardsville, 1984.

    Studies the principals' bases of power and teacher job satisfaction; tests the effect of teachers' age, length of service, and size of school on their perception of their principal's sources of power, loyalty to the principal, teacher job satisfaction and sense of powerlessness.

593. Harris, Patelle G., and others. The QUEST Concept: A Handbook on Planning and Implementation. 1980. ERIC, ED 207 945.

    Provides a plan for the development and implementation of a school-based teacher education program.

594. Henjum, Arnold E. "Recognizing Personality Differences Among Teachers Can Help Supervisors." NASSP Bulletin 68, no. 469 (February 1984): 50-55.

    Recognizes differences in personality among subject area preservice teachers and recommends that principals who became aware of the differences in their faculty will improve communication and their schools.

595. Herring Johnnan H. "The Moderating Effect of Role Ambiguity on the Relationship Between Leader Behavior and Teacher Satisfaction." Ed.D. dissertation, University of Houston, 1981.

    Addresses the relationship between principal leader behavior and teacher job satisfaction with role ambiguity as a moderating variable using the Principal Leader Description instrument, the Role Conflict/Ambiguity Questionnaire, and the Job Satisfaction Survey.

596. Hewitson, Mal. "Participative Decision Making for Teachers--Placebo or Panacea?" <u>Australian Journal of Education</u> 22, no. 2 (June 1978): 189-205.

    Examines teacher involvement in decision-making, teacher's feelings of rapport with the principal, and teacher's job satisfaction.

597. Holder, Courtroy Alphonso. "Principal Leadership Behavior and Teacher Job Satisfaction in Public Elementary Schools in Columbus." Ph.D. dissertation, The Ohio State University, 1984.

    Considers the influence of principal behavior on the job satisfaction of elementary school teachers using the Organizational Climate Description Questionnaire and the Index of Job Satisfaction.

598. Hoy, Wayne K., and David A. Sousa. "Delegation: The Neglected Aspect of Participation in Decision Making." <u>Alberta Journal of Educational Research</u> 30, no. 4 (December 1984): 320-331.

    Uses an index of shared decision making to study teacher job satisfaction and loyalty in relation to principal authority, and joint decision making.

599. Hsieh, Wen-Chyuan. "A Comparative Study of Relationships Between Principals' Leadership Style and Teachers' Job Satisfaction in the Republic of China and the State of Iowa in the United States." Ph.D. dissertation, The University of Iowa, 1976.

   Compares Chinese and American principals' leadership behavior, teachers' job satisfaction, and demographic variables using the Leader Behavior Description Questionnaire and the Minnesota Satisfaction Questionnaire.

600. Johnston, Gladys Styles, and Vito Germinario. "Relationship Between Teacher Decisional Status and Loyalty." <u>Journal of Educational Administration</u> 23, no. 1 (Winter 1985): 91-105.

   Examines the relationship between loyalty to the principal and teacher participation in decision making.

601. Jun, Sung-Yun. "Principal Leadership, Teacher Job Satisfaction and Student Achievement in Selected Korean Elementary Schools." Ph.D. dissertation, The Florida State University, 1981.

   Discusses teachers' job satisfaction, student achievement, and principals' leadership behavior using the Instructional Leadership Behavior Scale, the Instructional Systems Effectiveness Scale, and the Purdue Teacher Opinionaire.

602. Kim, Nam Il. "The Relationship Between School Principal Leadership Behavior and Teacher Stress, Satisfaction, and Performance in the Schools of Incheon, Korea." Ed.D. dissertation, University of Georgia, 1986.

   Describes principals' leadership styles, teachers' stress, job satisfaction, and job performance.

603. Klawitter, Pamela Amick. "The Relationship Between Principal's Leadership Style and Teacher Job Satisfacation." Ed.D. dissertation, West Virginia University, 1985.

    Explores the relationship between principals' leadership style and teachers' job satisfaction using the LEAD-Other and the Job Satisfaction Survey.

604. Knoop, Robert. The Alienated Teacher: A Profile. 1982. ERIC, ED 214 905.

    Examines personal-demographic factors, personal-psychological factors, situational-job characteristics, and job outcomes and its effects on teachers' alienation; recommends redesigning teachers' job and revising administrators' leadership behavior.

605. Knoop, Robert. Leadership Styles of Principals and Teachers' Job Satisfaction, Satisfaction with Supervision, and Participation in Decision Making. 1981. ERIC, ED 218 754.

    Surveys teachers about the effects of principals' leadership behavior on teachers' job satisfaction, satisfaction with supervision, and participation in decision-making using the Leader Behavior Description Questionnaire and scaled items on job satisfaction.

606. Koch, E. L. "Quality of Working Life (QWL): Some Potential Applications to Education." Urban Education 17, no. 2 (July 1982): 181-197.

    Describes the Quality of Working Life approach.

607. Krajewski, Robert J., and Norman L. McCumsey. How to Help Beginning Teachers. 1984. ERIC, ED 245 360.

    Describes the role of the principal in terms of beginning teachers' needs; discusses seven key areas.

608. Kuieck, Thomas John. "A Comparison of Three Operational Definitions of Job Satisfaction." Ed.D. dissertation, Western Michigan University, 1980.

   Focuses on the psychometric properties of the Need Satisfaction Questionnaire, the Quality of Employment Job Satisfaction Survey, and the Minnesota Satisfaction Questionnaire among teachers and administrators.

609. Kwak, Ray V. "The Chief School Officers' Role and Its Relationship to Teachers' Job Satisfaction." Ed.D. dissertation, State University of New York at Buffalo, 1978.

   Examines the influence of the chief school officer's roles on teachers' job satisfaction using the Purdue Teacher Opinionaire and an instrument developed by the researcher.

610. Landsmann, Leanna. "Is Teaching Hazardous to Your Health?" Today's Education 67, no. 2 (1978): 48-50.

   Summarizes the responses of teachers about teacher health and the role of the principal.

611. Landsmann, Leanna. "Warning to Principals: You May Be Hazardous to Your Teachers' Health." National Elementary Principal 57, no. 3 (March 1978): 69-72.

   Indicates that the principal can improve the physical environment of the school and reduce stress in teachers.

612. Laws, Sarah Monita Hooks. "Relationship Between Teacher Perceptions of the Principal Leader Behavior and Teacher Attitudes Toward Evaluation in Kentucky Public Schools." Ed.D. dissertation, University of Kentucky, 1985.

   Analyzes the relationship between principals' leadership behavior and teachers' attitudes about evaluation and job satisfaction using the Leader Behavior Description Questionnaire, the Teacher Evaluation Satisfaction instrument, and the Job Descriptive Index.

613. Leon Guerrero, Jose S., Jr. "A Study of an Administrator's Use of Authority as It Relates to Teacher Loyalty, Job Satisfaction, and Alienation in the Public Schools of Guam." Ed.D. dissertation, Western Michigan University, 1979.

   Investigates the relationship between administrators' use of informal and formal authority and teachers' job satisfaction, loyalty, and alienation using the Principal-Staff Inventory, the Teacher Alienation Inventory, the Teacher Loyalty Inventory, and the Teacher Job Satisfaction Inventory to form the Survey of Administrator's Use of Authority.

614. Lim, Sammy Bak Hong. "Job Satisfaction Factors of School Administrators and Teachers." Ed.D. dissertation, Brigham Young University, 1985.

   Compares the levels of job satisfaction among teachers and administrators; identifies factors leading to job satisfaction.

615. Lipham, James, and others. The Relationship of Decision Involvement and Principals' Leadership to Teacher Job Satisfaction in Selected Secondary Schools. 1981. ERIC, ED 207 129.

   Looks at participation in decision-making, principals' leadership behavior, and nine aspects of secondary school teachers' job satisfaction.

616. Ludolph, John Frederick. "An Examination of Participation in Decision Making and the Perceptions of Satisfaction for Elementary School Principals and Teachers in the State of Illinois." Ed.D. dissertation, Northern Illinois University, 1985.

Clarifies the relationship between participation in decision making and job satisfaction among teachers and principals in elementary schools using Herzberg's theory.

617. Marra, Peter Robert. "Principal's Leadership Behavior, Teacher's Decisional Participation, Teacher's Job Satisfaction and Student Achievement." Ed.D. dissertation, Fordham University, 1978.

Compares perceptions of elementary school teachers in terms of principals' leadership behavior, teachers' decisional participation, teachers' job satisfaction, and student achievement using the Executive Professional Leadership Questionnaire and the Decisional Participation Questionnaire.

618. Mattaliano, Anthony P. "Time for a Change: Theory X or Theory Y--What Is Your Style?" NASSP Bulletin 66, no. 456 (October 1982): 37-40.

Adapts McGregor's management theory to the school setting and contends that principals who have positive feelings about people will improve teacher motivation, creativity, and job satisfaction.

619. McBrayer, Brenda Joy. "The Effect of the Administrative Behavior of Secondary School Principals on the Participation and Influence of Teachers in School Decision-Making as Perceived by Teachers." Ed.D. dissertation, The University of Toledo, 1982.

Investigates the effects of administrative behavior on teacher participation in decision-making; examines teacher job satisfaction and morale using a questionnaire designed by Johnson (1976).

620. McCarthy, Timothy W. "The Relationships Among Trust, Job Satisfaction, and Teacher Perceptions of Principal Effectiveness." Ed.D. dissertation, Seattle University, 1986.

   Examines the relationships among teacher trust toward the principal, job satisfaction, and principal effectiveness using Kegan's Belief Scale, Bowling Green State University's Job in General, and Schutz's Perceptions of Administrative Interaction Questionnaire.

621. McCaskill, Edwin D., and others. A Research Study About Teachers' Perceptions of Job Satisfaction. 1979. ERIC, ED 184 205.

   Evaluates teachers' perceptions of job satisfaction and the supervision they receive from their principals using the Job Descriptive Index.

622. McEvoy, Barbara. "Twelve Terrific Teacher-Boosting Tips." Executive Educator 8, no. 9 (September 1986): 26, 30.

   Outlines ways for administrators to praise teachers.

623. Mendenhall, Diana Reed. "Relationship of Organizational Structure and Leadership Behavior to Staff Satisfaction in IGE Schools." Ph.D. dissertation, The University of Wisconsin-Madison, 1977.

   Studies the relationship between structural features of the school organization, leadership behavior, and teacher job satisfaction using the Structural Dimensions Questionnaire, the Decision Involvement Analysis Questionnaire, the Leadership Questionnaire, and the Job Satisfaction Questionnaire.

624. Mes, Cornelius John. "Principal Leadership Style and Its Relationship to Teacher Job Satisfaction as Moderated by Selected Contingency Factors." Ed.D. dissertation, University of La Verne, 1983.

    Tests the relationship between elementary school principal leadership behavior and teacher job satisfaction within the path-goal theory of leadership using the Leadership Behavior Description Questionnaire, the Job Descriptive Index, and a Likert-type scale to measure leader effectiveness.

625. Miskel, Cecil, and Melva Owens. Principal Succession and Changes in School Coupling and Effectiveness. 1983. ERIC, ED 231 081.

    Assesses the effects of principal turnover on school organizational structures and effectiveness (teacher job satisfaction and student achievement).

626. Miskel, Cecil, and David McDonald. Structure Coupling in Schools. 1982. ERIC, ED 214 247.

    Measures school effectiveness (adaptability, goal attainment, teacher job satisfaction, and student attitudes) and structural coupling (seven variables including teacher communication with principals) in elementary and secondary schools.

627. Morris, Monica B. The Public School as Workplace: The Principal as a Key Element in Teacher Satisfaction. A Study of Schooling in the United States. Technical Report Series, No. 32. 1981. ERIC, ED 214 899.

    Analyzes the data on school environments for "A Study of Schooling" to identify teacher perceptions; investigates principals' attitudes and roles and teacher job satisfaction.

628. Nelson, Mary Ann Elizabeth. "Leader Behavior and Its Relationship to Subordinate Job Satisfaction as Moderated by Selected Contingency Factors in Minnesota Public Schools: A Path-Goal Theory Approach." Ph.D. dissertation, University of Minnesota, 1980.

    Applies the path-goal theory of leadership to school settings and measures leaders' behaviors and teacher job satisfaction using the Schreisheim leader behavior scales, the Minnesota Satisfaction Questionnaire, a control for leniency measure, and a role clarity scale.

629. Nidich, Randi Jeanne, and Sanford I. Nidich. "A Study of School Organizational Climate Variables Associated with Teacher Morale." Clearing House 60, no. 4 (December 1986): 189-191.

    Identifies factors that contribute to teacher morale.

630. Nigro, Kirk A. Developing Confidence and Self-Motivation in Teachers: The Role of the Administrator. 1984. ERIC, ED 269 842.

    Describes ways principals can build confidence in teachers and improve teacher morale.

631. Nwaobasi, Jonathan Okezie. "Relationship Between Administrative Management System, Selected Demographic Variables and Level of Job Satisfaction: An Analysis of Principal-Teacher Perceptions." Ed.D. dissertation, Texas Southern University, 1982.

    Explores the relationship between elementary principals' management system (leadership behavior) and teacher job satisfaction using Likert's Profile of Organizational Characteristics and the Job Descriptive Index.

632. Padover, Wayne. "The Relationship Between Leadership of Elementary School Principals and Satisfaction of Elementary School Teachers During Declining Enrollment." Ph.D. dissertation, University of Oregon, 1982.

   Describes principals' leader behavior and elementary teacher job satisfaction during declining and non-declining enrollment using the Leader Behavior Description Questionnaire, the Overall Job Satisfaction Instrument, and the Principal's Questionnaire.

633. Parham, Carol Sheffey. "A Study of the Relationship Between Job Satisfaction/Dissatisfaction of Assistant Principals and Secondary School Teachers and Their Perceptions of the Bases of Power of Principals." Ed.D. dissertation, University of Maryland, 1985.

   Focuses on the relationship between assistant principals' and teachers' job satisfaction/dissatisfaction and the powerbases of their principals using the Educational Work Components Study and the Power Scale Index.

634. Pitner, Nancy J. "Substitutes for Principal Leader Behavior: An Exploratory Study." *Educational Administration Quarterly* 22, no. 2 (Spring 1986): 23-42.

   Examines the construct, Substitutes for Leadership, as a way of understanding and explaining the principals' influence potential and its effect on teachers' work, attitudes, and behavior.

635. Powers, Eileen Margaret. "Nevada Teachers' and Administrators' Perceptions of the Male Mid-Life Characteristics." Ed.D. dissertation, University of Nevada, Reno, 1981.

   Develops the PB Inventory Scale to identify the psychosocial characteristics and changes that influence male administrators' and teachers' job performance and satisfaction.

636. Powers, Neill MacMillan. "Congruence of Leadership Styles, Teacher Loyalty to Principal, and Teacher Job Satisfaction." Ed.D. dissertation, The University of North Carolina at Chapel Hill, 1976.

   Relates congruence of principals' leadership style to teachers' loyalty and job satisfaction using the Bachman short scale to rank-order the perceptions, the Hoy and Rees teacher loyalty instrument, and Bullock's job satisfaction scale.

637. Provence, Andrew Joseph. "The Relationship Between Secondary School Supervisors and Teacher Job Satisfaction." Ed.D. dissertation, Rutgers University, The State University of New Jersey (New Brunswick), 1978.

   Analyzes the relationship between secondary school supervisors' supervisory styles and teacher job satisfaction using the Teacher Perception of Supervisor Questionnaire and the Teacher's Need Satisfaction Questionnaire.

638. Quinn, Camille M. "A Correlational Study of Trust and Job Satisfaction in Education." Ed.D. dissertation, Oklahoma State University, 1984.

   Explores the relationship between trust in educational supervisors and high school teachers' job satisfaction.

639. Reddick, Thomas L., and Joseph C. Fields. <u>A Study of Professional Attitudes of Teachers in Five Public School Systems in Tennessee and Michigan.</u> 1978. ERIC, ED 161 863.

   Compares the effects of professional negotiations on job satisfaction, interpersonal trust, organizational commitment, and career dissatisfaction.

640. Richmond, Virginia P., and others. "Power Strategies in Organizations: Communication Techniques and Messages." Human Communication Research, 11, no. 1 (Fall 1984): 85-108.

 Examines teachers' perceptions of their use of power, their supervisors' use of power, and teacher job satisfaction.

641. Roach, David Robert. "Perceived Principal Effectiveness as a Function of the Relationship Between Leadership Style and Job Related Maturity of Elementary Teachers." Ph.D. dissertation, Ohio University, 1982.

 Applies the Hersey and Blanchard Life Cycle Theory of Leadership to elementary schools in order to measure job related maturity of elementary school teachers and principals' effectiveness using the Leader Behavior Description Questionnaire, the Teacher Description Questionnaire, and the Principal Effectiveness Scale.

642. Roberts, Kerry Lee. "An Analysis of the Relationship of Principals' Leadership Style to Teacher Stress and Job Related Outcome." Ph.D. dissertation, Washington State University, 1983.

 Studies the relationship between principals' leadership styles and teachers' job satisfaction, stress, performance, and absenteeism.

643. Rohman, Gary Bernard. "A Study of the Interaction of High School Principals' Leader Behaviors and the Locus of Control and Role Ambiguity of Teachers in Determining Their Job Satisfaction." Ed.D. dissertation, Rutgers University, The State University of New Jersey (New Brunswick), 1985.

 Investigates the interaction of high school principals' leadership behavior and overall and facet job satisfaction of teachers, role ambiguity, and teachers' locus of control using the Leader Behavior Description Questionnaire, the Role Ambiguity Scale, the Internal-External Scale, the Job Descriptive Index, and the Job in General Scale.

644. Ronnenkamp, Stephen Flint. "Organizational Climate and Job Satisfaction in Schools: A Relationship Study Conducted in Selected Schools in the Davis County School District, Utah." Ed.D. dissertation, Brigham Young University, 1984.

   Describes the relationship between organizational climate and job satisfaction among teachers and administrators using the Organizational Climate Description Questionnaire and the Job Description Index.

645. Rosenbach, William E.; Robert A. Gregory; and Robert L. Taylor. "Survey Feedback as an Organization Development Strategy in a Public School District." Education 103, no. 4 (Summer 1983): 316-325.

   Discusses differences in job satisfaction, psychological climate, social satisfaction, skill variety, autonomy, and feedback among teachers, administrators, and support personnel.

646. Salvi, Anthony Daniel. "Perceived Job Satisfaction and Organizational Structure in School Districts with High and Low Declining Enrollment." Ed.D. dissertation, Fordham University, 1981.

   Compares the organizational characteristics of secondary schools and the job satisfaction of teachers and administrators with high and low declining enrollment using the Profile of Organizational Characteristics and the Job Diagnostic Survey.

647. Sardana, Ranjana M. "Organizational Climate Related to Job Satisfaction and Loyalty of Teachers and Principals in Selected Rural and Urban High Schools in Punjab, India." Ed.D. dissertation, Texas Southern University, 1985.

   Studies the relationship between organizational climate and job satisfaction and loyalty among teachers and administrators using the Organizational Climate Description Questionnaire, the Minnesota Satisfaction Questionnaire, and Blau and Scott's measurement of subordinate loyalty.

648. Schroeder, Juanita Hellmers. "The Relationships Between Teacher Perception of Managerial Behavior, Teacher Satisfaction, and Teacher Absenteeism." Ed.D. dissertation, University of New Orleans, 1977.

   Examines teachers' perceptions of principals' leadership styles, job satisfaction, and absenteeism using the Leader Behavior Description Questionnaire and the Job Descriptive Index.

649. Senigaur, Edward. "The Teacher's Perception of the Principal's Leadership Behavior and Faculty Morale: Their Impact on Student Achievement." Ed.D. dissertation, University of Houston, 1981.

   Looks at the effects of principals' leadership behavior and teacher morale in student achievement using the Leader Behavior Description Questionnaire and the Ohio Inventory of Employee Morale.

650. Sharma, Motilal. "Social Climate and Its Relationship with Principal's Effectiveness and Teacher Satisfaction." Journal of Psychological Researches 21, no. 3 (September 1975): 105-107.

   Correlates school climate and secondary school teachers' job satisfaction and principal effectiveness using the Organizational Description Questionnaire.

651. Sidotti, Phillip. "A Study of the Elementary Principal's Use of Formal and Informal Authority as It Relates to Teacher Loyalty, Job Satisfaction, and Sense of Powerlessness." Ed.D. dissertation, Rutgers University, The State University of New Jersey, 1976.

   Considers the relationship between elementary school principals' source of authority and teacher job satisfaction, loyalty, and sense of powerlessness using a revised form of the Principal-Staff Authority Inventory, the Teachers Job Satisfaction Inventory, and the Teacher Alienation Inventory.

652. Singh, Indira. "The Effects of the Headmaster's Leadership on Teacher Job Satisfaction and Morale as Perceived by the Teachers in Nepal." Ed.D. dissertation, Columbia University Teachers College, 1984.

   Analyzes the impact of the headmasters' leadership on the job satisfaction and morale among secondary and vocational school teachers using the Headmaster Leadership Behavior Questionnaire and the Teacher Job Satisfaction and Morale Instrument.

653. Sinprasong, Sukanya. "A Study of the Relationships Between Leader Behavior of Private Secondary School Principals and Teacher Morale in Bangkok, Thailand." Ph.D. dissertation, North Texas State University, 1983.

   Examines principals' leader behavior and morale among private secondary teachers using the Leader Behavior Description Questionnaire and the Purdue Teacher Opinionaire.

654. Southerland, T. P. "Do You Have a Plan of Success for Your School?" Clearing House 57, no. 4 (December 1983): 158-162.

   Offers suggestions for administrators in developing good management procedures.

655. Stapleton, James C., and others. "The Relationship Between Teacher Brinkmanship and Teacher Job Satisfaction." Planning and Changing 10, no. 3 (Fall 1979): 157-168.

   Discusses the role of the principal as it relates to teacher brinkmanship and job satisfaction.

656. Stapleton, James C. Teacher Brinkmanship and Job Satisfaction. 1979. ERIC, ED 171 655.

   Considers the relationship between teacher brinkmanship and job satisfaction using the Teacher Job Satisfaction Inventory and the Teacher Brinkmanship Inventory.

657. Stapleton, James Clay. "Teacher Brinkmanship." Ed.D. dissertation, University of Houston, 1978.

   Develops the Teacher Job Satisfaction Inventory and the Teacher Brinkmanship Inventory in order to examine the relationship between teachers' job satisfaction and brinkmanship.

658. Stedt, Joe D., and Hugh W. Fraser. "A Checklist for Improving Teacher Morale." NASSP Bulletin 68, no. 470 (March 1984): 70-81.

   Describes the Behavioral Morale Checklist as a vehicle for assessing and improving teacher morale; includes recommendations for principals.

659. Stone, Vera. "Principal's Leadership Style, Situational Control and School Effectiveness." Ph.D. dissertation, University of California, Berkeley, 1979.

   Explores the interactions between principals' leadership style, teachers' job satisfaction and students' achievement in reading using Fiedler's contingency theory of leadership.

660. Suelter, Barbara L. "Building Administrator Participation in Special Education: A Factor in Special Education Teacher Job Satisfaction." Ed.D. dissertation, Illinois State University, 1986.

   Studies the relationship between administrators' participation in special education activities and the job satisfaction of special education teachers.

661. Sugg, William Grady. "A Study of Selected Attitudes of Superintendents, Principals, and Teachers and Their Relationship to the Job Satisfaction of Principals and Teachers." Ed.D. dissertation, George Peabody College for Teachers of Vanderbilt University, 1980.

   Explores administrators' views of the "nature of man" and its effect on teachers' job satisfaction using the KYX form and the Minnesota Satisfaction Questionnaire.

662. Sumbrall, Charlotte Claudia Hermann. "A Study of the Relationship Between the Leadership Behavior of Instructional Supervisors and the Job Satisfaction of Teachers in Texas." Ed.D. dissertation, University of Houston, 1976.

    Examines the relationship between instructional leaders' behavior and teachers' job satisfaction using the Job Descriptive Index, the Supervisory Behavior Description instrument, and the Leadership Opinion Questionnaire.

663. Sweeney, Jim, and Robert Pinckney. "Faculty Management: The Principal's Most Important Role." Spectrum, 1, no. 3 (Fall 1983): 3-6.

    Compares teachers' and principals' perceptions of the most important aspects of the principalship; reveals that human resource management impacts greatly on teacher job satisfaction.

664. "Teacher Enthusiasm Reaches Epidemic Proportions." Vocational Education Journal 61, no. 2 (March 1986): 32-33.

    Describes ways to improve teacher morale including greater administrative support and communication.

665. "Teacher's Counselor." Instructor 86, no. 1 (August-September 1976): 38-40.

    Discusses the conflict between a teacher and a principal over an informal and a structured classroom environment.

666. Theodory, George C. The Mediating Role of Principals' Situational Favorableness on School Effectiveness in Lebanon. 1982. ERIC, ED 214 298.

    Tests Fiedler's contingency theory that school effectiveness is related to the principals' leadership style among secondary schools; measures school effectiveness in terms of teacher job satisfaction and student achievement.

667. Theodory, George C. "Principals' Experience and Teachers' Satisfaction in Lebanese Secondary Schools." American Journal of Psychology 108, no. 1 (May 1981): 7-10.

   Supports Fiedler's contingency theory about the relationship between high and low Least Preferred Co-worker Scale scores of principals and teacher job satisfaction.

668. Tice, Paul Gary. "Teacher Job Satisfaction and the Personal Need for Control by Principals and Teachers." Ph.D. dissertation, George Peabody College for Teachers of Vanderbilt University, 1981.

   Focuses on the need for control by elementary school principals and teachers and teachers' job satisfaction using the Fundamental Interpersonal Relations Orientation-Behavior instrument and the Minnesota Satisfaction Questionnaire.

669. Vivian, Timothy Paul. "The Relationship Between Perceived Leadership Style, Size of School and Non-Instructional Time on Teacher Job Satisfaction." Ed.D. dissertation, University of South Carolina, 1983.

   Investigates the relationships between teachers' job satisfaction and principals' leadership style, size of the school, and the time engaged in non-teaching assignments.

670. Weller, L. David. "Principals, Meet Maslow: A Prescription for Teacher Retention." NASSP Bulletin 66, no. 456 (October 1982): 32-36.

   Discusses Maslow's hierarchy of needs as a way for principals to meet teachers' basic needs.

671. Wilhite, James Wesley. "The Congruence of Pupil Control Ideology Between Principals and Teachers as Related to Teacher Job Satisfaction." Ed.D. dissertation, Oklahoma State University, 1978.

   Examines the congruence of pupil control ideology between principals and teachers and its effect on teacher job satisfaction using the Purdue Teacher Opinionaire and the Pupil Control Ideology Form.

672. Williams, Patricia Ann Fontenot. "The Development and Testing of a Conceptual Model of Peer Supervision." Ed.D. dissertation, University of Houston, 1981.

Develops and tests a peer supervision model using the Teacher Attitudes Toward Supervision Instrument, the Hunter Teacher Appraisal Instrument, and the Minnesota Satisfaction Questionnaire.

673. Winkler, Abby Lynn. "The Relationships Between Elementary School Teacher Perceptions of Principal Leadership Style/Style Adaptability and Teacher Job Satisfaction/Satisfaction with Supervision." Ed.D. dissertation, The Catholic University of America, 1983.

Tests Hersey and Blanchard's Situational Leadership Theory within an elementary school setting using the Leadership Effectiveness and Adaptability Description to measure principals' leadership style and the Job Descriptive Index to measure teacher job satisfaction.

VIII. TEACHER STRESS AND BURNOUT

674. Abbott-Koch, Sarah. "Perceived Stress of Special Education Teachers and Regular Education Teachers Based on Task-Oriented, Role-Oriented, and Environment-Oriented Stress." Ed.D. dissertation, Texas Southern University, 1985.

    Validates the Job Stress in the School Setting instrument by comparing task-oriented stress, role-oriented stress, and environment-oriented stress among special education teachers and regular education teachers.

675. Alexander, Livingston, and others. A Factor Analytic Study of the Teaching Events Stress Inventory. 1983. ERIC, ED 237 545.

    Assesses the levels and sources of teacher stress using the Teaching Events Stress Inventory.

676. Alley, Robert D. "Stress and the Professional Educator." Action in Teacher Education 2, no. 4 (Fall 1980): 1-8.

    Describes conditions in the work environment that contribute to teacher stress and burnout.

677. Allie, Stephen Michael. "Organizational and Personal Life Stress and the Role of Moderator Variables in the Prediction of Burnout, Performance and Serious Illness." Ph.D. dissertation, The University of Texas at Dallas, 1982.

    Measures the effects of job stress and personal life stress on job performance, sick days used, burnout, serious illness, and teacher job satisfaction.

678. Altschuler, Alfred S., ed., and others. <u>Teacher Burnout</u>. Analysis and Action Series. 1980. ERIC, ED 201 640.

    Presents a series of articles that discuss the causes of teacher stress, methods for reducing stress, and a workshop guide; includes an annotated bibliography on stress.

679. Amodio, Toni. "An Analysis of Job-Related Stress and Dissatisfaction in the Teaching Profession." Ph.D. dissertation, Wayne State University, 1981.

    Identifies the most stressful areas in the teaching environment by using a stress inventory and identifies areas in the teaching environment that contribute to alienation using an alienation inventory.

680. Austin, Dean A. "The Teacher Burnout Issue." <u>Journal of Phyiscal Education, Recreation and Dance</u> 52, no. 9 (November-December 1981): 35-36.

    Describes causes and symptoms of teacher burnout and offers several coping strategies.

681. Barner, Ann E. "Do Teachers Like to Teach?" <u>Pointer</u> 27, no. 1 (Fall 1982): 5-7.

    Compares burnout and job satisfaction among regular and special education teachers.

682. Beasley, Carol R., and others. <u>On-the-Job Stress and Burnout: Contributing Factors and Environmental Alternatives in Educational Settings</u>. 1983. ERIC, ED 242 727.

    Compares stress, burnout and environmental factors among regular and special education teachers using the Maslach Burnout Inventory, the Stress Profile for Teachers, and a job-related questionnaire.

683. Beck, Cynthia L., and Richard M. Gargiulo. "Burnout in Teachers of Retarded and Nonretarded Children." Journal of Educational Research 76, no. 3 (January-February 1983): 169-173.

   Reports reduced stress among special education teachers in comparison to regular classroom teachers; offers recommendations for reducing stress.

684. Belcastro, Philip A., and Robert S. Gold. "Teacher Stress and Burnout: Implications for School Health Personnel." Journal of School Health 53, no. 7 (September 1983): 404-407.

   Identifies levels of teacher burnout and its relationship to somatic complaints and physical illnesses.

685. Belcastro, Philip A.; Robert S. Gold; and Leon C. Hays. "Maslach Burnout Inventory: Factor Structures for Samples of Teachers." Psychological Reports 53, no. 2 (October 1983): 364-366.

   Validates the factor structure of the Maslach Burnout Inventory using public school teachers.

686. Bensky, Jeffrey M., and others. P.L. 94-142 and Stress: An Analysis and Direction for the Future. 1979. ERIC, ED 171 028.

   Focuses on stress in relation to compliance with P.L. 94-142; finds that the more satisfied a teacher is in the professional role, the less the stress.

687. Birmingham, Judith Ann. "Job Satisfaction and Burnout Among Minnesota Teachers." Ph.D. dissertation, University of Minnesota, 1984.

   Examines teacher job satisfaction and burnout using the Minnesota Satisfaction Questionnaire and the Maslach Burnout Inventory.

688. Blase, Joseph J. "Teaching Coping and School Principal Behaviors." <u>Contemporary Education</u> 56, no. 1 (Fall 1984): 21-25.

   Discusses causes of teacher stress and suggestions for improving principal-teacher relations.

689. Broiles, Patricia Hope. "An Inquiry into Teacher Stress: Symptoms, Sources and Prevalence in Public Schools." Ph.D. dissertation, Claremont Graduate School, 1982.

   Studies job satisfaction, absenteeism, self-rating as a teacher, self-reported stress level, and desire to leave or remain teaching.

690. Bruno, James E. "Equal Educational Opportunity and Declining Teacher Morale at Black, White, and Hispanic High Schools in a Large Urban School District." <u>Urban Review</u> 15, no. 1 (1983): 19-36.

   Describes the low level of teacher morale in inner city schools and the conditions that cause teacher absenteeism and turnover.

691. Bruno, James E. "Morale-Affecting Stressors: An Analysis of Black, White, and Hispanic Elementary Schools." <u>Urban Education</u> 16, no. 2 (July 1981): 175-203.

   Reports on the causes of physical and mental stress among Black, White, and Hispanic elementary school teachers.

692. Bundy, O. Keith. "Everything You Always Wanted to Know About Professional Burnout But Were Afraid to Ask." <u>Contemporary Education</u> 53, no. 1 (Fall 1981): 9-11.

   Offers three solutions to the problem of teacher burnout.

693. Burden, Paul R. Personal and Professional Conflict: Stress for Teachers. 1982. ERIC, ED 218 272.

    Explores the interaction between teachers' personal and professional lives, difficulties in separating them, and stress from their jobs.

694. Burke, Robert E. "Take These Six Steps to Save a Troubled School." Executive Educator 6, no. 1 (January 1984): 21-22.

    Describes a six-step problem-solving process to improve teacher morale.

695. Burrell, Ann Glendinning. "An Examination of Variables Influencing the Perception of Stress Among Special Education Teachers." Ph.D. dissertation, Georgia State University, College of Education, 1982.

    Develops a questionnaire to identify sources of stress among special education teachers and their coping strategies; uses the Job Description Index to assess job satisfaction.

696. Burscemi, John N. "Practical Solutions for Administrators to Reduce Stress in the Classroom." Illinois School Research and Development 18, no. 1 (Fall 1981): 34-38.

    Reviews theories of organizational stress management and recommends techniques to reduce teacher stress.

697. Butt, Fairfield. "Teaching: How to Handle the Pollution." Pointer 24, no. 2 (Winter 1980): 22-23.

    Presents ways of dealing with teacher stress, including coping strategies.

698. Calabrese, Raymond L., and R.E. Anderson. "The Public School: A Source of Stress and Alienation Among Female Teachers." <u>Urban Education</u> 21, no. 1 (April 1986): 30-41.

   Examines the relationship between teacher stress and alienation among female teachers; presents suggestions for reducing stress through administrative policies.

699. Calder, Victoria Lynn. "Demographic and Work Environment Characteristics of Teachers as Predictors of Teacher Stress and Response to a Stress Intervention Program." Ph.D. dissertation, The University of Texas at Austin, 1984.

   Studies teachers who completed a stress intervention program in terms of physiological (blood pressure and total treadmill time) and psychological (well-being, job satisfaction, self-concept, energy-health, strain, job happiness, and happiness) measures of stress.

700. Cardinell, C.F. <u>Mid-Life Professional Crises: Two Hypotheses.</u> 1981. ERIC, ED 208 491.

   Presents a satisfaction-commitment conflict hypothesis among teachers based in Marlow's hierarchy of needs.

701. Cardinell, Charles F. "Teacher Burnout: An Analysis." <u>Action in Teacher Education</u> 2, no. 4 (Fall 1980): 9-15.

   Discusses the relationship between teacher burnout and job satisfaction.

702. Cherkes, Miriam, and Michael J. Fimian. <u>An Analysis of the Relationship Among Personal and Professional Variables and Perceived Stress of Mainstream and Special Education Teachers. Final Report.</u> 1982. ERIC, ED 244 486.

   Develops the Teacher Stress Survey to assess professional distress, discipline and motivation, emotional manifestations, behavioral manifestations, physiological manifestations, and fatigue manifestations among special education and mainstream teachers.

703. Cichon, Donald J., and Robert H. Koff. "Stress and Teaching." NASSP Bulletin 64, no. 434 (March 1980): 91-104.

    Presents the results of the Teaching Events Stress Inventory among Chicago teachers.

704. Cichon, Donald J., and Robert H. Koff. The Teaching Events Stress Inventory. 1978. ERIC, ED 160 662.

    Designs the Teaching Events Stress Inventory to assess the level of stress caused by thirty-six events associated with teaching.

705. Cohen, Jane A. "Stress and the Boarding School Teacher." Independent School 41, no. 3 (February 1982): 49-51.

    Discusses sources of stress among private boarding school teachers and coping strategies.

706. Colasurdo, Michael Modesto. "A Descriptive Survey of Professional Burnout Amongst Public School Teachers in San Diego, California." Ed.D. dissertation, United States International University, 1981.

    Researches the terms morale, stress, and alienation in order to define teacher burnout; selects specific personal and situational variables to examine the relationship between external conditions and teacher burnout.

707. Collingwood, Thomas R. "This Good-Health Regimen Keeps Employes Fit--And School Budgets Trim." American School Board Journal 171, no. 4 (April 1984): 48-49.

    Describes the Dallas School District's staff stress reduction program.

708. Cox, Tom, and Terence Brockley. "The Experience and Effects of Stress in Teachers." *British Educational Research Journal* 10, no. 1 (1984): 83-87.

    Reviews the literature on teacher stress and suggests that job satisfaction may reduce stress.

709. Crane, Stephen J., and Edward F. Iwanicki. "Perceived Role Conflict, Role Ambiguity, and Burnout Among Special Education Teachers." *Remedial and Special Education (RASE)* 7, no. 2 (March-April 1986): 24-31.

    Examines the relationship between role conflict and role ambiguity to teacher burnout among urban special education teachers.

710. Crase, Darrell. "Development Activities: A Hedge Against Complacency." *Journal of Physical Education and Recreation* 51, no. 9 (November-December 1980): 53-54.

    Lists suggestions for personal development activities for teachers to combat burnout.

711. Cunningham, William G. "Teacher Burnout: Stylish Fad or Profound Problem." *Planning and Changing* 12, no. 4 (Winter 1982): 219-244.

    Looks at the effects of teacher burnout on job satisfaction; discusses causes of teacher stress and ways of reducing burnout.

712. D'Acchioli, Anthony Louis. "Some Potential Effects of RIF-Related Job Actions on Public School Teachers." Ed.D. dissertation, Boston University, 1984.

    Explores the effects of job retention and locus of control on teacher job satisfaction and health using Rotter's I-E scale, the Job Diagnostic Survey, and Wahler's Physical Symptoms Inventory.

713. Daniels, Stephen F. "A Comparison of the Effects of a Cognitive Stress Management Program and a Relaxation Training Stress Management Program." Ph.D. dissertation, University of Southern Mississippi, 1984.

   Investigates the effects of a cognitive stress management program and a relaxation training stress management program on self-reported anxiety and teacher job satisfaction using the State-Trait Anxiety Inventory, the State Anxiety Scale, and the Global Rating of Job Satisfaction instrument.

714. Dawson, Grace Graves. "Causes of Stress in Teachers of the Hearing Impaired: A Comparison Between Itinerant Teachers and Self-Contained Classroom Teachers." Ph.D. dissertation, Southern Illinois University at Carbondale, 1985.

   Compares the causes of burnout between self-contained classroom teachers and itinerant teachers of the hearing impaired using the Maslach Burnout Inventory and the Minnesota Satisfaction Questionnaire.

715. Dedrick, Charles V., and others. "Teacher Stress: A Descriptive Study of the Concerns." NASSP Bulletin 65, no. 449 (December 1981): 31-35.

   Surveys teachers to identify sources of stress in teaching.

716. Dettmer, Peggy. "Preventing Burnout in Teachers of the Gifted." G/C/T, no. 21 (January-February 1982): 37-38, 40-41.

   Offers approaches to reduce burnout among teachers of the gifted.

717. DiTeodoro, Vincent A. "Sources of Teacher Satisfactions, Stress and Burnout in a Suburban School District." Ed.D. dissertation, Columbia University Teachers College, 1984.

   Investigates sources of job satisfaction, stress, and burnout among suburban teachers using the Farber Teacher Attitude Survey.

718. Dunham, Jack. *Stress in Teaching*. 1984. ERIC, ED 252 505.

   Identifies sources of teacher stress, teachers' coping strategies, role conflict and role ambiguity, and suggestions for strengthening personal, interpersonal, and organizational resources.

719. Dworkin, Anthony Gary. *When Teachers Give Up: Teacher Burnout, Teacher Turnover and Their Impact on Children*. 1985. ERIC, ED 273 575.

   Summarizes a sociological study of teacher burnout by examining teacher commitment, teacher turnover, social support, student achievement, and the decision to leave teaching.

720. Earl, Lorna Maxine. "Occupational Stress and Functioning Among Women Elementary School Teachers: A Model Including Personality Traits, Coping, Social Support and Life Stress." Ph.D. dissertation, The University of Western Ontario (Canada), 1986.

   Develops a questionnaire to examine teacher stress, social support, personality traits, coping mechanisms, major life events, and health status among female elementary school teachers.

721. Ellis, Joseph, and others. "A Statistical Analysis of Educator, Drop Out in Illinois Public Schools." *Illinois School Research and Development* 18, no. 2 (Winter 1982): 32-40.

   Studies teacher attrition, teacher job satisfaction, and teacher burnout.

722. Esteve, J.M., and A.F.B. Fracchia. "Inoculation Against Stress: A Technique for Beginning Teachers." *European Journal of Teacher Education* 9, no. 3 (1986): 261-269.

   Reviews the literature on the effects of stress on teacher morale.

723. Faas, Larry A. Characteristics and Stress Producing Factors in a Population of RIFFED Educators. 1982. ERIC, ED 232 243.

   Compares teachers who have and who have not been RIFFED in terms of thirty-eight stress factors.

724. Farber, Barry A. "Teacher Burnout: Assumptions, Myths, and Issues." Teachers College Record 86, no. 2 (Winter 1984): 321-338.

   Discusses the impact of teacher burnout on recruitment, retention, and teacher performance.

725. Farber, Barry A. "Stress and Burnout in Suburban Teachers." Journal of Educational Research 77, no. 6 (July-August 1984): 325-331.

   Assesses the sources of teacher job satisfaction, stress, and burnout among suburban teachers using a Teacher Attitude Survey.

726. Farber, Barry A. Teacher Burnout: Assumptions, Myths, and Issues. 1982. ERIC, ED 229 369.

   Examines several key issues regarding teacher burnout; concludes that teacher stress and teacher burnout are separate terms.

727. Farber, Barry A., and Julie Miller. "Teacher Burnout: A Psychoeducational Perspective." Teachers College Record 83, no. 2 (Winter 1981): 235-243.

   Discusses causes, conditions, symptoms, and treatment of teacher burnout.

728. Farrell, Edmund J. The Cycle of Renewal. 1983. ERIC, ED 225 168.

   Describes means of renewal for English teachers.

729. Federman, Deanna Goldstein. "An Exploratory Study into the Phenomenon of Teacher Burnout." Ph.D. dissertation, Temple University, 1984.

   Assesses the relationships between teacher burnout, attitude toward teaching, and demographic characteristics using the Teacher Burnout Inventory and the Teacher Perception Questionnaire.

730. Feinstein, Donald Jordan. "Teacher Burn-Out: An Investigation of the Relationship Among Locus of Control, Job Satisfaction, Self-Esteem and Depression of Teachers of the Emotionally Disturbed." Ph.D. dissertation, Loyola University of Chicago, 1982.

Addresses the issue of teacher burnout by studying job satisfaction, depression, self-esteem, locus of control, and years of teaching experience using the Minnesota Satisfaction Questionnaire, Depression Adjective Check List, Self-Perception Inventory-Teacher Form, and Rotter's Locus of Control Scale.

731. Feitler, Fred C., and Edward B. Tokar. <u>Teacher Stress: Sources, Symptoms and Job Satisfaction</u>. 1981. ERIC, ED 204 857.

Compares stress among American and British teachers using a survey questionnaire to assess teacher job satisfction, the causes, symptoms, and levels of teacher stress, and coping techniques.

732. Fibkins, William L. "Teacher Centering to Reduce Burn-Out and Isolation." <u>Action in Teacher Education</u> 2, no. 2 (Spring 1980): 31-36.

Describes the role of teacher centers in alleviating teacher burnout and isolation.

733. Fielding, Marianne A., and Meredith D. Gall. <u>Personality and Situational Correlates of Teacher Stress and Burnout</u>. 1982. ERIC, ED 219 353.

Measures junior high/middle school teachers' perceptions of: stress, burnout, locus of control, attitudes toward students, intolerance of ambiguity or change, and quality of the school as a work setting.

734. Fimian, Michael J. "Social Support and Occupational Stress in Special Education." *Exceptional Children* 52, no. 5 (February 1986): 436-442.

   Presents the findings of a study on the effects of teacher and administrative support on stress among special education teachers.

735. Fimian, Michael J. "The Development of an Instrument to Measure Occupational Stress in Teachers: The Teacher Stress Inventory." *Journal of Occupational Psychology* 57, no. 4 (December 1984): 277-293.

   Investigates the context validity, factorial validity, and internal consistency of the Teacher Stress Inventory among special education and regular teachers.

736. Fimian, Michael J. "Stress Reduction: Techniques for Teachers." *Pointer* 24, no. 2 (Winter 1980): 64-69.

   Outlines three steps to handle teacher stress, including identifying the problem, facing it, and developing personal and environmental management strategies.

737. Fimian, Michael J., and Linda P. Blanton. "Variables Related to Stress and Burnout in Special Education Teacher Trainees and First-Year Teachers." *Teacher Education and Special Education* 9, no. 1 (Winter 1986): 9-21.

   Studies role, stress, and burnout among special education trainees and beginning teachers; observes different problems at different levels of professional development.

738. Fletcher, Ben C., and Roy L. Payne. "Levels of Reported Stressors and Strains Amongst Schoolteachers: Some UK Data." *Educational Review* 34, no. 3 (November 1982): 267-278.

   Describes psychological stress and strain among teachers using job satisfaction, pressure, self-esteem, depression, anxiety, and somaticism variables.

739. Flint, Lowell. A Model for Understanding, Preventing and Controlling Burnout. 1982. ERIC, ED 212 630.

　　　Presents an interaction model of teacher job satisfaction and stress that generates three areas for discussion: measurement, stress management, and organizational development.

740. Forman, Judy S. "The Effects of an Aerobic Dance Program for Women Teachers on Symptoms of Burnout." Ed.D. dissertation, University of Cincinnati, 1983.

　　　Studies the impact of an aerobic dance program on female teacher burnout, absenteeism, stress, job satisfaction and morale using the Maslach Burnout Inventory, the Wilson Stress Profile for Teachers, and the Purdue Teacher Opinionaire.

741. Forman, Susan G. "Stress-Management Training: Evaluation of Effects on School Psychological Services." Journal of School Psychology 19, no. 3 (Fall 1981): 233-241.

　　　Finds that teacher satisfaction with the services of school psychologists increases after school psychologists participate in a stress management training program and inservice workshops.

742. Foster, Robert E. "Burnout Among Teachers of Severely Handicapped, Autistic Children." Pointer 24, no. 2 (Winter 1980): 24-28.

　　　Considers four stages of teacher burnout and a strategy for personal growth among teachers of the severely handicapped.

743. Foxworth, Marilyn D.; Frances A. Karnes; and Rex L. Leonard. "The Factorial Validity of the Teacher Occupational Stress Factor Questionnaire for the Teacher of the Gifted." Educational and Psychological Measurement 44, no. 2 (Summer 1984): 527-532.

　　　Validates the Teacher Occupational Stress Factor Questionnaire among elementary school teachers of the gifted.

744. Francis, D. "Communication Apprehension as a Cause of Stress and Low Morale." Unicorn, Bulletin of the Australian College of Education 10, no. 3 (August 1984): 255-260.

   Examines the causes and effects of communication apprehension.

745. Friesen, David. Overall Stress and Job Satisfaction as Predictors of Burnout. 1986. ERIC, ED 274 698.

   Examines the ability of overall job stress, job satisfaction, job challenge, and role clarity to predict teacher burnout using the Maslach Burnout Inventory.

746. Galloway, David, and others. "Mental Health, Absences from Work, Stress and Satisfaction in a Sample of New Zealand Primary School Teachers." Australian and New Zealand Journal of Psychiatry 18, no. 4 (December 1984): 359-363.

   Discusses the correlation between mental health and absenteeism using the General Health Questionnaire; correlates mental health and job satisfaction using the Satisfaction with Teaching Questionnaire among primary school teachers.

747. Galloway, David, and others. Teachers and Stress. Final Report, January 1981-May 1982. 1982. ERIC, ED 231 055.

   Reviews previous research on teacher stress and surveys teachers in terms of stress inventories, questionnaires on satisfaction with teaching, and general health.

748. Gentile, Lance M., and Merna M. McMillan. "Combating Burnout: A Must for Secondary Urban Reading Teachers." Reading World 19, no. 4 (May 1980): 332-338.

   Studies causes of burnout among secondary urban reading teachers and offers ways to reduce it.

749. Gibson, R. Oliver, and Donald W. Raw. <u>Burnout and Organization in Education: A Synthesis of Literature</u>. 1980. ERIC, ED 196 891.

   Describes teacher burnout in terms of system stress by viewing systems and their relationships at four levels: somatic, psychological, social, and cultural.

750. Gierbolini-Rodriguez, Angel Manuel. "The Development and Validation of a Burnout Measure--The Inventario de Extenuacion Personal (IEP)--in a Selected Group of Bilingual Special Education Teachers in Puerto Rico." D.Ed. dissertation, The Pennsylvania State University, 1984.

   Develops and validates a burnout instrument, the Inventario de Extenuacion Personal, among bilingual special education teachers in the areas of emotional exhaustion, personal fulfillment, personal feeling, and personal identification.

751. Ginsberg, Rick, and Albert Bennett. "'I Don't Get No Respect.'" <u>VocEd</u> 56, no. 8 (November-December 1981): 34-36.

   Studies causes and effects of teacher stress.

752. Gold, Yvonne. "The Factorial Validity of the Maslach Burnout Inventory in a Sample of California Elementary and Junior High School Classroom Teachers." <u>Educational and Psychological Measurement</u> 44, no. 4 (Winter 1984): 1009-1016.

   Validates the Maslach Burnout Inventory among junior high school teachers.

753. Goodall, Robert, and Les Brown. "Understanding Teacher Stress." <u>Action in Teacher Education</u> 2, no. 4 (Fall 1980): 17-22.

   Offers suggestions to reduce teacher stress; identifies discipline as the major source of stress.

754. Gress, James R., and Joan D. Inglis. <u>Implementation and Assessment of a School Staff Development Model for Changing School Climate and Teacher Stress.</u> Revised. 1982. ERIC, ED 214 868.

Describes a staff development project that was developed to improve school climate and alleviate teacher stress.

755. Grier, Kenneth Scott. "A Study of Job Stress in Police Officers and High School Teachers." Ph.D. dissertation, University of South Florida, 1982.

Describes sources of high school teachers' stress using the Teacher Stress Inventory, the Job Descriptive Index, the State-Trait Personality Inventory, the Biodata Questionnaire, and the Stress-Satisfaction Questionnaire.

756. Grossnickle, Donald R. "Teacher Burnout: Will Talking About It Help?" <u>Clearing House</u> 54, no. 1 (September 1980): 17-18.

Alerts the public to the problems of low morale, poor climate, and teacher stress.

757. Grossnickle, Richard. "A Life-Support System for Teachers." <u>Clearing House</u> 54, no. 3 (November 1980): 135-137.

Lists ways administrators affect school climate, change, teacher stress, and burnout.

758. Grubis, Steve. <u>Frozen and Forgotten: Stress Among Alaskan Bush Teachers.</u> 1982. ERIC, ED 230 537.

Describes the stress factors associated with teaching in rural Alaska by highlighting the cultural and environmental differences.

759. Hawkes, Richard R., and Charles V. Dedrick. "Teacher Stress: Phase II of a Descriptive Study." <u>NASSP Bulletin</u> 67, no. 461 (March 1983): 78-83.

Presents the results of a followup study on teacher stress; shows a change in teachers' concerns.

760. Hawley, Richard A. "Mr. Chips Revisited." Learning 12, no. 5 (December 1983): 70-71.

   Uses "Mr. Chips" as a role model for teachers who refuse to "burn out."

761. Heath, Douglas. Faculty Burnout, Morale, and Vocational Adaptation. 1981. ERIC, ED 201 057.

   Examines the relationship between job adjustment and personal fulfillment; indicates that low teacher morale means low vocational adaptation.

762. Henderson, David L., and others. Moonlighting, Salary, Morale, and the Approaching Teacher Shortage: A Follow-up Study. 1982. ERIC, ED 223 594.

   Reports the results of a 1982 statewide survey of public school teachers indicating that many teachers are considering leaving; compares the 1982 results with the 1980 survey.

763. Hittner, Amy. "Teachers in Stress: A Study of the Relationship Between Job Importance Perceptions of Stress and Life Satisfaction Among Selected Urban High School Teachers." Ph.D. dissertation, University of California, Berkeley, 1979.

   Examines the importance of teaching, stress, and life satisfaction among urban secondary school teachers within the framework of Lazarus' cognitive-phenomenological approach to stress.

764. Hoodecheck, Donald Joseph. "Occupational Stress of School Teachers in Four Rural Minnesota School Districts." Ph.D. dissertation, University of Minnesota, 1982.

   Examines the effects of teacher stress on self-esteem, job satisfaction, general well-being, and health among rural teachers using Needle's Occupational Stress, Coping and Health Problems of Teachers Questionnaire.

765. Hooper, Mary Lloyd. "The Relationship Between Selected Demographic Variables, Job Satisfaction and Teacher Burnout." Ed.D. dissertation, Mississippi State University, 1982.

> Analyzes the relationship between demographic characteristics, job satisfaction, and teacher burnout using the Purdue Teacher Opinionaire and the Maslach Burnout Inventory.

766. Hubert, John A., and others. *The Unit of Analysis in the Study of the Relationship of Teacher Stress to School Variables.* 1983. ERIC, ED 260 106.

> Studies the relationship between teacher stress and school sources of stress among high school teachers using the Porter Need Satisfaction Questionnaire and the Maslach Burnout Inventory.

767. Hudson, Floyd, and Kathleen Meagher. *Variables Associated with Stress and Burnout of Regular and Special Education Teachers. Final Report.* 1983. ERIC, ED 239 471.

> Develops eight scales to compare stress among regular and special education teachers: Stress Prone Personality Inventory, Life Experience Stress Level, Internal Coping Skills, External Supports, Perception of Stressors, Psychological Symptoms, Physiological Symptoms, and Reactions to Stress.

768. Hughes, Louise Bradley. "Teacher Morale and Perceptions of Organizational Characteristics in Public Schools Serving Handicapped Children." Ed.D. dissertation, Columbia University Teachers College, 1983.

> Explores the interaction between perceived organizational characteristics in schools serving handicapped students and teacher morale in terms of burnout, professional commitment, teaching gratification, and overall teaching stress using the Profile of Organizational Characteristics, the Role Conflict/Role Ambiguity Scales, the Educational Attitude Survey, and the Teacher Attitude Survey.

769. Ingram, Leslie A. <u>Teacher Burnout in Special Education: The Personal Perspective of a Classroom Teacher</u>. 1980. ERIC, ED 187 073.

    Recounts the experiences of a special education teacher in terms of the stages of burnout and ways to reduce it.

770. Iwanicki, Edward F., and Richard L. Schwab. "A Cross Validation Study of the Maslach Burnout Inventory." <u>Educational and Psychological Measurement</u> 41, no. 4 (Winter 1981): 167-174.

    Gives suggestions for improving the reliability of the depersonalization subscale of the Maslach Burnout Inventory.

771. Jackson, Bette Geller. "Burnout in Teachers Working with Educationally Handicapped Children." Ph.D. dissertation, University of Southern California, 1983.

    Investigates the relationship between job satisfaction and burnout; the relationship between self-concept and burnout among teachers of the educationally handicapped using the Maslach Burnout Inventory, the Job Satisfaction Questionnaire, the Tennessee Self-Concept Scale, and a list of stressors.

772. Johanson, Marilynn. "Managing the Load." <u>VocEd</u> 56, no. 8 (November-December 1981): 42-44.

    Offers suggestions to reduce stress among teachers by managing the noninstructional part of their lives.

773. Johnson, Judith Lefkow. "Stress as Perceived by Teachers of Hearing Impaired Children and Youth." Ph.D. dissertation, Gallaudet College, 1983.

    Describes sources, symptoms, and levels of stress among teachers of hearing impaired youngsters.

774. Jones, Mary Ann, and Joseph Emanuel. "There Is Life After Burnout." *High School Journal* 64, no. 5 (February 1981): 209-212.

    Lists the steps a teacher goes through from the beginning to the last stage of burnout.

775. Kaiser, Jeffrey S., and James J. Polczynski. "Educational Stress: Sources, Reactions, Preventions." *Peabody Journal of Education* 59, no. 2 (January 1982): 127-136.

    Discusses sources of teacher stress, reactions to stress, the effects of stress on teacher performance, and methods to prevent stress.

776. Kass, Sandra E. "Occupational Stress of Regular and Special Education Teachers." Ed.D. dissertation, University of Missouri-Saint Louis, 1985.

    Compares stress among regular elementary school teachers and special education teachers using the Hopkins Symptom Checklist and the Teacher Occupational Stress Factor Questionnaire.

777. Katz, Alexander I.J. "The Relationship of Individual Needs and Perceived Organizational Stress to Job Satisfaction in a Comparative Study of Elementary School Principals and Teachers in New York City." Ph.D. dissertation, New York University, 1980.

    Explores the relationship between organizational stress and job satisfaction among teachers and principals using the Role Conflict-Role Ambiguity Questionnaire, the Job Description Index, Vroom's Need for Independence Questionnaire, and a Self Description Questionnaire.

778. Kells, Patricia P., and others. *Study of Competencies Related to Stress Management and Ecological Concerns of Special Education Personnel*. Kansas Regent Institutions Special Project. Summary Report. 1982. ERIC, ED 232 332.

    Presents fifty ecological and stress management competencies that were designed as part of a plan to retain special education teachers; includes rating scales and a bibliography.

779. Kerr, Barbara J. "A Study of Job Satisfaction and Burnout of Special-Education Teachers in Selected Areas of Rural Kansas." Doctoral dissertation, University of Kansas, 1985.

   Investigates burnout and job satisfaction among rural special education teachers; compares special education teachers of self-contained classes and special education teachers of itinerant and resource rooms.

780. Kim, Young Mi, and others. <u>Job-Stress and Burnout of the Venezuelan Teachers: Related to Educational Systems Change (Educacion Basica)</u>. 1984. ERIC, ED 244 368.

   Compares stress and burnout among teachers in a conventional educational system and those in the new "Educacion Basica" system; provides a review of the literature on job-related teacher stress.

781. Kleinberg, Susan Beth. "Occupational Environments and Support Systems: Their Effects on Stress and Job Satisfaction of Home/Hospital Teachers." Ph.D. dissertation, University of Maryland, 1983.

   Focuses on role ambiguity, role overload, role insufficiency, stress, and job satisfaction among home/hospital teachers using the Osipow-Spokane Personal Strain Questionnaire, the Osipow-Spokane Personal Resources Questionnaire, Rahe's Recent Life Changes Questionnaire, and Hoppock's Job Satisfaction Blank.

782. Knowles, Barry Snidow. "Psycho-Social Correlates of Teacher Burnout: A Study of Absenteeism, Job Satisfaction, Job Stress, and Locus of Control Among Special Education Teachers in Selected Counties of West Virginia." Ed.D. dissertation, West Virginia University, 1980.

   Investigates job satisfaction, job stress, locus of control, and absenteeism among special education teachers using the Job Descriptive Index, the Job Stress Scale, and the I-E Locus of Control Scale.

783. Koonce, Glenn Lee. "The Effects of a Structured Wellness Program on Physical and Mental Well-Being of Public School Teachers and Staff Members." Ed.D. dissertation, Virginia Polytechnic Institute and State University, 1986.

Evaluates the effects of a wellness program on elementary school teachers using the General Well-Being Schedule, the Trait Anxiety Subscale of the State-Trait Anxiety Inventory, and the Brayfield and Rothe Job Satisfaction Index.

784. Kossack, Sharon W., and Sandra L. Woods. "Teacher Burnout: Diagnosis, Prevention, Remediation." Action in Teacher Education 2, no. 4 (Fall 1980): 29-35.

Includes changing the school environment and perspectives on teaching and teaching situations to diagnose, prevent, and reduce teacher burnout.

785. Kurtz, Sandra. An Annotated Bibliography of Literature Dealing with Stress in the Teaching Profession. 1980. ERIC, ED 187 707.

Presents an annotated bibliography on teacher stress and burnout; explores causes, characteristics, and coping techniques.

786. Lawrenson, Gary M., and Archie J. McKinnon. "A Survey of Classroom Teachers of the Emotionally Disturbed: Attrition and Burnout Factors." Behavioral Disorders 8, no. 1 (November 1982): 41-49.

Surveys special education teachers to assess their attrition rate, their major reason for leaving, their major job satisfaction, and sources of burnout.

787. Lawrenson, Gary, and Archie J. McKinnon. *Attrition, Burnout, and Job Satisfactions of Teachers of the Emotionally Disabled*. 1980. ERIC, ED 195 104.

   Surveys teachers of the emotionally disabled to get information about teacher characteristics, job satisfactions, dissatisfactions, and reasons for leaving; conducts followup telephone interviews to clarify initial findings.

788. Leck, Glorianne M. "Teacher Burnout and the Extinguishing of Civic Education." *Teacher Education Quarterly* 11, no. 2 (Spring 1984): 29-34.

   Suggests using interpretive, normative, and critical skills to solve problems found in the educational setting.

789. LeMaster, Frederick Alan. "The Relationships Between Teacher Stress, Attitudes Toward the Profession and Organizational Climate." Ed.D. dissertation, Oklahoma State University, 1981.

   Investigates stress, attitudes toward teaching, and organizational climate among elementary school teachers using the Minnesota Teacher Attitude Inventory, the Openness Index of the Organizational Climate Description Questionnaire, and the Organizational Leadership Stress Questionnaire.

790. Liebes, Sherry. *An Aging Teacher Corps: How Should School Systems Respond?* 1983. ERIC, ED 235 553.

   Examines staff development programs and intervention techniques to help administrators and teachers deal with burnout.

791. Litt, Mark D., and Dennis C. Turk. "Sources of Stress and Dissatisfaction in Experienced High School Teachers." *Journal of Educational Reearch* 78, no. 3 (January-February 1985): 178-185.

   Surveys high school teachers to find out sources of dissatisfaction and stress that may lead to the decision to leave teaching; creates a construct of teacher stress using role, school climate, coping resources, and work problems.

792. Little, Linda F. "Interpersonal Skills for Home Economics Educators: Four Strategies to Prevent Helper Burnout." *Journal of Home Economics* 77, no. 1 (Spring 1985): 22-25, 27.

    Presents case studies to demonstrate the use of interpersonal strategies to prevent teacher burnout.

793. Lynch, James J. *Beating Burnout*. 1981. ERIC, ED 218 532.

    Analyzes school counselors' stress and feels that teachers may need to learn stress management techniques as part of their preparation.

794. Manera, Elizabeth S., and Robert E. Wright. "Can You Identify Your Source of Stress?" *Clearing House* 55, no. 2 (October 1981): 53-58.

    Describes a fourteen-item Q-Sort instrument on stress in teaching and reports the rank order of the stress variables among different groups of educators.

795. Marchand, James Alfred. "Life Experience Commonalities That Exist Among Successful Teachers: Implications for Burnout." Ph.D. dissertation, The University of Connecticut, 1982.

    Explores the factors that distinguish teachers with high job satisfaction from teachers with stress.

796. Mattox, Keith E. "Why Teachers Quit." *Agricultural Education Magazine* 47, no. 6 (December 1974): 141-143.

    Discusses stress factors as contributing to the decision to leave teaching.

797. Mazer, Irene R., and Marjorie Griffin. *Perceived and Experienced Stress of Teachers in a Medium Sized Local School District*. 1980. ERIC, ED 186 379.

    Studies stress conditions among teachers and finds that involuntary transfer is the most stressful event.

798. McIntyre, Thomas C. "The Effect of Class Size on Perceptions of Burnout by Special Education Teachers." <u>Mental Retardation and Learning Disability Bulletin</u> 11, no. 3 (1983): 142-145.

   Analyzes the relationship between class size and six factors of burnout among special education teachers using the Maslach Burnout Inventory.

799. McIntyre, Thomas. <u>Factors Related to Burnout: A Review of Research.</u> 1982. ERIC, ED 218 908.

   Investigates the relationship between locus of control and burnout among special education teachers using the Maslach Burnout Inventory.

800. Meadow, Kathryn P. "Burnout in Professionals Working with Deaf Children." <u>American Annals of the Deaf</u> 126, no. 1 (February 1981): 13-22.

   Compares burnout, career motivation, and job satisfaction among teachers of deaf students and teachers of nonhandicapped students.

801. Meadow, Kathryn P. <u>Support for Parents and Professionals: A Key Issue for the Field of Deaf Education in the 1980's.</u> 1980. ERIC, ED 203 628.

   Suggests building support systems, changing job assignments, recognizing teachers' achievement and permitting time out from the classroom as ways of preventing teacher stress and burnout.

802. Meinke, Dean L., and others. <u>Perceived Stress Events by Teachers.</u> 1982. ERIC, ED 222 448.

   Develops and factor analyzes an instrument to assess teacher stress.

803. Mersky, Ronald. <u>Management Practices: A Major Cause of Stress Among Teachers.</u> 1983. ERIC, ED 253 918.

   Studies task-based stress among rural teachers using the Teaching Events Stress Inventory.

804. Miller, Sheryl L. Teacher Burnout. 1981. ERIC, ED 204 317.

   Reviews the literature on teacher stress and burnout, causes of stress, and coping techniques.

805. Milstein, Mike M., and Thomas J. Golaszewski. "Effects of Organizationally Based and Individually Based Stress Management Efforts in Elementary School Settings." Urban Education 19, no. 4 (January 1985): 389-409.

   Reports sources of stress among urban elementary school teachers and discusses the effectiveness of stress management intervention strategies.

806. Milstein, Mike M., and Thomas J. Golaszewski. Effects of Organizationally-Based and Individually-Based Stress Management Efforts in Elementary School Settings. 1984. ERIC, ED 244 378.

   Compares elementary school teachers at an individually based intervention site, an organizationally based intervention site, and a control site in terms of stress, effects of organizationally based stressors, and individual manifestations of teacher stress.

807. Milstein, Mike M., and Thomas J. Golaszewski. Organizationally-Based Stress: What Bothers Teachers (An End of Year Perspective). 1983. ERIC, ED 231 048.

   Reports the results of a survey across four school sites to assess organizationally based stress among elementary school teachers.

808. Milstein, Mike M., and others. "Organizationally Based Stress: What Bothers Teachers." Journal of Educational Research 77, no. 5 (May-June 1984): 293-297.

   Finds that teachers' stress is related more to classroom situations than to the school climate.

809. Moll, Marita. <u>Teacher Stress</u>. Bibliographies in Education. No. 75. 1982. ERIC, ED 222 459.

    Presents a bibliography on teacher stress that includes burnout, alienation, morale, and job satisfaction.

810. Moracco, John C., and others. "Comparison of Perceived Occupational Stress Between Teachers Who Are Contented and Discontented in Their Career Choices." <u>Vocational Guidance Quarterly</u> 32, no. 1 (September 1983): 44-51.

    Compares levels of stress among teachers who deplore their career choice and those who do not.

811. Moracco, John C., and others. <u>Stress in Teaching: A Comparison of Perceived Stress Between Special Education and Regular Teachers</u>. 1981. ERIC, ED 202 828.

    Compares the effects of stress on special education teachers and regular education teachers using the Teacher Occupational Stress Factor Questionnaire.

812. Murphy Gwendolyn. "Teacher Stress: Measurement and Management." Ed.D. dissertation, Boston University, 1984.

    Develops the Teacher Stress Inventory to measure sources of teacher stress and then designs a stress management program for teachers.

813. Murray, Ann. "Staff Development: Fine and Fit." <u>Educational Leadership</u> 40, no. 1 (October 1982): 57.

    Describes stress management training and morale building techniques.

814. Mykletun, Reider J. "Work Stress and Satisfaction of Comprehensive School Teachers: An Interview Study." <u>Scandinavian Journal of Educational Research</u> 29, no. 2 (June 1985): 57-71.

    Examines the relationship between teacher stress and job satisfaction using structured interviews.

815. Mykletun, Reidar J. "Teacher Stress: Perceived and Objective Sources, and Quality of Life." Scandinavian Journal of Educational Research 28, no. 1 (March 1984): 17-45.

   Studies the relationship between teacher stress and the quality of life using a seventy-four-item job stress rating scale and the General Health Questionnaire.

816. Needle, Richard H., and others. "Teacher Stress: Sources and Consequences." Journal of School Health 50, no. 2 (February 1980): 96-99.

   Outlines an inservice teacher workshop to identify stress and manage it.

817. Newbrough, Art. "Twelve Steps Toward Revitalization for Teachers." Education 103, no. 3 (Spring 1983): 270-273.

   Discusses twelve ways to deal with teacher burnout including professional support.

818. Newcomb, L.H., and others. "Extent of Burnout Among Teachers of Vocational Agriculture in Ohio." Journal of the American Association of Teacher Educators in Agriculture 28, no. 1 (Spring 1987): 26-33.

   Analyzes teacher burnout, job satisfaction, and coping ability among vocational agriculture teachers.

819. Newman, Katherine K., and others. Stress in Teachers' Midcareer Transitions: A Role for Teacher Education. 1980. ERIC, ED 196 868.

   Describes a graduate couarse to help teachers understand the stages and transitions in their teaching careers; provides case studies to examine the personal and emotional factors.

820. New York State United Teachers. <u>NYSUT Teacher Stress Survey</u>. NYSUT United Teachers Information Bulletin. 1979. ERIC, ED 180 985.

    Reports the results of a survey to identify sources of stress among urban, suburban, and rural teachers.

821. OFlynn-Comiskey, Alice I. "Coping with Stress: Ideas that Work." <u>Pointer</u> 24, no. 2 (Winter 1980): 70-72.

    Provides suggestions to reduce teacher stress that include identifying behavior response style.

822. Olson, Judy, and Patricia V. Matuskey. "Causes of Burnout in SLD Teachers." <u>Journal of Learning Disabilities</u> 15, no. 2 (February 1982): 97-99.

    Identifies six job related factors of stress among learning disabilities teachers.

823. <u>Options in Education. Teacher Burnout, Parts One and Two. Programs No. 248-249</u>. 1980. ERIC, ED 196 847.

    Conducts interviews with teachers to understand teacher burnout and presents the findings in this two-part transcript of a public radio broadcast.

824. Paine, Whiton Stewart. "The Burnout Phenomenon." <u>VocEd</u> 56, no. 8 (November-December 1981): 30-33.

    Defines teacher burnout and examines its causes, effects, and techniques to cope.

825. Partin, Ronald L., and Richard M. Gargiulo. "Burned Out Teachers Have No Class Prescriptions for Teacher Educators." <u>College Student Journal</u> 14, no. 4 (Winter 1980): 365-368.

    Recommends teaching beginning teachers how to recognize the early stages of stress before they become burned out.

826. Pattavina, Paul. "Bridging the Gap Between Stress and Support for Public School Teachers: A Conversation with Dr. William C. Morse About Teacher Burnout." Pointer 24, no. 2 (Winter 1980): 88-94.

   Summarizes an interview with William C. Morse on burnout among special education teachers.

827. Penny, James A. "Burnout." Science Teacher 49, no. 7 (October 1982): 46-49.

   Provides suggestions for dealing with teacher stress and avoiding burnout.

828. Pettegrew, Loyd S., and Glenda E. Wolf. "Validating Measures of Teacher Stress." American Educational Research Journal 19, no. 3 (Fall 1982): 373-396.

   Explores role-related stress, task-based stress, and environmental stress among secondary school teachers; validates a multivariate assessment instrument.

829. Pettegrew, Loyd S., and Glenda E. Wolf. Validating Measures of Teacher Stress. 1981. ERIC, ED 213 743.

   Uses a known groups approach to validate three stress measures among teachers: role-related stress, task-based stress, and environmental stress.

830. Portner, David Michael. "Reported Stress and Well-Being in Teachers and Student Teachers." Ph.D. dissertation, Saint Louis University, 1982.

   Investigates the relationship between stress, well-being, job satisfaction, and demographic variables among teachers and student teachers.

831. Pour, Barbara Hanna. "Who Speaks for Teachers? A Commentary on Teaching." Childhood Education 57, no. 5 (May-June 1981): 258-261.

   Identifies negative aspects of teaching that cause burnout and offers recommendations for making teaching more exciting.

832. Presley, Priscilla Henshaw. <u>Teacher Burnout in Special Education--Myth or Reality?</u> 1982. ERIC, ED 218 909.

   Measures teacher burnout among special education teachers using the Maslach Burnout Inventory; includes symptoms of burnout and recommendations for reducing it.

833. Radocy, Rudolf E., and George N. Heller. "Tips for Coping: The Music Educator and Stress." <u>Music Educators Journal</u> 69, no. 4 (December 1982): 43, 62-63.

   Discusses sources of stress among music teachers and coping strategies.

834. Rathbone, Charles, and Chaunce Benedict. <u>A Study of Teacher Burnout at the Junior High School Level.</u> 1980. ERIC, ED 190 547.

   Focuses on teacher burnout among junior high school teachers; categorizes interview data into five areas.

835. <u>Reduction in Force and Teacher Burnout.</u> 1984. ERIC, ED 259 474.

   Discusses reduction in force and teacher burnout; lists methods to cope with RIF and teacher stress.

836. Reese, Shirley Green. "Teacher Job Satisfaction and Job Stress of Urban Secondary School Physical Education Teachers." Ph.D. dissertation, The Florida State University, 1985.

   Studies the relationship between urban high school physical education teachers' job satisfaction and job stress using the Job Satisfaction Scale and the Job-Related Stress Scale.

837. Retish, Paul. "Burnout and Stress Among Special Educators and Others." <u>B.C. Journal of Special Education</u> 10, no. 3 (1986): 267-270.

   Discusses the effects of stress and burnout among special education teachers.

838. Riccio, Anthony C. "On Coping with the Stresses of Teaching." Theory into Practice 22, no. 1 (Winter 1983): 43-47.

   Suggests coping strategies for teachers; recommends the development of a strong, positive self-image.

839. Ricken, Robert. "Teacher Burnout--A Failure of the Supervisory Process." NASSP Bulletin 64, no. 434 (March 1980): 21-24.

   Offers suggestions to prevent teacher burnout by improving the supervisory process.

840. Riley, Bob E. Teacher Stress: A Workshop Approach. 1981. ERIC, ED 212 607.

   Describes a workshop approach to deal with teacher stress that defines stress, lists sources of stress, identifies positive and negative aspects of stress, and offers coping strategies.

841. Ryerson, Diane. "Organizational Strategies to Reduce the Risk." VocEd 56, no. 8 (November-December 1981): 40-41.

   Describes methods to alleviate teacher burnout, including participative decision making, flexible scheduling, advancement, and inservice training.

842. Sadler, James C., and James W. Cunningham. "Burnout and the Reading Teacher." Reading Horizons 23, no. 4 (Summer 1983): 223-229.

   Describes the cause of burnout among reading teachers and offers suggestions for preventing it.

843. St. Clair, Jack L. "Educator Stress in Terms of Selected Variables." Ed.D. dissertation, The Louisiana State University and Agricultural and Mechanical College, 1981.

   Develops the Sources of Stress Inventory to examine the interaction between grade level, years' experience, job satisfaction, and stressful work related events.

844. Santangelo, Sole, and David Lester. "Correlates of Job Satisfaction of Public School Teachers: Moonlighting, Locus of Control, and Stress." Psychological Reports 56, no. 1 (February 1985).

   Examines the relationship between teacher job satisfaction, stress, and locus of control using a job dissatisfaction scale, a measure of subjective perceived stress, and Rotter's Internal-External Locus of Control.

845. Sarros, James C. The Stress Stories of School Teachers and Administrators. 1986. ERIC, ED 270 409.

   Discusses aspects of the job that contribute to burnout among teachers and administrators using Maslach and Jackson's definition of burnout.

846. Saunders, Robert Ronald, and J. Foster Watkins. Teacher Burnout/Stress Management: An Exploratory Look in an Urban School System in Alabama. 1982. ERIC, ED 236 109.

   Develops a profile of teachers with high stress tendencies using a demographic questionnaire, the Teacher Occupational Stress Factor Questionnaire, and the Personal Lifestyle Survey.

847. Saunders, Ron, and J. Foster Watkins. Teacher Burnout/Stress Management Research: Implications for Teacher Preparation/Personnel Selection/Staff Development. 1980. ERIC, ED 225 940.

   Investigates the relationship between teacher personal and organizational variables and the types of stress using the Clark Teacher Occupational Stress Factor Questionnaire and the Everly Personal Lifestyle Survey.

848. Scharf, Sidney. "Factors Underlying the Measurement of Teacher Burnout." Ph.D. dissertation, Fordham University, 1984.

   Predicts that the same three factors can be identified in the Maslach Burnout Inventory and the Burnout-Tedium Measure and then correlates the Job Diagnostic Survey to the burnout factors.

849. Scherer, Marge. "Happy, Healthy Teaching. A Teacher's Guide to Do-It-Yourself Renewal." Instructor 92, no. 5 (January 1983): 44-46.

   Presents ideas to help teachers deal with problems involving teacher conditions, student behavior, burnout, and other sources of stress.

850. School Climate and Teacher Stress. Final Report of the Ohio Teacher Institute (1980-1981). 1981. ERIC, ED 225 953.

   Focuses on identifying sources of teacher stress, coping with stress, and understanding school climate on four levels: the teacher, the school, the classroom, and the student.

851. Schorr, Justin. "Toward a New Sense of Vocation." Art Education 35, no. 5 (September 1982): 24-26.

   Emphasizes the role that attitudes toward teaching play in coping with stress among art teachers.

852. Schwab, Richard L. "Teacher Burnout: Moving Beyond 'Psychobabble.'" Theory into Practice 22, no. 1 (Winter 1983): 21-26.

   Reviews the literature on teacher burnout and defines areas that require more research.

853. Schwab, Richard L., and Edward F. Iwanicki. "Perceived Role Conflict, Role Ambiguity, and Teacher Burnout." Educational Administration Quarterly 18, no. 1 (Winter 1982): 60-74.

   Finds a significant relationship between role conflict and emotional exhaustion and negative attitudes toward students; finds a significant relationship between role ambiguity and a lack of personal accomplishment.

854. Schwab, Richard L., and Edward F. Iwanicki. "Who Are Our Burned Out Teachers?" <u>Educational Research Quarterly</u> 7, no. 2 (Summer 1982): 5-16.

Examines the relationship between teacher background variables and burnout using the Maslach Burnout Inventory.

855. Schwanke, Dean, comp. <u>Teacher Stress: Selected ERIC Resources</u>. 1981. ERIC, ED 204 258.

Presents an annotated bibliography on teacher stress and burnout; includes research on teacher morale and job satisfaction.

856. Schwartz, Henrietta, and others. <u>School as a Workplace: The Realities of Stress. Volume I, Executive Summary; Volume II, School Site Case Studies and the Role of the Principal; Volume III, Methodology and Instrumentation</u>. 1983. ERIC, ED 239 009.

Examines the relationship between working conditions and teacher stress; includes a review of the literature, case studies, and instrumentation.

857. "77 Ways to Prevent Burnout." <u>VocEd</u> 56, no. 8 (November-December 1981): 49-51.

Offers seventy-seven ways to reduce teacher burnout and improve teacher morale.

858. Shaw, Stan F., and others. <u>Stress and Burnout: A Primer for Special Education and Special Services Personnel</u>. 1981. ERIC, ED 201 168.

Designs a primer to reduce burnout among special education teachers; focuses on assessing stress, inservice training, and various teacher and administrative roles.

859. Shaw, Stan, and others. <u>Preventing Teacher Burnout: Suggestions for Efficiently Meeting P.L. 94-142 Mandates and Providing for Staff Survival</u>. 1980. ERIC, ED 187 048.

    Considers burnout among special education teachers and suggests ways to reduce burnout.

860. Shaw, Stan, and others. "Strategies for Dealing with Burnout Among Special Educators." <u>Education Unlimited</u> 2, no. 4 (September-October 1980): 21-23.

    Suggests personnel and organizational management techniques to alleviate teacher burnout among special education teachers.

861. Shields-Kole, Joan E., and others. "Rediscovering the Joys of Teaching." <u>Association for Communication Administration Bulletin</u>, no. 45 (August 1983): 65-69.

    Provides a list of role-related needs and ways of satisfying these needs in order to minimize burnout, stress, and apathy.

862. Shoop, Linda. <u>Stress Management for School Personnel</u>. 1980. ERIC, ED 198 108.

    Outlines four approaches to deal with teacher stress.

863. Skinner, Michael G. "Combating the Effects of Debilitating Stress." <u>Pointer</u> 24, no. 2 (Winter 1980): 12-21.

    Reviews ways teachers react to stress, including rigidity, aggression, negativism, and withdrawal.

864. Smith, Dennie L., and Lana McWilliams. "Diagnostic-Prescriptive Approach to Reading Teacher Burnout." *Reading World* 20, no. 1 (October 1980): 53-56.

    Describes causes of burnout among reading teachers and offers suggestions to reduce burnout.

865. Smith, Sue Spratt. "Tell the Tomatoes to Get Along Without You." *English Journal* 70, no. 4 (April 1981): 28-29.

    Recommends attending summer conferences to revitalize English teachers.

866. Sny, Christopher L. "Stress and Its Relationship to the Educational Environment and Administration of Randomly Selected Wisconsin Public Schools." Ph.D. dissertation, The University of Wisconsin-Madison, 1984.

    Explains the relationship between job satisfaction of teachers and administrators and stress.

867. Sparks, Dennis C. "A Biased Look at Teacher Job Satisfaction." *Clearing House* 52, no. 9 (May 1979): 447-449.

    Administers a questionnaire during a Teacher Stress in-service workshop and discusses that 46 percent of the teachers present were dissatisfied with their job and would not choose teaching as a career if they could start all over.

868. Sparks, Dennis, and Janice Hammond. *Managing Teacher Stress and Burnout*. 1981. ERIC, ED 200 522.

    Offers a guide to identifying sources of stress, examining job satisfactions, and managing stress.

869. Stone, Jackie Alexander. "The Relationships Between Perceived Stress and Job Satisfaction, Locus of Control, and Length of Teaching Experience." Ed.D. dissertation, University of Houston, 1982.

   Examines the relationships between teacher stress, job satisfaction, locus of control, and length of teaching experience using the Job Descriptive Index, the Nowicki-Strickland Locus of Control instrument and the IPAT Anxiety Scale.

870. Stone, M.C. "Practical Observations Associated with Teacher Stress and Morale." Unicorn, Bulletin of the Australian College of Education 10, no. 3 (August 1984): 251-254.

   Points out causes for low morale and high stress among teachers.

871. Stubblefield, Phillip. "The Relationship Between Stress, Job Satisfaction, and Teaching Assignments Among Music Educators in the State of Michigan." Ph.D. dissertation, Michigan State University, 1983.

   Investigates the relationships between stress, job satisfaction, and teaching assignment among music teachers using the Stress-Related Questionnaire and the Job Description Index.

872. Sutton, Geoffrey, W., and Thomas J. Huberty. "An Evaluation of Teacher Stress and Job Satisfaction." Education 105, no. 2 (Winter 1984): 189-192.

   Compares stress and job satisfaction among regular education teachers and teachers of the severely handicapped in private schools using the Wilson Stress Profile for Teachers.

873. Swick, Kevin J., and Patricia E. Hanley. <u>Stress and the Classroom Teacher. What Research Says to the Teacher</u>. 1980. ERIC, ED 201 639.

    Discusses the positive and negative effects of teacher stress.

874. "Teacher Burnout." <u>USA Today</u> 113, no. 2479 (April 1985): 8-9.

    Predicts teacher burnout by studying participation in decision-making, job expectations, teacher autonomy, and role conflict.

875. <u>Teacher Satisfaction in Georgia and the Nation: Status and Trends. Teacher Burnout: Causes and Possible Cures</u>. Issues for Education Series. 1980. ERIC, ED 194 515.

    Identifies symptoms, causes, and consequences of teacher stress.

876. Thomas, Marcia Ann. "Observational Assessment of Stress-Related Behavior in Teacher Trainees: Development of an Instrument." Ed.D. dissertation, The George Washington University, 1984.

    Develops the Behavior Pattern Observation Scale for Teachers to assess stress-related behaviors in teacher trainees.

877. Thompson, Cathy Lynn. "A Comparison of Nonburned-Out and Burned-Out Teachers." Ph.D. dissertation, The Pennsylvania State University, 1985.

    Compares nonburned out elementary school teachers and burned out ones using the I-E Scale, the Role Ambiguity Scale, the Human Services Survey, and the Personal Opinion Questionnaire.

878. Treacy, Thomas Denis. "Teacher Perceptions Associated with Occupational Stress." Ed.D. dissertation, Temple University, 1983.

    Examines stress related physical illness, stress related psychological strain, sources of occupational stress, and burnout among teachers.

879. Trickett, Paul L. "Job Satisfaction of Teachers: The Impact of Rational Beliefs and Life Stress." Psy.D. dissertation, Rutgers University, The State University of New Jersey, G.S.A.P.P., 1981.

   Studies the effects of rational beliefs and non-occupational life stress on job satisfaction among elementary and middle school teachers using the Jones Irrational Beliefs Tests, the Social Readjustment Rating Scale, and seventeen items developed by E.A. Locke.

880. Triesen, David, and Mary-Jo Williams. "Organizational Stress Among Teachers." *Canadian Journal of Education* 10, no. 1 (Winter 1985): 13-34.

   Identifies sources of stress among teachers; finds that role overload, work load, relationships with peers, and relationships with students contribute to overall job stress.

881. Turner, Lana Gay. "Stress in Female Secondary Classroom Teachers." Ed.D. dissertation, Ball State University, 1985.

   Explores the relationship between stressful situations in the classroom and stress among female secondary school teachers using the Perceived Stress Questionnaire and the Perceived Needs in Stress Counseling instrument.

882. Van Hesteren, Frank. "The Counselor as a Stress Management Consultant to School Staffs." *Canadian Counsellor* 17, no. 1 (October 1982): 20-28.

   Provides a literature review and resource materials for stress management; describes the role of a counselor within the school setting.

883. Wangberg, Elaine G. "The Complex Issue of Teacher Stress and Job Dissatisfaction." *Contemporary Education* 56, no. 1 (Fall 1984): 11-15.

   Discusses teacher stress and job dissatisfaction in terms of societal, institutional, and personal variables.

884. Wangberg, Elaine G., and Justin E. Levitov. "Differences in Perceived Stress of Elementary Versus Secondary School Teachers." *Illinois School Research and Development* 20, no. 1 (Fall 1983): 33-37.

   Compares sources of stress among elementary and secondary school teachers.

885. Warnat, Winifred I. "Teacher Stress in the Middle Years: Crisis vs. Change." *Pointer* 24, no. 2 (Winter 1980): 4-11.

   Examines teacher stress among middle age teachers and believes that stress can either produce crisis or promote change.

886. Wechsler, Leonard David. "The Effects of Different Types of Stress as Perceived by Teachers in an Urban High School." Ed.D. dissertation, Columbia University Teachers College, 1983.

   Uses ethnographic techniques in an urban high school to examine the attitudes of academic and vocational teachers toward their jobs and students using the Farber Teacher Attitude Survey.

887. Wendt, Janice C. *Coping Skills: A Goal of Professional Preparation*. 1980. ERIC, ED 212 604.

   Describes the role that teacher education programs can play in reducing teacher stress by preparing beginning teachers for their new positions.

888. Werner, Anthony. "Support for Teachers in Stress: The Principal's Role." *Pointer* 24, no. 2 (Winter 1980): 54-60.

   Discusses the role of the principal in reducing teacher stress by offering emotional support.

889. Zabel, Mary Kay, and others. "Factors of Emotional Exhaustion, Depersonalization, and Sense of Accomplishment Among Teachers of the Gifted." *Gifted Child Quarterly* 28, no. 2 (Spring 1984): 65-69.

   Examines burnout among teachers of the gifted using the Maslach Burnout Inventory.

890. Zabel, Robert H., and Mary Kay Zabel. "Factors in Burnout Among Teachers of Exceptional Children." *Exceptional Children* 49, no. 3 (November 1982): 261-263.

   Surveys junior high school level special education teachers in terms of occupational stress and burnout.

891. Zabel, Robert H., and Mary Kay Zabel. *Factors Involved in Burn-Out Among Teachers of Emotionally Disturbed and Other Types of Exceptional Children.* 1981. ERIC, ED 204 943.

   Examines teacher burnout among special education teachers using three burnout measures.

892. Zabel, Robert H., and Mary Kay Zabel. "Burnout: A Critical Issue for Educators." *Education Unlimited* 2, no. 2 (March 1980): 23-25.

   Defines teacher burnout among special education teachers and provides suggestions for alleviating burnout.

893. Zahn, Jane. "Burnout in Adult Educators." *Lifelong Learning: The Adult Years* 4, no. 4 (December 1980): 4-6.

   Describes the characteristics, sources, and solutions to the problem of burnout among adult educators.

894. Zahner, Mary Catherine. "Differential Well-Being of Educators." Ph.D. dissertation, Saint Louis University, 1980.

   Investigates levels and types of stress, well-being, and job satisfaction among teachers using a questionnaire about different aspects in their work experience, in their well-being, and demographic characteristics.

IX. TEACHING

895. Adams, Ronald D., and Carl Martray. <u>Teacher Development: A Study of Factors Related to Teacher Concerns for Pre, Beginning, and Experienced Teachers</u>. 1981. ERIC, ED 200 591.

   Assesses teacher concerns using the Teacher Concerns Checklist; correlates concerns with levels of experience.

896. Adams, Ronald D., and Carl R. Martray. <u>Correlates of Teacher Perceived Problems</u>. 1980. ERIC, ED 195 567.

   Develops the Teacher Preparation Evaluation Inventory to identify problems encountered by teachers; correlates the four identified factors with the F-scale, the Rokeach Dogmatism Scale, and the Teacher Concerns Checklist.

897. Anand, Usha, and T.S. Sohal. "Relationship Between Some Personal Traits, Job Satisfaction and Job Performance of Employees." <u>Journal of Psychological Researches</u> 25, no. 3 (September 1981): 159-163.

   Investigates the relationships among personal and job-related characteristics, job performance, and four aspects of job satisfaction (institutional participation, recognition, environment, and affiliation with work).

898. Appelgryn, A.E., and C. Plug. "Application of the Theory of Relative Deprivation to Occupational Discrimination Against Women." South African Journal of Psychology 11, no. 4 (1981): 143-147.

   Tests the theory of relative deprivation by examining teacher job satisfaction using the Job Description Index, the Bem Sex-Role Inventory, and the Wilson-Patterson Attitude Inventory.

899. Arndt, Charles Richard. "Correlates of Teacher Effectiveness: Environmental Robustness and Other Teacher Characteristics." Ph.D. dissertation, Bowling Green State University, 1981.

   Examines teacher in-school environmental robustness, teacher out-of-school environmental robustness, teacher self-concept, and teacher job satisfaction using the Robustness Semantic Differential scales, the Acceptance of Self and Others Scales, and the Purdue Teacher Opinionaire.

900. Atkin, J. Myron. "Who Will Teach in High School?" History Teacher 15, no. 2 (February 1982): 225-242.

   Looks at the reasons why high-achieving college students are not becoming high school teachers.

901. Barber, Patricia Ann. "Job Satisfaction of Elementary and Secondary Teachers." Ed.D. dissertation, Rutgers University, The State University of New Jersey (New Brunswick), 1980.

   Studies the relationship between general, intrinsic, and extrinsic teacher job satisfaction and demographic variables using a modified version of the Minnesota Satisfaction Questionnaire.

902. Barter, Richard F. "Rejuvenating Teachers." Independent School 43, no. 3 (February 1984): 37-42.

   Reviews research on teacher effectiveness and makes recommendations to meet teachers' needs.

903. Bell, T. H. The Peer Review Model for Managing a Career Ladder/Master Teacher/Performance Pay Program for Elementary and Secondary Schools. 1983. ERIC, ED 242 097.

   Describes a career ladder system for teachers.

904. Bentley, Ralph R., and Averno M. Rempel. Changing Teacher Morale: An Experiment in Feedback of Identified Problems of Teachers and Principals. Final Report. 1967. ERIC, ED 021 779.

   Uses the Purdue Teacher Opinionaire to measure high school teachers' morale.

905. Bentzen, Mary M., and others. "A Study of Schooling: Adult Experiences in Schools." Phi Delta Kappan 61, no. 6 (February 1980): 394-397.

   Provides information about teachers' experiences in schools using the "Study of Schooling."

906. Bilsky, Dorothy Gartner. "An Analysis of the Relationship of Teachers' Job Satisfaction and Teachers' Union Attitudes in a Large Midsouthern City." Ed.D. dissertation, Memphis State University, 1982.

   Examines the relationship between teachers' job satisfaction and teachers' attitudes toward collective bargaining; investigates the effects of personal and external factors on teachers' attitudes toward collective bargaining.

907. Boardman, Randolph Melvin. "The Relationship Between Life Satisfaction and Job Satisfaction Among Teachers in Four Midwestern States." Ed.D. dissertation, The University of Nebraska-Lincoln, 1985.

   Explores the relationship between life satisfaction and teacher job satisfaction in terms of leisure time, family life, health, government, life off the job, working conditions, pay, recognition, supervision, and the job in general.

908. Bogad, Carolyn McWilliams. <u>The Process of Deciding "Not" to Become a Teacher</u>. 1983. ERIC, ED 230 515.

   Identifies three categories of reasons for not choosing a teaching position among students in a five-year credential program using interviews and case studies.

909. Book, Michael Dell. "Collective Bargaining, Teachers and Job Satisfaction." Ed.D. dissertation, Drake University, 1982.

   Compares teacher job satisfaction among schools with certified bargaining units and those without using the Minnesota Satisfaction Questionnaire.

910. Bouie, Ann Sherrell. "The Relationship Between Teacher Career Aspirations, Job Satisfaction and School Socioeconomic Status." Ph.D. dissertation, Stanford University, 1977.

   Develops a four-part questionnaire to study the relationships between school socioeconomic status, elementary school teacher's job satisfaction, career aspirations, and the utility of the master's degree for horizontal or vertical mobility.

911. Bradley, Kath. "Recruitment to the Teaching Profession." <u>Educational Research</u> 25, no. 2 (June 1983): 116-124.

   Compares teaching as a career choice among those who were actually teaching and those who decided against teaching.

912. Bridges, Edwin M. "Job Satisfaction and Teacher Absenteeism." <u>Educational Administration Quarterly</u> 16, no. 2 (Spring 1980): 41-56.

   Investigates the relationship between teacher job satisfaction and absenteeism.

913. Butler, John Kenrick. "Some Effects of Role-Value Congruence on Job Satisfaction." D.B.A. dissertation, The Florida State University, 1977.

   Studies the effects of personal work values on job satisfaction among teachers using Super's Work Values Inventory, the Minnesota Satisfaction Questionnaire, the Marlowe-Crowne Social Desirability Scale, the Dull vs. Bright scale of Cottell's Sixteen Personality Factor Questionnaire, and questions developed by the researcher.

914. Calder, Paula Holzman. Role Conflict and Its Correlates in an Educational Setting. Final Report. 1969. ERIC, ED 033 454.

   Explores the relationship between teacher satisfaction and role dissensus.

915. Caram, Dorothy Farrington. "An Analysis of Factors Associated with Job Dissatisfaction and Quitting Behavior Among Urban Public School Teachers." Ed.D. dissertation, University of Houston, 1982.

   Develops two models (restricted and less restricted) to predict teacher alienation and quitting behavior.

916. Carey, Jane Frances. "A Study of Dissonance in the Classroom Setting: Its Relationship to Teacher Job Satisfaction, Student Achievement and School Satisfaction." Ph.D. dissertation, University of Maryland, 1974.

   Develops the Teacher Role Perception Scale to measure student expectations for teachers and studies dissonance from unfulfilled teacher and student expectations in relation to teacher job satisfaction.

917. Carillon, James W., and Robert I. Sutton. "The Relationship Between Union Effectiveness and the Quality of Members' Worklife." Journal of Occupational Behaviour 3, no. 2 (April 1982): 171-179.

   Examines the relationship between teacher job satisfaction and union effectiveness.

918. Catney, Robert T. "A Study of the Relationships Among (1) Job Satisfaction and (2) Teacher Attitude and Involvement in a Teacher Center." Ed.D. dissertation, Syracuse University, 1976.

   Investigates the relationships among elementary school teachers' job satisfaction, teacher attitudes, and participation in a teacher center using the Minnesota Satisfaction Questionnaire and a semantic differential test designed by the researcher to assess attitudes toward the components of the teacher center.

919. Chapman, David W. "Career Satisfaction of Teachers." Educational Research Quarterly 7, no. 3 (Fall 1982): 40-50.

   Relates teachers' career satisfaction to skills, values, and accomplishments using Holland's Theory of Occupational Choice.

920. Chapman, David W., and Malcolm A. Lowther. "Teachers' Satisfaction with Teaching." Journal of Educational Research 75, no. 4 (March-April 1982): 241-247.

   Proposes a conceptual scheme to study the relationship between attitudes, values, and accomplishments and teachers' career satisfaction.

921. Chapman, Jack. "The Heuristicism of the Self-Actualized Teacher." Ed.D. dissertation, University of Kansas, 1978.

   Looks at teacher self-actualization, creativity, personal growth, and job satisfaction among teachers using the California Q-sort method to develop a personality profile and a psychological job description.

922. Chatelain, Timothy D. "The Relationship Between Rate of Verbal Participation in Shared Decision Making and Teacher Job Satisfaction." Ed.D. dissertation, Brigham Young University, 1985.

    Examines the relationship between rate of verbal participation in shared decision making and teacher job satisfaction using a record of verbal responses and the Teacher Job Satisfaction Survey.

923. Chen, Wen-Shyong. "The Job Satisfaction of School Teachers in the Republic of China as Related to Personal and Organizational Characteristics." Ph.D. dissertation, University of Minnesota, 1977.

    Studies teacher job satisfaction in terms of satisfied and dissatisfied teachers using the Minnesota Satisfaction Questionnaire.

924. Clarke, Robert, and others. "Age as a Factor in Teacher Job Satisfaction." Psychology: A Quarterly Journal of Human Behavior 22, no. 2 (1985): 19-23.

    Studies the effect of age on teacher job satisfaction.

925. Clarken, Rodney Hal. "Congruency as a Predictor of Job Choice and Satisfaction for Teachers." Ph.D. dissertation, Wayne State University, 1983.

    Tests Holland's congruency hypothesis to predict job choice for teacher education students and job satisfaction for teachers using the Vocational Preference Inventory and the Hoppock Job Satisfaction Blank No. 5.

926. Cobb, Sara Frances Head. "Job Satisfaction of Teachers in a Selected County as Measured by the Purdue Teacher Opinionaire." Ed.D. dissertation, University of Southern Mississippi, 1986.

    Compares teacher job satisfaction among elementary and secondary school teachers using the Purdue Teacher Opinionaire.

927. Cole, Dennis Wyman. "An Analysis of Job Satisfaction Among Elementary, Middle Level, and Senior High School Teachers." Ed.D. dissertation, University of Colorado at Boulder, 1977.

   Compares job satisfaction among elementary, middle, and senior high school teachers using the Job Description Index.

928. Conroy, Joseph Patrick. "The Effect on the Job Descriptive Index Used for Measuring Teacher Job Satisfaction When a Student Area Is Added." Ed.D. dissertation, University of Denver, 1979.

   Develops a student area subscale and adds it to the Job Descriptive Index to create the Teacher Job Descriptive Index.

929. Cooper, Gary Robert. "Collegial Supervision: The Feasibility of Implementation and Particular Effectiveness on Teacher Attitudes and Job Satisfaction." Ed.D. dissertation, University of Pennsylvania, 1983.

   Describes the effectiveness of a collegial supervision program on teachers' attitudes and job satisfaction using recorded interviews, informal conversations, teacher logs, attendance records, and attitude surveys.

930. Coughlan, Robert J. "Job Satisfaction in Relatively Closed and Open Schools." *Educational Administration Quarterly* 7, no. 2 (1971): 40-59.

   Investigates the effects of teachers' work values on their job satisfaction in closed and open systems.

931. Crawford, John Haley. "Teacher Recruitment and Retention in a Rural School District: A Case Study." Ph.D. dissertation, Georgia State University--College of Education, 1986.

   Explores the relationships among low student achievement, teacher job satisfaction, morale, recruitment, and retention among rural school teachers using the Teacher Performance Assessment Instrument and the Organizational Commitment Questionnaire.

932. Davidson, Wilma, and Susan Kline. "Job Sharing in Education." Clearing House 52, no. 5 (January 1979): 226-228.

   Presents the advantages of job sharing for all school personnel; discusses programs in three states.

933. Deever, R. Merwin, and H. Allen Shockley. Job Satisfaction of Teachers in Selected Extended School Year Program. Research Reports on Educational Administration, Volume 5, Number 5. 1975. ERIC, ED 181 583.

   Summarizes a doctoral dissertation that discusses teacher job satisfaction in extended school year programs.

934. DeFazio, Richard Joseph. "A Study of the Relationships Among Teacher Job Satisfaction, Teacher Militancy, and School District Conflict." Ed.D. dissertation, Syracuse University, 1978.

   Examines the relationships among teacher job satisfaction, teacher militancy, and school district conflict using the Minnesota Satisfaction Questionnaire and the Index of Activity Inventory.

935. DeLong, Thomas J. "Career Orientations of Rural Educators: An Investigation." Rural Educator 4, no. 2 (Winter 1982): 12-16.

   Surveys rural teachers to assess eight career orientations using the Career Orientations Inventory; discusses reasons why rural teachers quit.

936. Denton, Jon J. Employment and Academic Characteristics of Former Undergraduate Education Students. 1983. ERIC, ED 227 058.

   Compares employment patterns and academic profiles among education and agriculture graduates.

937. Devlin, Barbara Seeley. "Teacher Participation in Decision-Making and Its Relationship to the Variables, Job Satisfaction, Organizational Commitment, Job Tension, and Attitudinal Militancy." Ph.D. dissertation, University of Minnesota, 1978.

　　Examines the relationships between extent and nature of teacher participation in decision-making and teacher job satisfaction, organizational commitment, job tension, and attitudinal militancy among secondary teachers using the School and Faculty Information Profile, the Survey of Principal Attitudes, and the Teacher View of the School Organization instrument; considers mediating variables.

938. deVoss, Gary, and Carol Phelps. <u>Follow-Up of a Random Sample of 1975/78 Graduates at The Ohio State University's College of Education Teacher Certification Program</u>. Technical Report No. 4. 1979. ERIC, ED 201 617.

　　Reports on the career choices of education graduates who are teaching or who chose not to teach; asks questions about attitudes toward the job, current problems, and patterns they think their careers will follow.

939. Dewar, A. M., and H. A. Lawson. "The Subjective Warrant and Recruitment into Physical Education." <u>Quest</u> 36, no. 1 (1984): 15-25.

　　Describes recruitment and perceptions of skills and abilities for physical education teachers.

940. Dickinson, Damon J. "The Relation Between the Evaluation of Teachers and Job Satisfaction and Teachers' Views on the Evaluation of Teachers." Ph.D. dissertation, University of Oregon, 1986.

　　Describes teachers' views of evaluation practices, teachers' overall job satisfaction, and teachers' professional orientation among teachers in grades kindergarten through eight.

941. Dillon, Roy D. "Identification of Factors Influencing Vocational Agriculture Teachers to Leave Teaching." <u>Journal of the American Association of Teacher Educators in Agriculture</u> 19, no. 3 (November 1978): 34-39.

    Identifies sixteen factors for leaving teaching among agricultural education teachers using personal interviews.

942. Divers, Arthur Jesse. "An Analysis of the Relationship of Teacher Job Satisfaction and Teacher Union Activism in the Detroit Public School System." Ph.D. dissertation, The University of Michigan, 1980.

    Explores the relationship between teacher job satisfaction and participation in union activities; considers the effect of demographic variables.

943. Dodge, Joan Moir. "Perceived Organizational and Personal Factors Related to Job Satisfaction in Public School Teachers." Ph.D. dissertation, University of Maryland, 1982.

    Examines the effects of participation in decision-making, teaching anxiety, social support (organizational variables), job involvement, years of teaching experience, age and sex (personal variables) on teacher job satisfaction.

944. Doran, Madeleine S. "The Relationship of Selected Variables to Teacher Absenteeism." Ed.D. dissertation, University of South Florida, 1986.

    Compares high- and low-absence groups in terms of teacher job satisfaction using the Job Descriptive Index.

945. Dowell, Billie Fann. "The Relationship Between Certain Personality Types and Level of Job Satisfaction for a Selected Group of Elementary, Middle, and Secondary Public School Teachers in the Northeast Texas Area." Ed.D. dissertation, East Texas State University, 1985.

   Studies the relationship between personality and teacher job satisfaction using the Myers-Briggs Type Indicator (Form F) and the Minnesota Satisfaction Questionnaire.

946. Eckard, Hubert Brown, Jr. "The Relationship Between Teacher Absenteeism and Selected Personal, Status, and Situational Factors." Ed.D. dissertation, University of Virginia, 1983.

   Investigates the relationship between teacher absenteeism and age, sex, tenure, health status, job satisfaction, school size, level of school taught, and other personal, status, and situational variables.

947. Egan, John Robert. "Absenteeism and Job Satisfaction of Wisconsin Public School Teachers." Ph.D. dissertation, The University of Wisconsin-Madison, 1984.

   Looks at the relationship between teacher absenteeism and teacher job satisfaction using the Job Description Index.

948. Farmer, Michael Joseph. "The Relationship of Teachers' Job Satisfaction and Teachers' Job Dissatisfaction to Teachers' Union Attitudes." Ed.D. dissertation, New York University, 1976.

   Approaches teachers' attitudes toward unionization in terms of Herzberg's two-factor theory of satisfaction-dissatisfaction using the Teacher Opinionnaire and a modified version of the Industrial Relations Center Union Attitude Scale.

949. Fawley, Shirley M. "Personality Characteristics and Job Satisfaction Among Teachers on the Elementary, Middle, and Secondary Levels." Ph.D. dissertation, University of South Carolina, 1979.

    Examines the relationship between personality and teacher job satisfaction using the Comrey Personality Scales and the Minnesota Satisfaction Questionnaire.

950. Fevurly, James Robert. "Organizational Structure, Climate and School Effectiveness." Ed.D. dissertation, University of Kansas, 1977.

    Predicts teacher job satisfaction, loyalty, and organizational effectiveness in terms of bureaucratic structure and climate using the Structural Properties Questionnaire, the Profile of a School, the Index of Organizational Effectiveness, and a job satisfaction and a loyalty scale developed by the researcher.

951. Finch, Gary Arnold. "Why Teachers Resign." Ph.D. dissertation, The University of Wisconsin-Milwaukee, 1982.

    Compares resignees and non-resignees in order to explain why teachers resign using demographic information, a survey form, and personal interviews with nine resignees.

952. Fountain, Patricia Anne Johns. "What Teaching Does to Teachers: The Teacher as Worker." Ph.D. dissertation, Yale University, 1975.

    Interviews suburban secondary school teachers about levels of job satisfaction and their political, social, and ideological attitudes.

953. Friedler, Maruta Eisenberg. "A Quality Circle in an Urban K-8 Public School." Psy.D. dissertation, Rutgers University, The State University of New Jersey, G.S.A.P.P., 1986.

    Studies the effects of a pilot Quality Circle on the morale, job satisfaction, and performance of teachers in an urban K-8 public school.

954. Fruth, Marvin J., and others. <u>Commitment to Teaching: Teachers' Responses to Organizational Incentives</u>. Report from the Program on Student Diversity and School Processes. 1982. ERIC, ED 223 557.

    Addresses the question of organizational incentives and teacher satisfaction with students, curricula, and classroom procedures.

955. Furey, Robert Andreas, Jr. "I Still Love to Teach; I Just Hate Being a Teacher: An Investigation of the Relationship Between Life Cycle Theory and Dissatisfaction in Teaching." Ed.D. dissertation, University of Massachusetts, 1984.

    Investigates the relationship between life cycle theory and dissatisfaction with teaching among midlife males.

956. Gaetino, Joseph Q. "Teacher Attitudes Toward Early Retirement Incentive Plans." Ed.D. dissertation, The Pennsylvania State University, 1980.

    Assesses teachers' attitudes toward early retirement incentive plans and teachers' background characteristics; discusses the relationships between sex, job satisfaction, and early retirement.

957. Garcia, Gonzalo, Jr. "The Relationship of Job Satisfaction and Selected Demographic Variables with the Desire to Change Careers of Vocational Teachers." Ph.D. dissertation, The Ohio State University, 1980.

    Studies the relationship between job satisfaction and demographic factors among vocational education teachers using the Short-Form Minnesota Satisfaction Questionnaire and a Career Change Scale; identifies reasons and barriers to career change.

958. Ghonaim, Ahmed Ali A. "A Study of the Relationship Between Organizational Climate, Job Satisfaction, and Educational District Size, and the Differences in Their Perception by Male Administrators and Teachers in Saudi Arabia." Ph.D. dissertation, Michigan State University, 1986.

   Investigates the relationship between organizational climate, job satisfaction, school size, district size, and educational experience using the Organizational Climate Description Questionnaire and the Teacher Job Satisfaction Questionnaire.

959. Gilson, Thomas Q., and Elias T. Ramos. "Public School Teacher Attitudes Toward Unionization." Journal of Collective Negotiations in the Public Sector 7, no. 2 (1982): 145-154.

   Surveys teachers about their attitudes toward unionization and job related issues of satisfaction and supervisory relationships.

960. Goertz, Margaret E., and others. The Impact of State Policy on Entrance into the Teaching Profession. Final Report. 1984. ERIC, ED 255 515.

   Identifies types of policies and points of policy intervention in a 50-state survey about entry of people into teaching.

961. Goodlad, John I. "Teaching: An Endangered Profession. Response to Donna Kerr." Teachers College Record 84, no. 3 (Spring 1983): 575-578.

   Compares his proposals for educational reform with those of Donna Kerr; points to three reasons why students decide not to become teachers.

962. Grandjean, Burke Dorn. "Autonomy and Authority Among Professional Educators." Ph.D. dissertation, The University of Texas at Austin, 1976.

   Tests Argyris' personality and organization theory in Catholic high schools.

963. Greenwood, Gordon E., and Robert S. Soar. "Some Relationships Between Teacher Morale and Teacher Behavior." *Journal of Educational Psychology* 64, no. 1 (1973): 105-108.

    Explores the relationship between teacher morale and verbal teacher behavior among female elementary school teachers using the Purdue Teacher Opinionaire and the Reciprocal Category System.

964. Grimm, W. Jeffrey. "Existential Meaning in the Professional Life of Teachers and Its Relationship to Teacher Job Satisfaction." Ed.D. dissertation, University of Idaho, 1984.

    Explores the relationship between job satisfaction and purpose in professional life for teachers.

965. Gustafson, Mary C. "Factors Influencing Decisions of Schoolteachers to Leave Education." Ed.D. dissertation, University of Cincinnati, 1981.

    Compares satisfied, dissatisfied, and former teachers in terms of possible reasons for leaving education using the California Personality Inventory and the Internal-External Locus of Control scale.

966. Hange, Jane. *Teachers in Their Fifth Year: An Analysis of Teaching Concerns from the Perspectives of Adult and Career Development*. 1982. ERIC, ED 214 906.

    Conducts a followup study four years after "The First Year Teacher Study" to focus on adult developmental issues; discusses the results in six areas.

967. Harrison, William A. *Attracting and Retaining Qualified Teachers*. An Issue Brief of the Education and Job Training Program. 1984. ERIC, ED 250 832.

    Outlines the problems of attracting and retaining teachers in terms of current research, policy options, implications, and conflicting factors.

968. Harwood, William. "The Relationship Between Job Satisfaction and Life Satisfaction of Educators in an Urban Public School System." Ph.D. dissertation, University of New Orleans, 1986.

    Measures job and life satisfaction among urban teachers using the Job Descriptive Index; discusses four models that relate to job and life satisfaction.

969. Heckert, Joseph Wayne. "Pupil Control Ideology-Pupil Control Behavior Congruence and the Job Satisfaction of Public School Teachers." Ed.D. dissertation, The Pennsylvania State University, 1976.

    Studies teacher job satisfaction, teacher pupil control ideology, and pupil control behavior using the Brayfield-Rothe Index of Job Satisfaction, the Pupil Control Ideology Form, and the Pupil Control Behavior Form.

970. Hedley, Harold Hastings. "The Relationship of Job Preview to Absenteeism, Turnover, and Job Satisfaction of Public School Teachers." Ed.D. dissertation, The College of William and Mary in Virginia, 1985.

    Investigates the relationship between job preview (information about teaching) and absenteeism, turnover, and teacher job satisfaction among newly hired teachers using the Job Descriptive Index and the Job in General measure.

971. Henderson, David L., and Karen L. Henderson. <u>Moonlighting, Salary, and Morale: The Texas Teachers Story</u>. 1986. ERIC, ED 269 374.

    Indicates that four out of ten teachers are considering leaving the teaching profession and almost one-fourth moonlight to supplement their income.

972. Hillson, John, and Gale Hagee. Study to Determine Influencing Factors for Selecting Agricultural Education as a Career. Final Report. 1980. ERIC, ED 195 707.

   Describes those factors that influence undergraduate students to choose a career in agricultural education; cites economic/social and personal reasons.

973. Hinkley, Nancy Emily Engstrom. "The Relationship Between Sex and Intrinsic Job Satisfaction of Adult Educators." Ed.D. dissertation, North Carolina State University at Raleigh, 1975.

   Develops an instrument to measure higher level need fulfillment (Maslow) among adult educators.

974. Holdaway, Edward A. Satisfaction of Teachers in Alberta with Their Work and Working Conditions. Report of a Study. 1978. ERIC, ED 151 948.

   Examines teacher job satisfaction and its relationship to age, sex, and experience using Herzberg's classification of satisfaction and dissatisfaction.

975. Holifield, Mitchell Lane. "Variation in Job Satisfaction and Dissatisfaction Among Missouri's Beginning, Mid-Career, and Retired Elementary and Secondary Public School Teachers." Ph.D. dissertation, Southern Illinois University at Carbondale, 1985.

   Designs the Survey of Teacher Satisfaction/ Dissatisfaction to measure thirteen job dimensions among beginning, mid-career, and retired teachers.

976. Hooks, James Byron, Jr. "Conflict and Conflict Resolution in Relationship with Job Satisfaction in Teaching." Ph.D. dissertation, Northwestern University, 1975.

   Investigates the effects of nine factors of conflict in the teacher's environment with nine factors of teacher's job satisfaction.

977. Horner, Douglas Leroy. "The Relationship of Job Satisfaction to Values Consensus of an Organization and Its Members." Ph.D. dissertation, Southern Illinois University at Carbondale, 1981.

   Identifies the factors that affect teacher job satisfaction; reports twelve value rankings of teachers and for the district.

978. Hutcherson, Shirlie Jean. "The Relationship of the Job Satisfaction of Classroom Teachers to Student Perceptions of Classroom Satisfaction." Ed.D. dissertation, The University of Nebraska-Lincoln, 1981.

   Compares teachers with high, average, and low levels of job satisfaction and student perceptions of satisfaction using the Work Environment Scale and the Classroom Environment Scale.

979. Irondi, Emezuo Ogbonna. "Factors Influencing Teacher Mobility in Nigeria." Ph.D. dissertation, University of Illinois, 1985.

   Studies teachers' perceptions of teaching, job change, inter-school mobility, and demographic variables that influence their decisions to quit.

980. Jamentz, Catherine C. "Merit Pay: The Impact on Teachers and Schools." Ed.D. dissertation, Harvard University, 1985.

   Analyzes four performance-based financial incentive programs and explores some basic assumptions about merit pay and its effects on teachers and working conditions.

981. Jantzen, J. Marc. "Why College Students Choose to Teach: A Longitudinal Study." Journal of Teacher Education 32, no. 2 (March-April 1981): 45-49.

   Conducts a survey of college students to determine the reasons why they chose to become teachers; cites service, interest in children, and leadership as three reasons.

982. Keene, Douglas Laird. "Personality Factors Related to Career Choice and Job Satisfaction Among Female Elementary and Secondary Teacher Education Alumni." Ph.D. dissertation, The University of Texas at Austin, 1983.

    Contacts education alumni and administers the Self Report Inventory, the Adjective Self Description instrument, and the Hoppock Job Satisfaction Blank to identify personality traits that influence career choice and job satisfaction.

983. Keith, Pat M., and others. "Teacher Education Graduates: Sex, Career Plans, and Preferences for Job Factors." Urban Education 18, no. 3 (October 1983): 361-375.

    Looks at the impact of sex, career plans, and teaching level on preferences for job factors.

984. Kennard, Margaret Anne. "A Study of the Relationship Between Teachers' Perceptions of Self-Actualization Needs and the Perceptions of Satisfaction with the Teaching Profession." Ed.D. dissertation, Western Michigan University, 1983.

    Develops an instrument to assess teachers' perceptions of self-actualization and teachers' perceptions of job satisfaction.

985. Kephart, Charles Allen. "The Relationships of Teacher Militancy to Organizational Structure and Job-Satisfaction." Ed.D. dissertation, New York University, 1981.

    Explores the relationships of teacher militancy to organizational structure and job satisfaction/dissatisfaction using the Structural Properties Questionnaire IV, the Teacher Opinionnaire Item Scale, and the Attitudinal Militancy Scale-III.

986. Keppel, Francis. "A Field Guide to the Land of Teachers." Phi Delta Kappan 68, no. 1 (September 1986): 18-23.

    Compares the Holmes Group report and the Carnegie Task Force report.

987. Kirkwood, Kristian John. "An Examination of Some of the Determinants Affecting Teacher Absenteeism." Ed.D. dissertation, University of Toronto (Canada), 1980.

>Identifies the factors related to teacher absenteeism using the Job Description Index.

988. Kladder, Fred William, Jr. "Teacher Participation in Decision Making: An Investigation of Staff Development and Job Satisfaction." Ph.D. dissertation, Indiana University, 1982.

>Uses a discrepancy model to study teacher participation in decision making and its relationship to staff development and teacher job satisfaction.

989. Knight, James A. "Why Vocational Agriculture Teachers in Ohio Leave Teaching." *Journal of the American Association of Teacher Educators in Agriculture* 19, no. 3 (November 1978): 11-17.

>Surveys vocational education teachers to ascertain reasons for resigning; cites poor salary and lack of advancement opportunities.

990. Knoop, Robert. "Age and Correlates of Locus of Control." *Journal of Psychology* 108, no. 1 (May 1981): 103-106.

>Explores the relationship between locus of control and education, sex, income, self-esteem, job involvement, job satisfaction, and alienation using Rotter's I-E Locus of Control Scale.

991. Kowalczyk, Robert Stephen. "Local Teacher Organizations: The Relationship Between Teachers' Perceptions of Their Union and Job Satisfaction." Ph.D. dissertation, The University of Michigan, 1982.

>Examines the relationship between union performance and teacher job satisfaction.

992. Krohn, Eric Wilson. "Perceived Organizational Structure and the Pupil Control Ideology and Job Satisfaction of Elementary and Secondary School Teachers." Ph.D. dissertation, The University of North Carolina at Chapel Hill, 1979.

   Investigates the relationships between teacher-perceived organizational structure and teacher attitudes toward pupil control and job satisfaction using the Structural Properties Questionnaire IV, the Pupil Control Ideology Form, and the Job Description Index.

993. Kuhn, Barbara J. "Teacher Personality Type and Job Satisfaction." Ed.D. dissertation, The University of Florida, 1981.

   Describes the relationship between teacher personality type and job satisfaction using the Myers-Briggs Type Indicator and the Minnesota Satisfaction Questionnaire.

994. Kuhns, Alice Pauline. "A Study of the Relationship Between a Participatory Management Model and Selected Variables." Ed.D. dissertation, Virginia Polytechnic Institute and State University, 1986.

   Studies participatory management, job satisfaction, job-related tension, intention-to-leave, absenteeism, sex, and years of experience among middle school teachers.

995. Laber, Robert Keith. "Occupational Adaptation Among Career Elementary and Secondary Teachers." Ed.D. dissertation, Columbia University Teachers College, 1982.

   Develops a questionnaire to investigate adult developmental stage theory, support in teaching, and professional development in the schools.

996. Lamb, Patricia G. "Are You Coming Back Next Year?" Today's Education 69, no. 2 (April-May 1980): 56-57.

   Focuses on the emotional rewards of teaching.

997. Laurento, Louis Michael. "A Study Designed to Investigate the Relationship Between the Strength of the Professional Employee's Contract and the Degree of Teacher Job Satisfaction." Ed.D. dissertation, Temple University, 1980.

    Compares one school system with a strong professional employee's contract and one school system with a weak professional employee's contract and the levels of teacher job satisfaction.

998. Lester, Paula E. "Development of an Instrument to Measure Teacher Job Satisfaction." Ph.D. dissertation, New York University, 1984.

    Develops the Teacher Job Satisfaction Questionnaire to assess nine areas of teacher satisfaction.

999. Leveille, Martha Ferrell. "Characteristics of High- and Low-Teacher Morale: In-Depth Interviews with Teachers." Ed.D. dissertation, University of Southern California, 1981.

    Determines the characteristics of high- and low-teacher morale among elementary school teachers using the Purdue Teacher Opinionaire and unstructured interviews.

1000. Lipka, Richard P., and L. R. Goulet. "Age and Intergroup Differences in Attitudes Toward the Teaching Profession: How Do Teachers and Students View Themselves and Each Other?" Contemporary Educational Psychology 6, no. 1 (January 1981): 12-21.

    Looks at attitudes toward teaching among teachers and students at different ages in teacher education programs.

1001. Little, Nina. "A Study of Teacher Participation in Curriculum Development and Teacher Job Satisfaction." Ph.D. dissertation, The University of Nebraska-Lincoln, 1985.

   Correlates elementary school teachers' involvement in curriculum development and teacher job satisfaction using an instrument designed by the researcher.

1002. Lofland, Gretchen Dickens. "The Study of the Relationship Between Organizational Climate and Job Satisfaction of Teachers in Selected Schools in the District of Columbia." Ed.D. dissertation, The George Washington University, 1985.

   Studies the relationship between organizational climate and teacher job satisfaction using the Organizational Climate Description Questionnaire and the Minnesota Satisfaction Questionnaire.

1003. Lombard, Cheryl Ruth. "A Study of the Correlation Between Job Satisfaction and Values for Public and Non-Public School Teachers Currently Teaching in South Florida Schools." Ed.D. dissertation, Florida Atlantic University, 1985.

   Examines the relationship between teacher job satisfaction and values using the Minnesota Satisfaction Questionnaire and the Allport-Vernon-Lindzey Study of Values Scale.

1004. Lopez, Elsa Margarita. "Job Satisfaction and Need Importance: Race, Sex, and Occupational Group." Ph.D. dissertation, Stevens Institute of Technology, 1977.

   Uses the need fulfillment and reference group models of job satisfaction with urban teachers.

1005. Lowther, Malcolm A., and others. The Mid-Career
Malaise of Teachers: An Examination of Job Attitudes and the Factors Influencing Job Satisfaction
in the Middle Years. Final Report. 1982. ERIC,
ED 218 280.

Examines the quality of teachers' work lives,
teachers' job satisfaction, and the relationship
between teachers' work experiences and life experiences using data from three national surveys.

1006. Maddux, Cleborne D., and others. A Survey of Texas
Public School Teachers. 1980. ERIC, ED 212 559.

Develops a questionnaire to explore teacher
job satisfaction, teacher behavior, and other
factors that affect teachers' lives.

1007. McDonald, David G. "Structural Coupling and School
Outcomes: Job Satisfaction Student Attitudes and
Perceptions of School, Student Achievement in Reading, Student Achievement in Mathematics, and Perceived Organizational Effectiveness." Ph.D. dissertation, University of Kansas, 1982.

Explores the relationship between structural
coupling and organizational effectiveness as measured by teacher job satisfaction, student attitudes and perceptions of school, and student achievement in reading and math.

1008. McGowan, James Robert. "An Investigation of the
Relationship Between Certain Situational Variables,
Personality Variables and Job Satisfaction Within
the Path-Goal Model of Management Among Public
School Teachers." Ph.D. dissertation, University
of Maryland, 1980.

Tests the applicability of the Path-Goal Model
of Leadership to predict teacher job satisfaction
using the Job Descriptive Index, the Job Diagnostic
Survey, the Participation in Decision Making Scale,
the Adorno F-Scale, and the Job Involvement Survey.

1009. McGrath, Edmund Roy, Jr. "The Exodus Syndrome: Factors Affecting Teacher Career Change." Ed.D. dissertation, Boston University, 1986.

   Focuses on identifying the factors that contribute to the decision to leave teaching; examines organizational and personal variables among secondary school teachers.

1010. Meacham, Douglas J. "A Comparison of Levels of Job Satisfaction Among Selected Groups of Employees in Public School Education, Provo, Utah, 1984-85." Ed.D. dissertation, Brigham Young University, 1986.

   Compares job satisfaction/dissatisfaction among elementary, junior high, and senior high school teachers using a questionnaire that measures motivator and hygiene factors.

1011. Meeker, Eleanor Marie. "A Study of Five Aspects of Job Satisfaction Among Teacher Resignees." Ed.D. dissertation, Oklahoma State University, 1983.

   Addresses the issue of teacher job satisfaction and voluntary resignation by focusing on five areas of job satisfaction and personal variables.

1012. Miller, John P., and others. _Teachers in Transition: Study of an Aging Teaching Force_. Informal Series/44. 1982. ERIC, ED 220 988.

   Groups teachers by age according to the adult developmental stages outlined by Levinson and Sheehy to study teacher job satisfaction, dissatisfaction, and aspirations.

1013. Miller, Marvin Harry. "The Relation of Teacher Job Satisfaction to Participation in the Decision-Making Process in Mississippi." Ed.D. dissertation, University of Southern Mississippi, 1984.

   Examines the relationship between teacher job satisfaction and participation in decision-making using the Decision Involvement Analysis Instrument.

1014. Miskel, Cecil G., and others. "Organizational Structures and Processes, Perceived School Effectiveness, Loyalty, and Job Satisfaction." Educational Administration Quarterly 15, no. 3 (Fall 1979): 97-118.

Describes the characteristics of effective schools using the Index of Effectiveness, the Profile of a School, and the Structural Properties Questionnaire.

1015. Moore, Barbara McGregor. "Satisfaction with Teaching as a Job and as a Career." Ph.D. dissertation, Claremont Graduate School, 1986.

Discusses the differences between job satisfaction and career satisfaction; presents a model of teacher job satisfaction.

1016. Moore, Gary E., and William G. Camp. "Why Vocational Agriculture Teachers Leave the Profession: A Comparison of Perceptions." Journal of the American Association of Teacher Educators in Agriculture 20, no. 3 (November 1979): 11-18.

Surveys vocational agriculture teachers who replaced leaving teachers to find out the reasons for leaving the profession.

1017. Moseley, Kenneth Stewart. "Development of a Multi-Dimensional Instrument for Measuring Teacher Morale." Ed.D. dissertation, Duke University, 1977.

Develops and validates the Teacher Opinionaire to measure seven factors that contribute to teacher morale.

1018. Moss, Jeffrey W., and Gary E. Briers. Relationship of Attitudes of Vocational Student Teachers to Their Plans to Teach. 1982. ERIC, ED 224 993.

Looks at the attitudes of vocational student teachers and investigates an alternative method of scoring the Purdue Student-Teacher Opinionaire.

1019. Nabors, James Joseph. "Vocational Satisfaction in Holland's Theory of Careers." Ph.D. dissertation, University of Kansas, 1980.

   Uses Holland's theory of careers to study vocational satisfaction and the relationship of satisfaction to congruence, consistency, and differentiation among elementary school teachers using the Job Descriptive Index and Holland's Self-Directed Search.

1020. National Study of School Evaluation. <u>Teacher Opinion Inventory. Instructions for Use. Part A. Part B.</u> 1975. ERIC, ED 155 185.

   Develops the Teacher Opinion Inventory to assess teachers' attitudes toward their schools.

1021. "NEA Survey Investigates Teacher Attitudes, Practices." <u>Phi Delta Kappan</u> 62, no. 1 (September 1980): 49-50.

   Reports the results of a national survey on finance, job security, job satisfaction, student discipline, and testing.

1022. Negrete, Edward, Jr. "Teacher Perceptions for Increasing Staff Stability at Difficult to Staff Schools in a Large Urban School District: Analysis of Pecuniary and Nonpecuniary Benefits." Ed.D. dissertation, University of California, Los Angeles, 1983.

   Investigates the relationship between financial and non-financial rewards as a means to increase teacher stability at difficult to staff urban schools.

1023. Nelson, Suzanne J. "Professional Negotiations and Teachers' Decisional States." Ed.D. dissertation, The University of Oklahoma, 1983.

   Compares non-negotiating school districts with negotiating school districts in relation to teachers' participation in decision making.

1024. Nevels, Ralph W. "A Study of the Relationship Between Teachers' Attitude Toward Professionalism and Teachers' Satisfaction/Dissatisfaction with Their Jobs." Ed.D. dissertation, University of Kentucky, 1984.

   Explores the relationship between teacher professionalism and teacher job satisfaction using the Teacher Professionalism Scale and the Minnesota Satisfaction Questionnaire.

1025. Nixon, Mary, and L.R. Gue. "Women Administrators and Women Teachers: A Comparative Study." <u>Alberta Journal of Educational Research</u> 21, no. 3 (September 1975): 196-206.

   Reviews the literature on professionalism and sex-role orientation; compares satisfaction among teachers and administrators.

1026. Nwagwu, Nicholas. "The Impact of Changing Conditions of Service on the Recruitment of Teachers in Nigeria." <u>Comparative Education</u> 17, no. 1 (March 1981): 81-86.

   Replicates a 1972 survey to see if improvements in teaching conditions and benefits influenced high school graduates' attitudes toward elementary school teaching as a career.

1027. Olstad, Roger G., and Jack L. Beal. "The Science and Mathematics Teacher Shortage: A Study of Recent Graduates." <u>Science Education</u> 68, no. 4 (July 1984): 397-402.

   Compares the responses of certified science and mathematics education graduates who never taught, left teaching, and remained in teaching.

1028. O'Shea, Richard Anthony. "The Effects of Personality and Situational Variables on Teachers' Perceptions of Need-for-Involvement in Decision Making." Ph.D. dissertation, The University of Connecticut, 1976.

   Examines teachers' need for involvement in decision making, authoritarianism, risk taking, interpersonal trust (personality factors), level of teaching, location of school, length of service, staff size (situational factors), job satisfaction and bureaucracy.

1029. Owuamanam, Donatus O. "Providing for Job Tenure, Job Satisfaction and Productivity in Teachers." Adolescence 19, no. 73 (Spring 1984): 221-224.

Presents a theoretical analysis of the relationship between teacher job satisfaction, tenure, and performance.

1030. Pellicer, Leonard O. "Job Satisfaction--Its Impact upon Teacher Attendance." NASSP Bulletin 68, no. 475 (November 1984): 44-47.

Identifies sources of teacher satisfaction and dissatisfaction in an attempt to improve teacher attendance.

1031. Poll, Carol. It's a Good Job for a Woman (and a Man): Why Males and Females Choose to Be Elementary School Teachers. 1979. ERIC, ED 183 562.

Interviews male and female elementary school teachers to find out when they decided to enter teaching and why they chose teaching as a career.

1032. Porter, Franklin Harold. "The Relationship of Personality Traits to Job Satisfaction of Teacher Education Majors Who Chose Teaching or Non-Teaching Careers." Ed.D. dissertation, Mississippi State University, 1980.

Compares personality characteristics between teacher education graduates who entered teaching and those who did not using Cattell's 16PF Questionnaire; examines levels of job satisfaction between the two groups using the Job Descriptive Index.

1033. Pound, Winsdon Norwood Montresseur. "The Relationship Between School Calendar and Teacher Job Satisfaction." Ed.D. dissertation, Virginia Polytechnic Institute and State University, 1975.

   Investigates the relationship between type of school calendar and teacher job satisfaction using the Minnesota Satisfaction Questionnaire and a Personal/Situational Data Form.

1034. Pusateri, Paul David. "A Study of the Relationships Between Self-Actualization and Job Satisfaction in Teaching." Ph.D. dissertation, Loyola University of Chicago, 1976.

   Explores the relationship between self-actualization and teacher job satisfaction using Shostrom's Personal Orientation Inventory and the Index of Job Satisfaction; uses Maslow's theory of human motivation.

1035. Rayder, Nicholas F., and Bart Body. The Educational Forces Inventory: A New Technique for Measuring Influences on the Classroom. 1975. ERIC, ED 179 580.

   Field tests the Educational Forces Inventory that describes the influence of thirteen factors on teacher morale and classroom effectiveness.

1036. Ream, Marsha A. Status of the American Public School Teacher, 1975-76. 1977. ERIC, ED 159 163.

   Presents ten chapters that describe teachers during the 1975-1976 school year; describes reasons for becoming a teacher, plans to remain in teaching, sources of job satisfaction, and problem areas.

1037. Reddish, Marvin LaDelle. "The Relationship of Selected Mississippi Public School Teachers' Locus of Control to Their Perceptions of Job Satisfaction." Ed.D. dissertation, Mississippi State University, 1983.

   Assesses the relationship between teachers' locus of control and job satisfaction using Rotter's Internal-External Locus of Control Scale and the Minnesota Satisfaction Questionnaire (Short Form).

1038. Reed, Donald B., and Dennis A. Conners. "The Paradox of 'Making It': Teachers and Collective Bargaining." Peabody Journal of Education 59, no. 2 (January 1982): 118-120.

   Discusses teacher job satisfaction and collective bargaining.

1039. Rippe, Kenneth Lee. "The Relationships of Role Conflict and Role Ambiguity to Job Satisfaction of Nebraska Public School Administrators and Teachers." Ed.D. dissertation, The University of Nebraska-Lincoln, 1983.

   Correlates teacher job satisfaction, role conflict, and role ambiguity using Bullock's Job Satisfaction Scale and the Rizzo, House, and Lirtzman instrument to measure role conflict and role ambiguity.

1040. Robinson, John P., and others. Measures of Occupational Attitudes and Occupational Characteristics. Appendix A to Measures of Political Attitudes. 1971. ERIC, ED 059 922.

   Reviews the research on job satisfaction and presents scales to measure general job satisfaction, job satisfaction in certain careers, and specific job satisfaction categories.

1041. Rosenholtz, Susan J., and Mark A. Smylie. "Teacher Compensation and Career Ladders." Elementary School Journal 85, no. 2 (November 1984): 149-166.

   Addresses the issues of why teachers enter and leave the profession, the incentives that help teachers improve, and skill acquisition and development.

1042. Saad Sulayman, Nimir Sulayman. "The Relationship Between Teachers' Attitudes Toward Educational Change and Their Job Satisfaction in Sudan." Ed.D. dissertation, University of California, Los Angeles, 1984.

   Explores the relationship between educational change and teacher job satisfaction using the Educational Change Scale (Osman) and the Job Satisfaction Scale based on Kalleberg's theory.

1043. Sarason, Seymour B. "Again, the Preparation of Teachers: Competency and Job Satisfaction." Interchange on Educational Policy 10, no. 1 (1978): 1-11.

   Discusses the importance of preparing teachers for the reality of the classroom.

1044. Savwoir, Audrey Johnson. "Conditions Associated with Early Retirement Decisions." Ed.D. dissertation, Columbia University Teachers College, 1986.

   Studies the relationship between early retirement incentive plans and age, sex, and teaching assignment, as well as the relationship between involvement in decision-making, job satisfaction, and plans to retire among teachers with twenty or more years of teaching.

1045. Seifert, Kelvin. The Achievement of Care: Men Who Teach Young Children. 1983. ERIC, ED 231 542.

   Interviews male early childhood teachers about their job satisfaction, teaching history and career plans, and attitudes about male participation in early childhood teaching.

1046. Sheikh Attari, Mohammad Hossein. "Relationships Between Job Satisfaction and Self-Actualization Among Teachers in the San Diego City Schools." Ph.D. dissertation, United States International University, 1985.

    Assesses the relationship between teacher job satisfaction and self-actualization using the Purdue Teacher Opinionnaire and the Personal Orientation Inventory; compares satisfied with dissatisfied teachers.

1047. Smith, Don L. "An Empirical Study of Whether the Direct Involvement of Classroom Teachers in the Decision-Making Process of a Public School District in Conjunction with Their Locus of Control Orientation Effects Their Perceptions of Job Satisfaction." Doctoral dissertation, North Texas State University, 1985.

    Studies the impact of participation in decision-making and locus of control on teacher job satisfaction using Rotter's Internal-External Locus of Control Scale and the Job Descriptive Index.

1048. Smith, Harold Dean. "Teacher Voluntary Absenteeism and Perceptions of the Professional Environment, Job Satisfaction and Impact of Collective Bargaining." Ed.D. dissertation, Seattle University, 1982.

    Looks at teacher voluntary absenteeism, job satisfaction, collective bargaining, and personal and demographic variables.

1049. Srivastava, R.C. "Participation and Decision-Making: Review of Researches." *Indian Educational Review* 18, no. 1 (January 1983): 47-77.

    Reviews the literature on the effects of teacher participation in decision-making; finds a positive relationship between participation and job satisfaction and morale.

1050. Stark, Joan S., and others. _Teacher Certificate Recipients at the University of Michigan 1946 Through 1976: A 1980 Follow-Up Study._ 1980. ERIC, ED 209 209.

   Compares career teachers and non-educators in relation to initial employment, future career plans, satisfaction with life, satisfaction with their education, and the appropriateness of their education.

1051. Stretton, Thomas Richard, Jr. "Staff Development: Design, Implementation, and Assessment of a Comprehensive Program." Ed.D. dissertation, University of Pennsylvania, 1982.

   Develops a staff development program to address the issues of teacher burnout, staff morale, job satisfaction, aging teachers, and organizational effectiveness.

1052. Tabb, Stuart Michael. "The Organizational Climate of Public Schools: A Human Services Approach." Ph.D. dissertation, University of Maryland, Baltimore Professional Schools, 1984.

   Investigates the relationship between teacher job satisfaction and organizational climate among high school teachers; develops a model for school social work practice.

1053. Torres, Saul. "Perceived Family Emotional Relationships, Person Orientations, and Expected-Job-Satisfaction Among Teachers in Training in Mexico: A Test of Anne Roe's Theory of Vocational Interest and Choice with the General Culture Group." Ed.D. dissertation, Andrews University, 1983.

   Tests Roe's theory of vocational interest and choice among teachers using the Family Relations Inventory, the Biographical Questionnaire Subtest VI, the Person Interest Inventory, and the Job Satisfaction Blank No. 5.

1054. Trotter, John Rhodes. "What Teachers Like and Dislike About Teaching." Ed.D. dissertation, University of Georgia, 1984.

    Administers the Teaching Likes and Dislikes Survey in order to develop the Teaching Likes Index and the Teaching Dislikes Index; reports the most frequently cited likes and dislikes.

1055. Valdez, Diana Marie. "The Contribution of Background and Role Factors in the Prediction of Job Satisfaction for Chicano and Anglo Teachers." Ph.D. dissertation, University of California, Riverside, 1983.

    Examines differences in job satisfaction among Anglo and Chicano teachers using the Purdue Teacher Opinionaire and background variables.

1056. Watkins, David. "Self-Esteem as a Moderator in Vocational Choice: A Test of Korman's Hypothesis." Australian Psychologist 10, no. 1 (March 1975): 75-80.

    Tests Korman's hypothesis about vocational choice among elementary school student teachers using a self-concept instrument from the Adjective Check List, the Marlowe-Crown Social Desirability Scale, an occupational needs instrument developed by Trusty and Sergiovanni, and a scale to assess their ability as teachers.

1057. Wiggins, James D., and others. "Job Satisfaction Related to Tested Congruence and Differentiation." Journal of Vocational Behavior 23, no. 1 (August 1983): 112-121.

    Studies personality-environment congruence and differentiation among teachers using the Vocational Preference Inventory; relates these variables to teacher job satisfaction.

1058. Winters, Linda Lee. "A Meta-Analysis of Bureaucratic Structure and Teacher Job Satisfaction." Ed.D. dissertation, University of Kansas, 1983.

   Provides a historical review for this research on the relationship between bureaucratic structure and teacher job satisfaction.

1059. Wippich, Barbara J. "Analysis of Communication and Job Satisfaction in an Educational Setting." Ph.D. dissertation, University of Kansas, 1983.

   Analyzes the relationship between communication and teacher job satisfaction using the Communication Satisfaction Survey, the Personal Report of Communication Apprehension, and the Job Satisfaction Measure.

1060. Wisniewski, Richard, and Paul Kleine. "Teacher Moonlighting: An Unstudied Phenomenon." Phi Delta Kappan 65, no. 8 (April 1984): 553-555.

   Presents the results of a teacher survey that shows the prevalence of moonlighting.

1061. Yarworth, Joseph Seitzinger. "The Relationship Between Personal Factors, Role Ambiguity, Role Conflict and Teacher Job Satisfaction." Ph.D. dissertation, The University of Connecticut, 1978.

   Examines the relationship between role ambiguity and role conflict and their impact on teacher job satisfaction using an instrument adapted from the work of Rizzo, House, and Lirtzman and the Minnesota Satisfaction Questionnaire (Short Form).

1062. Zak, Itai. "Continuous Self-Selection Processes in Teacher Education: The Way for Survival." Journal of Education for Teaching 7, no. 3 (October 1981): 263-273.

   Describes three selection stages in the process to go into teaching; suggests that personality traits play a bigger part than cognitive ability in career choice.

1063. Zimmerman, Karen W., and others. "Career Involvement and Job Satisfaction as Related to Job Strain and Marital Satisfaction of Teachers and Their Spouses." Home Economics Research Journal 8, no. 6 (July 1980): 421-427.

   Explores the relationship between job status, job satisfaction, and marital satisfaction among home economic teachers using the Locke Wallace Marital Adjustment Scale.

AUTHOR INDEX

Abbott-Koch, S.; 674
Abdul Malek, A.P.B.; 193
Abelson, A.G.; 194
Abreu, J.R.; 314
Adams, R.D.; 895, 896
Ageel, H.A.; 315
Agte, L.; 316
Ahmed, S.H.; 132
Aiken, L.H.; 383
Alden, S.E.; 317
Alder, C.E.; 318
Alexander, L.; 675
Alexander, L.L.; 319
Allen, D.I.; 52
Allen, R.E.; 320
Allie, S.M.; 677
Altschuler, A.S.; 678
Amirtash, A.-M.; 195
Amodio, T.; 679
Anand, S.P.; 133
Anand, U.; 897
Anderson, R.E.; 698
Andrew, H.O., Jr.; 134
Andrew, L.D.; 555
Antonecchia, D.; 135
Appelgryn, A.E.; 898
Araghi, M.A.K.; 321
Arndt, C.R.; 899
Arulefela, O.A.; 136;
Asad, S.W.E.-D.; 323
Askar, A.G.; 196
Asmussen, C.B.; 322
Atkin, J.M.; 900
Attuwaybi, O.B.; 197
Austin, D.A.; 680

Azinger, A.T.; 490

Baber, W.C.; 202
Baird, L.L.; 324
Baker, C.P.; 556
Balazadeh, G.; 325
Balkin, D.B.; 380
Bandy, H.; 1
Barahimi, I.; 137
Barber, P.A.; 901
Barker, J.D.; 198
Barlar, D.G.; 326
Barnard, B.; 2
Barner, A.E.; 681
Barnes, E.L.; 327
Bartek, J.A.; 54
Barter, R.F.; 902
Barth, R.S.; 558
Beal, J.L.; 1027
Beasley, C.R.; 682
Beatty, G.J.; 150
Beck, C.L.; 683
Beck, T.M.; 500
Becvar, R.J; 3
Bednar, A.S.; 328
Behrman, E.H.; 138
Belcastro, P.A.; 684, 685
Bell, T.H.; 903
Bembry, S.A.; 199
Benedict, C.; 834
Bennett, A.; 751
Bensky, J.M.; 686
Benson, J.; 559
Bentley, R.R.; 904

Bentzen, M.M.; 905
Berman, M.; 385
Bernard, J.S.; 557
Bessai, F.; 14
Bhella, S.K.; 560
Bilsky, D.G.; 906
Bina, M.J.; 200, 201
Binnie, D.G.; 491
Birmingham, J.A.; 687
Blackbourn, J.M.; 561
Blackburn, R.T.; 339, 340
Blair, A.K.; 4
Blanton, L.P.; 737
Blase, J.; 562, 688
Bledsoe, J.C.; 139, 202
Block, I.G.; 563
Bloemaker, D.A.; 203
Bloland, P.A.; 140
Bloom, S.E.; 492
Bluedorn, A.C.; 359
Boardman, R.M.; 907
Boberg, A.D.; 329
Body, B.; 1035
Boeck, D.G.; 204
Bogad, C.McW.; 908
Bolding, J.T.; 330
Bonjean, C.M.; 383
Book, M.D.; 909
Bouie, A.S.; 910
Bowen, B.E.; 331
Bowers, R.J.; 205
Bowman, D.C.; 493
Boyd, C.R.; 206
Boyenga, K.W.; 332
Boynton, P.; 564
Bradley, K.; 911
Brassard, M.R.; 141
Braswell, R.E., Jr.; 207
Brewer, F.G.; 565
Bridges, E.M.; 55, 912
Briers, G.E.; 1018
Briscoe, M.L.; 333
Brockley, T.; 708
Brod, R.S.; 208
Brodinsky, B.; 494, 566
Broesamle, J.J.; 334

Brogdon, R.; 5
Broiles, P.H.; 689
Brookes, M.C.T.; 335
Brown, H.D.; 209
Brown, L.; 753
Bruno, J.E.; 690, 691
Buchmann, M.; 119
Buffer, J.J., Jr.; 245
Buford, C.T.; 567
Buhmeyer, K.J.; 336
Bullock, J.A.; 210
Bulls, B.S.; 337
Bundy, O.K.; 692
Burcham, S.P.; 211
Burden, P.R.; 6, 56
Burke, J.S.; 568
Burke, R.E.; 694
Burrell, A.G.; 695
Burscemi, J.N.; 696
Butler, J.K.; 913
Butt, F.; 697
Button, R.I.; 917
Buxton, M.M.; 57

Cain, B.L.; 7
Calabrese, R.L.; 698
Calder, P.H.; 914
Calder, V.L.; 699
Calhoun, C.C.; 212
Cammarata, J.J.; 495
Camp, W.G.; 1016
Campbell, J.M.G.; 338
Caram, D.F.; 915
Cardinell, C.F.; 700, 701
Cares, R.C.; 339
Carey, D.; 496
Carey, J.F.; 916
Carillon, J.W.; 917
Carlile, C.; 569
Carlson, R.V.; 262
Carter, L.; 351
Cartwright, R.; 351
Casey, C.E.; 213
Cassara, S.; 341
Catney, R.T.; 918
Chan, R.C.-M.; 342

Author Index

Chandler, J.B.; 407
Chapey, G.M.; 343
Chapman, D.W.; 919, 920
Chapman, J.; 921
Charters, W.W., Jr.; 497
Chatelain, T.D.; 922
Chen, C.-Z.; 214
Chen, W.-S.; 923
Cherkes, M.; 702
Christian, P.L.; 344
Cichon, D.J.; 703, 704
Clark, K.J.; 570
Clark, N.I.; 498
Clark, S.M.; 346, 347
Clarke, R.; 924
Clarke, R.L.; 142
Clarken, R.H.; 925
Clay, T.; 215
Cobb, S.R.H.; 926
Cohen, J.A.; 705
Cole, D.W.; 927
Coley, T.G.; 58
Collingwood, T.R.; 707
Collins, J.R.; 216
Coltrin, S.; 345
Conners, D.A.; 1038
Conroy, J.P.; 928
Cooper, G.R.; 929
Cooper, L.; 571
Corcoran, M.; 346, 347
Cortis, G.; 8
Cote, M.M.; 348
Coughlan, R.J.; 930
Cowan, C.A.; 349
Cox, T.; 708
Craig, L.V.; 572
Crane, S.J.; 709
Crase, D.; 710
Crawford, J.H.; 931
Craycraft, K.R.; 59
Croft, J.C.; 573
Cruz-Rodriguez, A.; 499
Cunningham, J.W.; 842
Cunningham, W.G.; 711
Cupo, A.F.; 350

D'Acchioli, A.L.; 712

D'Alonzo, B.; 217
Daly, R.E.; 143
Daniels, S.C.; 574
Daniels, S.F.; 713
Dansie, L.J., Jr.; 575
Davidson, W.; 932
Davis, F.G.T.; 144
Davis, F.W.; 218
Davis, L.R.; 351
Dawson, G.G.; 714
Dawson, J.A.; 9
Decker, J.D.; 219
Dedrick, C.V.; 715, 759
Deever, R.M.; 933
DeFazio, R.J.; 934
De Frain, J.A.H.; 352
de Guzman, R.M.; 419
DeHart, A.R.; 353
DeLong, T.J.; 935
Demps, H.W.; 145
Dempsey, M.A.; 146
Denton, J.J.; 936
Deschamp, P.A.; 500
Dettmer, P.; 716
Deverin, D.G.; 576
De Ville, L.M.; 60
Devlin, B.S.; 937
Devore, M.A.; 220
deVoss, G.; 10, 938
Dewar, A.M.; 939
Dickinson, D.J.; 940
Diener, T.; 355
Dill, G.A.; 356
Dillon, R.D.; 941
Dinkel, S.K.; 221
DiPasquale, N.A.; 61
DiTeodoro, V.A.; 717
Divers, A.J.; 942
Dobson, C.; 357
Dodds, L.K.; 577
Dodge, J.M.; 943
Donahue, J.M.; 358
Doran, M.S.; 944
Dougherty, T.W.; 359
Douglas, J.M.; 360
Dowell, B.F.; 945
Driscoll, A.; 11, 12

Driscoll, J.W.; 361
Drummond, R.J; 13
Dryden, B.J.; 578
Duffour, R.P.; 579
Duke, P.O'N.; 222
Duke, W.H.; 580
Dunham, J.; 718
Dunwell, R.R.; 501
Dupuis, M.M.; 223
Dvorak, J.; 581
Dworkin, A.G.; 719

Earl, L.M.; 720
Earls, N.F.; 224
Earp, W.A., Sr.; 362
Easterly, J.L; 62
Eckard, H.B., Jr.; 946
Ecker, M.A.; 582
Edmonds, E.L; 14
Egan, J.R.; 947
Ejiogu, A.M.; 363
Elliott, R.C.; 583
Ellis, D.J.; 15
Ellis, J.; 721
Ellis, J.R.; 15, 16
Ellis, T.I.; 502
Emanuel, J.; 774
Engel, R.A.; 584
Engelking, J.L.; 503, 504
Eriksson, K.H.; 225
Erlandson, D.A.; 505, 536
Espy, A.McD.; 585
Esteve, J.M.; 722
Even, M.J.; 226

Faas, L.A.; 723
Fagen, M. M.; 17
Fair, J.W.; 227
Farber, B.A.; 724, 725, 726, 727
Farber, J.H.; 228
Fareri, C.; 506
Farmer, M.J.; 948
Farrell, E.J.; 728
Fawley, S.M.; 949

Feagan, S.Y.; 63
Fearnow, C.D.; 364
Federman, D.G.; 729
Feild, H.S.; 365, 378, 379
Feinstein, D.J.; 730
Feitler, F.C.; 731
Felder, J.B.; 229
Feldman, N.O.; 99
Fevurly, J.R.; 950
Fibkins, W.L.; 732
Fielding, M.A.; 733
Fields, J.C.; 639
Fimian, M.J.; 702, 734, 735, 736, 737
Finch, G.A.; 951
Findley, B.F., Jr.; 366
Finger, S.G.; 64
Fink, L.D.; 367, 368, 369
Fitzgerald, S.M.; 65
Flaningam, R.B.; 370
Flannery, D.M.; 147
Fleming, K.P.; 66
Fletcher, B.C.; 738
Flint, L.; 739
Fordham, W.M., Jr., 371
Forman, J.S.; 740
Forman, S.G.; 741
Forrer, K.; 571
Foster, Robert E.; 742
Fountain, P.A.J.; 952
Fox, G.C.; 373
Fox, J.H., Jr.; 586
Fox, W.M.; 507
Foxworth, M.D.; 67, 743
Fowler, D.L.; 372
Fracchia, A.F.B.; 722
Francis, D.; 744
Frank, A.; 68
Frank, T.G.; 69
Franklin-Rier, A.L.; 148
Fraser, H.W.; 658
Fraser, K.P.; 587
Frataccia, E.V.; 508
Freedman, S.; 70
Freeman, N.S.; 374

Author Index

Freeman, P.; 351
Friedlander, J.; 375
Friedler, M.E.; 953
Friesen, D.; 745
Fruth, M.J.; 954
Fuller, J.; 376
Funk, F.; 5
Furey, R.A., Jr.; 955

Gaetino, J.Q.; 956
Gaite, A.J.H.; 377
Galanter, W.L.; 71
Gall, M.D.; 733
Galloway, D.; 72, 746, 747
Gana, B.; 149
Garcia, G., Jr.; 957
Gardner, D.C.; 150
Gargiulo, R.M.; 683, 825
Garskof, M.S.; 509
Gechman, A.S.; 73, 129
Gemmill, G.R.; 395
Gentile, L.M.; 748
Germinario, V.; 600
Ghanavi, G.; 151
Ghonaim, A.A.A.; 958
Gibson, R.O.; 749
Gierbolini-Rodriguez, A.M.; 750
Giles, W.F.; 365, 378, 379
Gilson, T.Q.; 959
Ginsberg, R.; 751
Gist, R.C.; 74
Glickman, C.D.; 588
Glueck, W.F.; 345
Gnecco, D.R.; 75
Goertz, M.E.; 960
Goetsch, D.L.; 18
Golaszewski, T.J.; 805, 806, 807
Gold, R.S.; 684, 685
Gold, Y.; 752
Gomez, Meijia, L.R.; 380
Gonnet, K.A.M.; 381
Goodall, R.; 753
Goodlad, J.I.; 961

Goodwin, D.H.; 382
Gordon, P.A.; 510
Gorrell, J.J.; 19
Gould, P.A.; 76
Goulet, L.R.; 1000
Grady, T.L.; 230, 231
Grandjean, B.D.; 383, 962
Grant, J.O.C.; 77
Greenwood, G.E.; 963
Gregor, T.G.; 246
Gregory, M.D.; 232
Gregory, R.A.; 645
Greiner, J.M.; 513
Gress, J.R.; 754
Grier, K.S.; 755
Griffin, M.; 797
Grigsby, C.J.; 589
Grimm, W.J.; 964
Grossnickle, D.R.; 756, 757
Grubis, S.; 758
Guagulwong, T.; 78
Gue, L.R.; 1025
Guerrieri, S.I.; 79
Gupta, K.; 152
Gustafson, M.C.; 965

Habashi, M.; 590
Haberman, M.; 20
Hadaway, F.J.; 233
Hadbai, M.; 124;
Hafford, H.M.; 511
Hagensee, T.E.; 591
Hages, G.; 972
Haji-Hashim, A.B.; 384
Haller, E.J.; 80
Hammer, T.H.; 385
Hammond, D.W.; 592
Hammond, J.; 868
Handley, H.M.; 234
Hange, J.; 966
Hanley, P.E.; 873
Hanser, L.M.; 386, 387
Harder, W.M.; 512
Harris, P.G., 593
Harrison, M.G.; 388

Harrison, R.; 81
Harrison, W.A.; 967
Harshberger, R.F.; 389
Hartley, C.W.; 82
Harvey, P.L.; 83
Harwood, W.; 968
Hashemi, A.S.; 390
Hatoff, B.; 21
Hatry, H.P.; 513
Haughey, M.L.; 235
Hauser, P.; 84
Hawk, D.; 10
Hawkes, R.R.; 759
Hawley, R.A.; 760
Hays, L.C.; 685
Haywood, G.D.; 139, 153
Heath, D.; 761
Heather, D.D.; 154
Hebert, E.A.; 514
Heckert, J.W.; 969
Heckman, M.G.; 236
Hedley, H.H.; 970
Heller, G.N.; 833
Heller, L.E.; 532
Helm, D.G.; 515
Henderson, C.H., Jr., 85
Henderson, D.L.; 762, 971
Henderson, K.L.; 971
Henderson, L.F.; 86
Henderson, R.L.; 155
Henjum, A.E.; 594
Hennington, I.; 508
Herring, J.H.; 595
Herwood, M.C.; 22
Hewitson, M.; 596
Higgs, C.; 391
Hill, E.A.; 392, 393
Hill, M.D.; 394
Hillson, J.; 972
Hinckley, N.E.E.; 973
Hittner, A.; 763
Holcomb, J.; 516
Holdaway, E.A.; 974
Holder, C.A.; 597
Holifield, M.L.; 975

Holley, C.S.; 237
Hollon, C.J.; 395
Holmes, C.T.; 527
Holt, F.G.; 396
Hoodecheck, D.J.; 764
Hooks, J.B., Jr.; 976
Hooper, M.L.; 765
Hopkins, C.E.; 397
Horn, J.G.; 238
Horner, D.L.; 977
Hoth, E.K.; 398
Hough, M.J.; 156
Hoy, W.K.; 598
Hsieh, W.-C.; 599
Hubert, J.A.; 766
Huberty, T.J.; 872
Hudson, F.; 767
Hudson, L.R.; 399
Hughes, L.B.; 768
Hunt, H.H.; 336
Hunter, J.K.; 239
Hunter, M.; 400
Hutcherson, S.J.; 978
Hutchison, T.; 544
Hutton, J.B.; 401
Hyder, C.R.; 240
Hyler, L.R.; 525

Ibrahim, J.M.; 402
Indiresan, J.; 403, 404, 405
Inglis, J.D.; 754
Ingram, L.A.; 769
Irondi, E.O.; 979
Iwanicki, E.F.; 709, 770, 853, 854

Jackson, B.G.; 771
Jackson, N.A.; 406
Jackson, W.K.; 407
Jamentz, C.C.; 980
Jantzen, J.M.; 981
Jeffs, A.; 517
Jobe, M.E.; 401
Johnson, J.L.; 773
Johnson, J.R.; 87
Johnston, G.S.; 600

Author Index

Johnston, R.L.; 241
Jones, J.W.; 242
Jones, M.A.; 774
Joo, S.H.; 88
Jorde-Bloom, P.; 243
Jun, S.-Y.; 601

Kaiser, J.S.; 775
Kaminetzky, B.S.; 518
Kanu, I.N.; 244
Kaplan, L.E.; 408
Karnes, F.A.; 67, 743
Karoonlanjakorn, S.; 409
Karugu, G.K.; 519
Kass, S.E.; 776
Kasten, K.L.; 89
Katz, A.I.J.; 777
Kaufman, A.H.; 245, 410
Kaufman, J.W.; 520
Kazanas, H.E.; 246
Keaveny, T.J.; 320
Keene, D.L.; 982
Keith, P.M.; 983
Kells, P.P.; 247, 778
Kelsay, J.D.; 248
Kennard, M.A.; 984
Keon, T.L.; 359
Kephart, C.A.; 985
Kepner, H.S., Jr.; 23
Keppel, F.; 986
Kerr, B.J.; 779
Kesselheim, A.J.; 249
Key, J.P.; 250
Khillah, K.(L.)R.; 521
Kim, J.S.; 411
Kim, N.I.; 602
Kim, Y.M.; 780
King, D.J.; 24
King, J.C.; 108
King, W.; 250
Kirkwood, K.J.; 987
Kirtdum, A.; 90
Kladder, F.W., Jr.; 988
Klapachan, P.; 412
Klawitter, P.A.; 603
Kleinberg, S.B.; 781
Kleine, P.; 1060

Kline, J.D.; 239
Kline, S.; 932
Klosterman, K.J.; 25
Knight, J.A.; 989
Knold, J.A.; 251
Knoop, R.; 413, 522, 604, 605, 990
Knopp, R.; 91
Knowles, B.S.; 782
Koch, E.L.; 606
Koff, R.H.; 703, 704
Kohan, A.R.; 252
Koonce, G.L.; 783
Kossack, S.W.; 784
Kotrlik, J.W.; 253
Kovacevich, D.A.; 254
Kowalczyk, R.S.; 991
Krawewski, R.J.; 607
Kreis, K.; 157, 158, 523
Kremier, J.H.; 92
Krohn, E.W.; 982
Krupp, J.-A.; 26
Kuhn, B.J.; 993
Kuhns, A.P.; 994
Kuieck, T.J.; 608
Kulpa, C.M.; 183
Kurtz, S.; 785
Kutie, R.C.; 255
Kwak, R.V.; 609

Laber, R.K.; 995
Lacewell, W.E.; 414
Ladd, E.C., Jr.; 415
Ladipo, B.; 524
Lamb, P.G.; 996
Landsmann, L.; 610, 611
Lasley, T.J.; 27
Laurento, L.M.; 997
Lawrenson, G.M.; 786, 787
Laws, S.M.H.; 612
Lawson, H.A.; 939
Lebovitz, G.; 256
Lebowitz, R.; 93, 94
Leck, G.M.; 788
Lee, J.S.; 257
Lee, K.-H.; 159

LeMaster, Frederick A.; 789
Lenz, O.V., Jr.; 95
Leo, K.B.; 258
Leonard, R.L.; 743
Leon Guerrero, J.S., Jr.; 613
Lester, D.; 844
Lester, P.E.; 998
Leveille, M.F.; 999
Levitov, J.E.; 884
Lewis, A.L.F.; 96
Liebes, S.; 790
Ligon, J.A.; 160
Lim, S.B.H.; 614
Lindsey, R.H.; 161
Lipham, J.; 615
Lipka, R.P.; 1000
Litt, M.D.; 791
Little, L.F.; 792
Little, N.; 1001
Lofland, G.D.; 1002
Lombard, C.R.; 1003
Lopez, E.M.; 1004
Losik, R.C.; 416
Lovett, M.T.; 28
Lowther, M.A.; 920, 1005
Ludolph, J.F.; 616
Lynch, J.J.; 793

Mack, K.P.; 162
MacPhail-Wilcox, B.; 525
Macqueen, L.W.; 259
Maddux, C.D.; 1006
Mahan, J.M.; 29
Malek, A.P.; 253
Manera, E.S.; 794
Manning, T.L.; 163
Marchand, J.A.; 795
Marion, R.A.; 164
Mark, D.H.; 260
Markello, R.; 436
Marozas, D.S.; 526
Marra, P.R.; 617
Marshall, R.L.; 261
Martray, C.; 895, 896
Mastrian, L.; 108

Mathews, G.; 16
Mattaliano, A.P.; 618
Mattes, W.A.; 262
Matthews, K.M.; 527
Mattox, K.E.; 796
Matuskey, P.V.; 822
Mawter, P.T.; 97
May, B.R.; 417
May, D.C.; 526
Mayfield, J.R.; 437
Mazer, I.R.; 797
McArthur, J.T.; 30, 31
McBrayer, B.J.; 619
McCarthy, T.W.; 620
McCaskill, E.D.; 621
McCumsey, N.L.; 607
McDonald, D.; 626
McDonald, D.G.; 1007
McElroy, L.A.; 165
McEvoy, B.; 622
McGowan, J.M.; 528
McGowan, J.R.; 1008
McGrath, E.R., Jr.; 1009
McIntyre, T.C.; 798, 799
McKinnon, A.J.; 786; 787
McMillan, M.M.; 748
McNair, B.S.; 418
McWilliams, L.; 865
Meacham, D.J.; 1010
Meadow, K.P.; 800, 801
Meagher, K.; 767
Meek, B.L.; 98
Meeker, E.M.; 1011
Mehta, M.; 529
Meinke, D.L.; 802
Melendez, W.A.; 419
Mellinger, G.P.; 420
Mendenhall, D.R.; 623
Mersky, R.; 803
Mes, C.J.; 624
Metzdorf, V.A.; 166
Meyers, C.; 263
Milgram, R.M.; 99
Miller, G.A.; 421
Miller, J.; 727
Miller, J.P.; 1012

Author Index

Miller, L.E.; 32, 264, 265
Miller, M.H.; 1013
Miller, S.L.; 804
Milliken, W.J.; 266, 309
Milstein, M.; 523, 805, 806, 807, 808
Miskel, C.; 531, 532, 625, 626
Miskel, C.G.; 1014
Misko, G.; 100
Mitchum, M.D.; 422
Modiano, R.; 267
Mohnson, M.; 772
Mokry, A.-I.; 167
Moll, M.; 809
Moller, L.E.; 268
Moore, B.McG.; 1015
Moore, G.E.; 1016
Moracco, J.C.; 810, 811
Morgan, T.D.; 423
Morioka, H.N.; 424
Morris, B.N.; 101
Morris, E.A.; 168
Morris, J.E.; 33
Morris, M.B.; 627
Morrow, P.C.; 357
Morton, D.S.; 102
Mosley, K.S.; 1017
Moss, J.W.; 1018
Muchinsky, P.M.; 386
Mulligan, K.; 34
Muncrief, M.; 269, 270
Murphy, D.L.H.; 103
Murphy, G.; 812
Murphy, P.J.; 235, 593
Murray, A.; 813
Murray, M.L.; 425
Myers, L.B.; 426
Mykletun, R.J.; 814, 815

Nabors, J.J.; 1019
National Study of School Evaluation; 1020
Nederveen, P.; 271
Needle, R.H.; 816
Neely, J.H.; 427

Neely, J.R.; 272
Negrete, E., Jr.; 1022
Neill, S.B.; 494
Nelson, M.A.E.; 626
Nelson, R.W.; 23
Nelson, S.J.; 1023
Neumann, L.; 428
Neumann, Y.; 428
Nevele, R.W.; 1024
Newbrough, A.; 817
Newcomb, L.H.; 818
Newcombe, E.; 533
Newman, K.K.; 819
Newton, T.A.; 429
New York State United Teachers; 820
Nicholson, J.H.; 273
Nickel, B.B.; 274
Nidich, R.J.; 629
Nidich, S.I.; 629
Nigro, K.A.; 630
Nisha, B.; 152
Nixon, M.; 1025
Nolan, C.J.; 430
Norvell, C.A.; 275
Nwagwu, N.; 1026
Nwaobasi, J.O.; 631

Oakes, J.; 276
Oberlin, M.H.; 277
Obi-Akatchak, E.E.O.; 169
OFlynn-Comiskey, A.I.; 821
Oladebo, S.A.; 170
Olanya, P.; 104
Olasiji, T.D.; 431
Olson, J.; 822
Olson, R.R.; 278
Olstad, R.G.; 1027
Openshaw, H.; 432
O'Reilly, R.R.; 91
Ornstein, A.C.; 534, 535
O'Shea, R.A.; 1028
O'Such, T.G.; 279
Owens, M.; 625
Owuamanam, D.O.; 1029

Pacheco, A.; 433
Packard, J.S.; 105, 106
Padover, W.; 632
Paibulnukulkij, A.; 35
Paine, W.S.; 824
Panrat-Isra, S.; 434
Parham, C.S.; 633
Parkay, F.W.; 171
Parker, P.J.B.; 107
Partin, R.L.; 825
Pascale, P.J.; 108
Pastor, M.C.; 505, 536
Pastor, M.C.B.; 172
Pattavina, P.; 826
Pauley, T.R.; 173
Pauli, J.L.; 174
Payne, R.L.; 738
Pearson, D.A.; 435, 460
Peek, T.R.; 280
Pellicer, L.O.; 1030
Penny, J.A.; 827
Perko, L.L.; 537
Peters, A.S.; 436
Peters, D.S.; 437
Pettegrew, L.S.; 828, 829
Phelps, C.; 938
Phelps, T.K.; 281
Phillips, H.; 438
Pierce, A.; 36
Pinckney, R.; 663
Pitner, N.J.; 634
Plant, W.T.; 464
Plesman, C.K.S.; 282
Plihal, J.; 109, 110
Plug, C.; 898
Poindexter, J.O'N; 439
Polczynski, J.J.; 775
Polejewski, S.A.S.; 440
Poll, C.; 1031
Pook, M.E.P.; 175
Porter, F.H.; 1032
Portner, D.M.; 830
Pound, W.N.M.; 1033
Pour, B.H.; 831
Powell, J.P.; 441
Power, P.G.; 37

Powers, E.M.; 635
Powers, N.MacM.; 636
Prachedetsuwat, N.; 442
Prescott, W.; 443
Presley, P.H.; 832
Price, G.G.; 111
Provence, A.J.; 637
Pusateri, P.D.; 1034

Quinn, C.M.; 638

Rabinowitz, S.; 470
Radocy, R.E.; 833
Ramos, E.T.; 959
Ramsden, P.A.; 444
Ramsey, J.K.; 445, 446
Randklev, B.S.; 112
Raschke, D.B.; 113
Rathbone, C.; 834
Ravin, N.; 284
Raw, D.W.; 749
Rayder, N.F.; 1035
Ream, M.A.; 1036
Reddick, T.L.; 639
Reddish, M.LaD.; 1037
Reed, D.B.; 1038
Rees, M.A.; 447
Reese, S.G.; 836
Reid, E.J.; 176
Reiss, M.A.; 448
Rempel, A.M.; 904
Retish, P.; 837
Riccio, A.C.; 838
Richards, C.J.; 285
Richmond, V.P.; 640
Ricken, R.; 839
Riday, G.E.; 449, 450
Ridnour, R.E.; 451
Riley, B.E.; 840
Rinehart, R.L.; 452
Rippe, K.L.; 1039
Roach, D.R.; 641
Roberts, K.L.; 642
Robinson, D.C.; 114
Robinson, J.P.; 1040
Rochelle, W.J.; 177
Rodriguez, R.A.; 286

Author Index

Rogers, R.E.; 538
Rohman, G.B.; 643
Romero, D.; 287
Ronnenkamp, S.F.; 644
Rosenbach, W.E.; 645
Rosenfeld, D.J.; 453
Rosenholtz, S.J.; 1041
Ross, N.P.; 115
Rotheram, M.J.; 454
Ryerson, D.; 841

Saad Sulayman, N.S.; 1042
Sadler, J.C.; 842
Saidian, M.; 288
St. Clair, J.L.; 843
Salit, V.L.; 289
Salvi, A.D.; 646
Santangelo, S.; 844
Sarason, S.B.; 1043
Sardana, R.M.; 647
Sarros, J.C.; 845
Saunders, R.R.; 846, 847
Savoie, R.J.; 290
Savwoir, A.J.; 1044
Sayer, B.; 187
Schackmuth, T.G.; 116, 117
Schaefer, B.M.; 118
Scharf, S.; 848
Scherer, M.; 849
Schmidt, G.L.; 539
Schmidt, W.H.; 119
Schneider, G.T.; 178
Schoorman, F.D.; 455
Schorr, J.; 851
Schroeder, J.B.; 648
Schultheis, R.A.; 179
Schuster, J.H.; 456
Schwab, R.L.; 770, 852, 853, 854
Schwanke, D., 855
Schwartz, H.; 856
Schwartz, T.A.; 291
Scott-Miller, S.J.; 180
Seibert, M.L.; 457
Seidman, E.; 458, 459
Seifert, K.; 1045

Seiler, R.E.; 435, 460
Selby, T.J.; 140
Senigaur, E.; 649
Severe, S.F.; 292
Sharma, M.; 650
Shaw, S.F.; 858, 859, 860
Sheely, H.H.; 293
Sheikh Attari, M.H.; 1046
Shepherd, J.M.; 38
Sherwin, B.J.; 461
Shields-Kole, J.E.; 861
Shill, J.F.; 234
Shirey, D.C.; 12
Shish, Y.-S.; 294
Shobe, R.E.; 120
Shockley, H.A.; 933
Shoop, L.; 862
Sidotti, P.; 651
Silver, P.F.; 540
Silvester, T.J.; 295
Simmons, J.; 296
Singh, I.; 652
Sinprasong, S.; 653
Sistrunk, P.D.; 462
Skalak, C.H.; 463
Skinner, M.G.; 863
Smilansky, J.; 121
Smith, C.B.; 541
Smith, D.B.; 464
Smith, D.L.; 864, 1047
Smith, F.D.; 122
Smith, H.D.; 1048
Smith, S.S.; 865
Smolen, B.W.; 465
Smylie, M.A.; 1041
Sny, C.L.; 866
Soar, R.S.; 963
Sohal, T.S.; 897
Solasurdo, M.M.; 706
Sonpon, T.N.; 297
Sousa, D.A.; 598
Southerland, T.P.; 654
Spaedy, M.A.S.; 542
Sparani, E.F.; 39
Sparks, D.; 543, 867, 868

Spector, B.S.; 298
Speed, N.E.; 181
Spencer, W.; 5
Srivastava, R.C.; 1049
Srivastava, S.K.; 182
Stafford, C.R.; 40
Stapleton, J.C.; 655, 656, 657
Stark, J.S.; 1050
Stealey, P.A.T.; 300
Stecklein, J.E.; 466
Stedt, J.D.; 658
Steinbach, G.M.; 301
Steitz, J.A.; 183
Stembridge, A.F.; 467
Stern, W.A.; 184
Stewart, J.J.; 41
Stillwell, J.L; 42
Stitt, W.L.; 468
Stone, J.A.; 869
Stone, M.C.; 870
Stone, M.G.; 123
Stone, V.; 659
Story, M.W.; 302
Stratton, T.R., Jr.
Stubblefield, P.; 871
Stumpf, S.A.; 469, 470
Stunard, S.-L.L.; 303
Sudsawasd, S.; 471
Suelter, B.L.; 660
Sugg, W.G.; 661
Sullivan, M.M.; 397
Sumbrall, C.C.H.; 652
Sutton, G.W.; 872
Sweeney, J.; 185, 186, 663
Swick, K.J.; 873
Sylvia, R.D.; 544
Szura, J.P.; 545

Tabachnick, B. R.; 43
Tabb, S.M.; 1052
Taylor, G.A., III; 546
Taylor, G.H.; 187
Taylor, R.L.; 645
Taylor, S.V.; 370

Theodory, G.C.; 124, 666, 667
Thierbach, G.L.; 188
Thomas, M.A.; 876
Thompson, A.P.; 189
Thompson, C.L.; 877
Thompson, L.N.; 125
Thornton, D.K.; 472
Tice, P.G.; 658
Tisher, R.P.; 44, 45
Tokar, E.B.; 731
Torbati, M.B.T.M.; 473
Torres, S.; 1053
Treacy, T.D.; 878
Treacy, T.J.; 304
Trickett, P.L.; 879
Trinca, C.E.; 474
Trotter, J.R.; 1054
Tucci, A.W.; 547
Turk, D.C.; 791
Turner, L.G.; 881

Uncapher, B.W.; 475

Valdez, D.M.; 1055
Van Berkum, C.; 305
VandenBoogert, C.A.; 126
Vandett, N.J.; 306
Van Hestern, F.; 862
Van Patten, J.J.; 330
Van Wijk, A.; 476
Vatthaisong, A.; 477
Veenman, S.; 46
Vermillion, M.E.; 545
Villeme, M.G.; 47
Vivian, T.P.; 669

Walsh, E.J.; 478
Walter, G.; 17
Wangberg, E.G.; 127, 883, 884
Wangphanich, P.; 479
Warnat, W.I.; 885
Warner, W.M.; 128
Warren, D.L.; 548
Washington, E.M.; 480

Author Index

Waters, R.G.; 48
Watkins, D.; 1056
Watkins, J.F.; 846, 847
Watts, H.; 549
Weber, C.J.M.; 481
Weber, W.F.; 190
Wechsler, L.D.; 886
Weiner, A.M.; 307
Weiner, N.; 454
Weinroth, E.D.; 550
Weiser, H.E., Jr.; 191
Weller, L.D.; 670
Wellington, J.; 308
Wendt, J.C.; 887
Werner, A.; 888
Western Australian Education Department; 49
Whaples, G.C.; 309
White, J.D.; 551
Wiener, Y.; 73, 129
Wiggins, J.D.; 310, 311, 1057
Wilcox, K.E.; 552
Wilhite, J.W.; 671
Wilkes, S.T.; 561
Wille, J.H.; 482
Williams, D.; 483
Williams, F.P.; 484
Williams, J.A.; 130
Williams, M.-J.; 880
Williams, P.A.F.; 672

Willie, R.; 466
Wilson, L.C.; 312
Wilson, S.R.; 553
Winkler, A.L.; 673
Winkler, L.D.; 485
Winters, L.L.; 1058
Wippich, B.J.; 1059
Wiseman, D.E.; 217
Wiseman, J.W.; 486
Wisniewski, R.; 1060
Wittenauer, M.A.; 487
Wolf, G.E.; 828, 829
Womack, S.T.; 50
Woods, S.L.; 784
Wright, G.R.; 51
Wright, M.D.; 313
Wright, R.E.; 794
Wu, J.-S.; 131

Yarworth, J.S.; 1061
Young, M.G.; 192

Zabel, M.K.; 889, 890, 891, 892
Zabel, R.H.; 488, 890, 891, 892
Zahn, J.; 893
Zahner, M.C.; 894
Zak, I.; 1062
Zaremba, J.P.; 554
Zimmerman, K.W.; 1063
Zimmerman, W.W.; 489

TITLE INDEX

Absenteeism and Job Satisfaction of Wisconsin Public School Teachers, 947
Academic Health Educators Demographic and Professional Descriptors, Levels of Job Satisfaction and Professional Attitudes, 408
Academic Turbulence and the Crisis of Professional Satisfaction, 334
Accounting Educators: Characteristics, Attitudes, Job Satisfaction and Commitment of Faculties Housed in Degree Granting Programs in a Select Area of the State of Minnesota, 440
Achievement of Care: Men Who Teach Young Children, The, 1045
Actual and Desired Roles of the High School Learning Disability Resource Teacher, 217
Administrator's Handbook for Improving Faculty Morale, 555
Adult Basic Education Teacher Survey, 1975, 226
Advisers to Rural Schools. A Survey of the Advisory Service Which Is Specially Provided for Small Rural Schools in New England, 4
Again, the Preparation of Teachers: Competency and Job Satisfaction, 1043
Age and Correlates of Locus of Control, 990
Age and Intergroup Differences in Attitudes Toward the Teaching Profession: How Do Teachers and Students View Themselves and Each Other?, 1000
Age as a Factor in Teacher Job Satisfaction, 924
Aging Teacher Corps: How Should School Systems Respond?, An, 790
Agricultural Education: Review and Synthesis of the Research, 257
Alienated Teacher: A Profile, The, 604
Alternative Career Options of Unemployed and Underemployed Graduates of Teacher Preparation Programs and the Implications for Teacher Supply, 22

American Elementary Teacher Today: Results of Instructor's First National Teacher Poll, The, 53

Analysis of Career Motivations and Job Satisfactions Among Public Community College Faculty in Selected States, An, 482

Analysis of Communication and Job Satisfaction in an Educational Setting, 1059

Analysis of Communication Satisfaction in Four Rural School Systems, 242

Analysis of Communication Satisfaction in an Urban School System, 273

Analysis of Factors Associated with Job Dissatisfaction and Quitting Behavior Among Urban Public School Teachers, An, 915

Analysis of Job Satisfaction Among Academic Staff of Universities in Malaysia, An, 384

Analysis of Job Satisfaction Among Elementary, Middle Level, and Senior High School Teachers, An, 927

Analysis of Job Satisfaction and Participation in Inservice Education Programs of Wisconsin Post-Secondary Business and Office Education Teachers, An, 244

Analysis of Job-Related Stress and Dissatisfaction in the Teaching Profession, The, 679

Analysis of Perceived Stress in Elementary and Secondary Student Teachers and Full-Time Teachers, An, 19

Analysis of the Relationship Among Personal and Professional Variables and Perceived Stress of Mainstream and Special Education Teachers. Final Report, An, 702

Analysis of the Relationship of Perceived Professionalism and Perceived Complexity of Organizational Environment to Job Satisfaction Among Elementary School Teachers, 66

Analysis of the Relationship of Principals' Leadership Style to Teacher Stress and Job Related Outcomes, An, 642

Analysis of the Relationship of Teacher Job Satisfaction and Teacher Union Activism in the Detroit Public School System, 942

Analysis of the Relationship of Teachers' Job Satisfaction and Teachers' Union Attitudes in a Large Midsouthern City, An, 906

Analysis of the Relationships Among Control Variables, Organizational Climate, Job Satisfaction, Teacher Absenteeism, and Teacher Turnover in the Secondary Public School, An, 165

Analysis of Relationships Among Teacher Autonomy, Contact with the Principal, and Teacher Job Satisfaction, 575
Analysis of Role Perceptions of Title I Project Teachers, An, 289
Analysis of Sex and Departmental Differences in the Perceptions of Assistant Professors Regarding Work Environments, Mentoring, and Academic Employment, An, 372
Analysis of Stress and Its Relationship to the Satisfaction of Secondary Home Economics Teachers in Alabama, An, 237
Analysis of Teachers' Perceived Sources of Job Satisfaction at the Monrovia Consolidated School System: A Public School District in Liberia, An, 297
Androgyny, Stress, and Satisfaction: Dual-Career and Traditional Relationships, 454
Annotated Bibliography of Literature Dealing with Stress in the Teaching Profession, An, 785
Application of Herzberg Theory of Job Satisfaction to Iowa Public School Teachers, The, 528
Application of Herzberg's Theory of Motivation to Work to Public Elementary School Teachers in Puerto Rico, The, 499
Application of the Motivator-Hygiene Theory of Job Satisfaction and Job Dissatisfaction Among Administrators and Academic Staff of a Selected University in Nigeria, 431
Application of the Theory of Relative Deprivation to Occupational Discrimination Against Women, 898
Are Rural Teachers Satisfied with the Quality of Their Work Life, 235
Are There Any Rewards for Teaching?, 437
Are You Coming Back Next Year?, 996
Aspects of the Social Self of Nigerian Primary School Teachers, 104
Assessment of the Effectiveness of Summer Workshops for Training Teachers to Use the Materials of the Industrial Arts Curriculum Project, An, 240
Assessment of the Effects of a Reading Workshop on Job Satisfaction of Elementary School Teachers, An, 115
Assessment of Job Satisfaction of Industrial Arts Teacher Educators, An, 245
Attitudes of Student Teachers toward Selected Areas of Teaching, 42
Attitudes of Teachers Toward the 9-13 Middle School, 187
Attracting and Retaining Qualified Teachers. An Issue Brief of the Education and Job Training Program, 967

Attrition, Burnout, and Job Satisfactions of Teachers
    of the Emotionally Disabled, 787
Authoritarianism and Attitudes Toward Teaching in Teaming
    and Non-Teaming Situations, 59
Autonomy and Authority Among Professional Educators, 962

Basic Survival Guide for New Teachers, A, 564
Beating Burnout, 798
Beginning Teachers' Perception of Their Difficulties with
    Performance of Professional Roles, 16
Biased Look at Teacher Job Satisfaction, A, 867
Bridging the Gap Between Stress and Support for Public
    School Teachers: A Conversation with Dr. William
    C. Morse About Teacher Burnout, 826
Building Administrator Participation in Special Education:
    A Factor in Special Education Teacher Job Satisfaction,
    660
Building Morale. Motivating Staff: Problems and Solutions,
    494
Bureaucratic Nature of Schools and Teacher Job Satisfaction,
    The, 559
Bureaucratic Orientation and Job Satisfaction: A Cross
    Cultural Study of British and Indian Engineering
    Teachers, 403
Burned-Out Community College Humanities Instructor: Causes
    and Cures, The, 316
Burned Out Teachers Have No Class Prescriptions for Teacher
    Educators, 825
Burnout, 827
Burnout Among Teachers of Severely Handicapped, Autistic
    Children, 742
Burnout and Organization in Education: A Synthesis of
    Literature, 749
Burnout and the Reading Teacher, 842
Burnout and Stress Among Special Educators and Others,
    837
Burnout: A Critical Issue for Educators, 892
Burnout in Adult Educators, 893
Burnout in Professionals Working with Deaf Children, 800
Burnout in Teachers of Retarded and Nonretarded Children,
    683
Burnout in Teachers Working with Educationally Handicapped
    Children, 771
Burnout: The New Academic Disease. ASHE-ERIC Higher
    Education Research Report No. 9, The, 419
Burnout Phenomenon, The, 824

Can You Identify Your Source of Stress?, 794
Care and Feeding of Part-Time Teachers, The, 438
Career Involvement and Job Satisfaction as Related to Job Strain and Marital Satisfaction of Teachers and Their Spouses, 1063
Career Needs and Satisfactions of Teachers: A Replication Study, 65
Career Orientations of Rural Educators: An Investigation, 935
Career Roles, Psychological Success, and Job Attitudes, 469
Career Satisfaction of Teachers, 919
Career Stage as a Moderator of Performance Relationships with Facets of Job Satisfaction and Role Perceptions, 470
Causal Analysis of Satisfaction, Performance, Work Environment and Leadership in Selected Secondary Schools, A, 143
Causal Model of Turnover of Postsecondary Vocational Instructors Incorporating Demographic Factors, Work-Related Variables, and Job Satisfaction, A, 319
Causes of Burnout in SLD Teachers, 822
Causes of Stress in Teachers of the Hearing Impaired: A Comparison Between Itinerant Teachers and Self-Contained Classroom Teachers, 714
Challenge to the Charges: A Junior High School Self-Improvement Study, 239
Changing Teacher Morale: An Experiment in Feedback of Identified Problems of Teachers and Principals. Final Report, 904
Characteristics and Stress Producing Factors in a Population of RIFFED Educators, 723
Characteristics of High- and Low-Teacher Morale: In-Depth Interviews with Teachers, 999
Characteristics of Perceived Leadership, Job Satisfaction, and Central Life Interests in High-Achieving, Low-Achieving, and Improving Chapter I Schools, 275
Checklist for Improving Teacher Morale, A, 658
Chief School Officers' Role and Its Relationship to Teachers' Job Satisfaction, The, 609
Classroom Conflict Management and Secondary Teachers' Job Satisfaction, 135
Cognitive Style Compatibility and Job Satisfaction of University Personnel: An Exploratory Study, 426
Collective Action and Unionism Among Secondary School Teachers, 151

Collective Bargaining and the Quality of Work Life, Faculty Election Results Still Undecided, the Decennium Conference, a Modest Attitudinal Survey on Ten Years of Collective Bargaining, 360
Collective Bargaining, Teachers and Job Satisfaction, 909
College Faculty Satisfaction and Institutional Identification, 322
College Teachers' Work Motivation, Central Life Interests, and Voluntarism as Predictors of Job Satisfaction and Job Performance, 352
Collegial Environment Vitality, 452
Collegial Supervision: The Feasibility of Implementation and Particular Effectiveness on Teacher Attitudes and Job Satisfaction, 929
Combating Burnout: A Must for Secondary Urban Reading Teachers, 748
Combating the Effects of Debilitating Stress, 863
Commitment: A Behavioral Approach to Job Involvement, 129
Commitment to Teaching: Teachers' Responses to Organizational Incentives, 954
Communication Apprehension as a Cause of Stress and Low Morale, 744
Communication Patterns, Commitments, and Satisfactions of Faculty in a Geographically-Divided Multicampus University, 475
Communication Satisfaction in Private, Church-Related Schools, 258
Communication Satisfaction of Business Education Teachers in an Urban School System, 222
Comparative Analysis of a Four- and Five-Day Workweek Among Community College Faculty with Respect to Job Satisfaction, A, 364
Comparative Analysis of the Job Satisfaction Determinants of Two Groups of Secondary Vocational Education Teachers, A, 227
Comparative Analysis of Perceived Job Satisfaction Among Graduate and NCE Post-Primary School Teachers in Ogoja, Nigeria, A, 169
Comparative Attitudinal Analysis of Selected Business Teachers in Iowa Public Secondary Schools Concerning Their Current Job Satisfaction, A, 199
Comparative Study of the Morale of Regular and Special Education Teachers, A, 254

Comparative Study of Motivation to Work and Job Satisfaction Between Male and Female Faculty Members at a Midwestern Regional University, A, 325

Comparative Study of the Perceptions of Faculty and Administrators Regarding the Importance of Selected Factors in Determining Faculty Job Satisfaction in the Alabama Public Junior Colleges, A, 382

Comparative Study of Relationships Between Principals' Leadership Style and Teachers' Job Satisfaction in the Republic of China and the State of Iowa in the United States, A, 599

Comparison of Components in the Employment Satisfaction of General and Special Class Teachers, A, 279

Comparison of Concerns of Secondary and Elementary Student Teachers, A, 29

Comparison of the Effects of a Cognitive Stress Management Program and a Relaxation Training Stress Management Program, A, 713

Comparison of Factors Influencing Job Satisfaction and Dissatisfaction of Nursing Faculty with Faculty in Other Departments of Selected Private Liberal Arts Colleges in the Midwest, A, 358

Comparison of Job Satisfaction of South Carolina Teachers Involved in Two Different Systems of Instructional Organization, A, 295

Comparison of the Leadership Styles of Principals and Factors of Organizational Climates of Selected Open Space Suburban Elementary Schools, A, 591

Comparison of Levels of Job Satisfaction Among Selected Groups of Employees in Public School Education, Provo, Utah, 1984-85, A, 1010

Comparison of Nonburned-Out and Burned-Out Teachers, A, 877

Comparison of Perceived Occupational Stress Between Teachers Who Are Contented and Discontented in Their Career Choices, 810

Comparison of Teacher Job Satisfaction Between Predominantly Black and White Schools, A, 60

Comparison of Three Operational Definitions of Job Satisfaction, A, 608

Complex Issue of Teacher Stress and Job Dissatisfaction, The, 883

Concept and Determinants of Job Satisfaction: An Exploratory Study in the Colleges of Applied Arts and Technology in Ontario, 354

Conditions Associated with Early Retirement Decisions, 1044
Conditions for Practice: The Reasons Teachers Selected Rural Schools, 262
Conflict and Conflict Resolution in Relationship with Job Satisfaction in Teaching, 976
Congruence of Leadership Styles, Teacher Loyalty to Principal, and Teacher Job Satisfaction, 636
Congruence of Pupil Control Ideology Between Principals and Teachers as Related to Teacher Job Satisfaction, The, 671
Congruency as a Predictor of Job Choice and Satisfaction for Teachers, 925
Content Area Reading Project: An Inservice Education Program for Junior High School Teachers and Teachers of Adults, Appendix A, The Instruments and Their Development: Presentation and Analysis of the Findings. Final Report, The, 223
Continuous Self-Selection Processes in Teacher Education: The Way for Survival, 1062
Contribution of Background and Role Factors in the Prediction of Job Satisfaction for Chicano and Anglo Teachers, The, 1055
Coping Skills: A Goal of Professional Preparation, 887
Coping with Stress: Ideas that Work, 821
Correlates of Job Satisfaction of Public School Teachers: Moonlighting, Locus of Control, and Stress, 844
Correlates of Teacher Effectiveness: Environmental Robustness and Other Teacher Characteristics, 899
Correlates of Teacher Perceived Problems, 896
Correlates of University Faculty Interest in Unionization: A Replication and Extension, 320
Correlation of Selected Variables with the Morale of Virginia Teachers of Agricultural Education, 264
Correlational Study of Trust and Job Satisfaction in Education, A, 638
Counselor as a Stress Management Consultant to School Staffs, The, 882
Creating Conditions for Professional Practice in Education, 23
Creating a Healthy Organizational Climate, 330
Creating and Maintaining Staff Morale: The Personnel Administrator's Role in a Time of Ferment in Education, 584
Creating Job Satisfaction in a Static Teacher Market, 116

Title Index

Creativity as a Predictor of Teachers' Effectiveness, 99
Cross Validation Study of the Maslach Burnout Inventory, A, 770
Cycle of Renewal, The, 728

Decision Involvement and Job Satisfaction in Middle and Junior High Schools, 188
Decision Involvement and Job Satisfaction in Wisconsin Elementary Schools, 128
Decision Participation and Staff Satisfaction in Middle and Junior High Schools that Individualize Instruction, 181
Delegation: The Neglected Aspect of Participation in Decision Making, 598
Demographic and Work Environment Characteristics of Teachers as Predictors of Teacher Stress and Response to a Stress Intervention Program, 699
Descriptive Analysis of Factors Which Contribute to Job Dissatisfaction Among Secondary School Band Directors, A, 232
Descriptive Study of the Isolate Sister-Teacher and the Quality of Community Life Among Roman Catholic Teaching Sisters, A, 213
Descriptive Study of the Perceived Influence of Institutional Interruptions on the Morale and Work of Teachers and Pupils in Elementary Schools, A, 81
Descriptive Survey of Professional Burnout Amongst Public School Teachers in San Diego, California, 706
Determinants of Job Satisfaction Among Public Special School Teachers in Taiwan, the Republic of China, 294
Determinants of Job Satisfaction Among Selected Male High School Physical Educators in the City of Tehran, Iran, 195
Developing Confidence and Self-Motivation in Teachers: The Role of the Administrator, 630
Development Activities: A Hedge Against Complacency, 710
Development and Evaluation of a Collaborative and Goal-Focused Staff Development Intervention, The, 83
Development and Test of a Typology of Control, The, 82
Development and Testing of a Conceptual Model of Peer Supervision, The, 672

Development and Validation of a Burnout Measure--The Inventario de Extenuacion Personal (IEP)--in a Selected Group of Bilingual Special Education Teachers in Puerto Rico, The, 750
Development and Validation of an Elementary School Substitute Teacher Questionnaire, The, 108
Development of Guidelines for Policy-Relevant Studies of Faculty Vitality Through an Institutional Case Study, 347
Development of an Instrument to Measure Occupational Stress in Teachers: The Teacher Stress Inventory, The, 735
Development of an Instrument to Measure Teacher Job Satisfaction, 998
Development of a Multi-Dimensional Instrument for Measuring Teacher Morale, 1017
Development of a Rating Scale for Measurement of the Concept of Modal Organizational Orientation and the Prediction of Work Satisfaction on the Basis of Personal/Organizational Congruence, 461
Development of a Structure for Interpreting Human Relations Constructs in Higher Education, The, 343
Development of Teacher Perspectives, The, 43
Diagnostic-Prescriptive Approach to Reading Teacher Burnout, 864
Differences in Perceived Stress of Elementary Versus Secondary School Teachers, 884
Differences in Perceived Teacher-Coach Job Attitudes as Identified by Senior High School Principals and Teacher-Football Coaches (Role-Conflict), 207
Differential Well-Being of Educators, 894
Dimensions of Faculty Members' Sensitivity to Job Satisfaction Items, 365
Distinctive Physical Education Teachers: Personal Qualities, Perceptions of Teacher Education and the Realities of Teaching, 224
Do Teachers Like to Teach?, 681
Do You Have a Plan of Success for Your School?, 654
Do You Hear What I Hear? A Response to Faculty Perceptions, 356

Educational Forces Inventory: A New Technique for Measuring Influences on the Classroom, The, 1035
Educational Stress: Sources, Reactions, Preventions, 775
Educator Stress in Terms of Selected Variables, 843

Title Index

Effect of the Administrative Behavior of Secondary School Principals on the Participation and Influence of Teachers in School Decision-Making as Perceived by Teachers, The, 619

Effect of Class Size on Perceptions of Burnout by Special Education Teachers, The, 798

Effect of Faculty Gender on Job Satisfaction in Selected Sex-Typed Units Within Institutions of Higher Education, The, 486

Effect of Faculty Participation in the Decision Making Process upon Perceptions of Organizational Climate and Job Satisfaction, 465

Effect of Leadership Roles on the Satisfaction and Productivity of University Research Professors, The, 345

Effect of Organizational Structure of Schools and Role Orientation of Teachers on Job Satisfaction of Teachers, The, 130

Effect of Participation in Collaborative Supervision on Cooperating Teachers' Job Satisfaction and on Their Evaluation of Fellow Teachers, Student Teachers, and Supervisors as Sources of New Instructional Ideas, The, 362

Effect of Role Perception of Regular and Special Education Teachers on Job Satisfaction (Role Conflict, Ambiguity, Intolerance), The, 146

Effect on the Job Descriptive Index Used for Measuring Teacher Job Satisfaction When a Student Area Is Added, The, 928

Effects of an Aerobic Dance Program for Women Teachers on Symptoms of Burnout, The, 740

Effects of Amount, Format, and Location of Demographic Information on Questionnaire Return Rate and Response Bias of Sensitive and Nonsensitive Items, 378

Effects of Associate Teaching on Teacher Morale, The, 5

Effects of Career Orientation on Retirement Attitudes and Retirement Planning, 357

Effects of Defensiveness and Self-Actualization of a Herzberg Replication, 545

Effects of Demographic and Personality Factors on Job Satisfaction of Self-Contained Classroom Teachers and Open-Area Team Teachers, The, 103

Effects of Different Types of Stress as Perceived by Teachers in an Urban High School, The, 886

Effects of the Headmaster's Leadership on Teacher Job Satisfaction and Morale as Perceived by the Teachers in Nepal, The, 652

Effects of Individual and Job Characteristics on Job Satisfaction of Supplementary and Hebrew Day Schools' Hebrew Teachers, The, 284

Effects of the Institutional Structure of Schools on Teachers. Final Report, The, 70

Effects of Leadership on Perceived Job Satisfaction and Influence Among Intermediate School District Special Education Personnel in Michigan, 277

Effects of Mentoring and Support Training Groups upon Job Satisfaction, Attitudes, Needs, Performance, and Morale of Beginning Teachers, The, 24

Effects of Organizational Climate and Leadership Behavior on Teacher Job Satisfaction in Selected Schools, The, 572

Effects of Organizationally Based and Individually Based Stress Management Efforts in Elementary School Settings, 805, 806

Effects of Personality and Person-Environment Congruence on Job Satisfaction of Community College Faculty and Professional Staff, 327

Effects of Personality and Situational Variables on Teachers' Perceptions of Need-for-Involvement in Decision Making, The, 1028

Effects of Reduction in Force on the Morale of Elementary Classroom Teachers, The, 95

Effects of Role Agreement on Resource Specialist Job Satisfaction and Mainstreaming Learning Disabled Students, 228

Effects of a Structured Wellness Program on Physical and Mental Well-Being of Public School Teachers and Staff Members, The, 783

Efficacy of Institutionally Dispensed Rewards in Elementary School Teaching, The, 89

Electronic Office--Educator's Input Outside the Classroom, The, 255

Elementary School Staff Support System Effects on Program Implementation and Job Satisfaction, 71

Elementary Teacher Perceptions of Certain Organizational Processes and Job Satisfaction in Schools with Self-Contained and Differentiated Staffing Classrooms, 87

Elementary Teacher Satisfaction and Morale and Perceived Participation in Decision-Making, 86

Elements of Job Dissatisfaction Associated with Performance Evaluation, 493
Empirical Study of Whether the Direct Involvement of Classroom Teachers in the Decision-Making Process of a Public School District in Conjunction with Their Locus of Control Orientation Effects Their Perceptions of Job Satisfaction, An, 1047
Employee Information Environments and Job Satisfaction: A Closer Look, 387
Employment and Academic Characteristics of Former Undergraduate Education Students, 936
English Departmental Student Achievement, Organizational Climate and Job Satisfaction in Selected New York City High Schools, 304
Environmental Satisfiers in Academe, 435
Equal Educational Opportunity and Declining Teacher Morale at Black, White, and Hispanic High Schools in a Large Urban School District, 690
Evaluation of the Beginning Teacher Supervision Program Conducted by the Department of Agricultural and Extension Education at the Pennsylvania State University, An, 48
Evaluation of Teacher Stress and Job Satisfaction, An, 872
Everything You Always Wanted to Know About Professional Burnout But Were Afraid to Ask, 692
Examination of Administrative Leadership Style in the Public High School, An, 580
Examination of Field Instructor Turnover in Relation to Agency and University Support, Job Satisfaction, and Intrinsic Satisfaction, An, 453
Examination of Participation in Decision Making and the Perceptions of Satisfaction for Elementary School Principals and Teachers in the State of Illinois, An, 616
Examination of Some of the Determinants Affecting Teacher Absenteeism, An, 987
Examination of Variables Influencing the Perception of Stress Among Special Education Teachers, An, 695
Existential Meaning in the Professional Life of Teachers and Its Relationship to Teacher Job Satisfaction, 964
Exodus Syndrome: Factors Affecting Teacher Career Change, The, 1009
Expectancy Motivation Theory and School Outcomes, 492
Experience and Effects of Stress in Teachers, The, 708

Exploratory Study into the Phenomenon of Teacher Burnout, An, 729
Exploratory Study of Male Primary Teachers: Their Perceptions of Professional Status and Potential for Increasing Their Number, An, 98
Exploratory Study of the Relationship of Job Satisfaction to Work Values in the Maryland Cooperative Extension Service, An, 309
Extent of Burnout Among Teachers of Vocational Agriculture in Ohio, 818
External and Internal Correlates of Teachers' Satisfaction and Willingness to Report Stress, 121

Factor-Analytic Study of Job Satisfaction Among Special Educators, A, 194
Factor Analytic Study of the Teaching Events Stress Inventory, A, 675
Factor Invariance in the Measurement of Job Satisfaction, 202
Factorial Validity of the Maslach Burnout Inventory in a Sample of California Elementary and Junior High School Classroom Teachers, The, 752
Factorial Validity of the Teacher Occupational Stress Factor Questionnaire and Psychological Measurement, The, 743
Factors Associated with Career Change among Secondary School Teachers: A Review of the Literature, 140
Factors Associated with the Retention of Industrial Educators, 203
Factors in Burnout Among Teachers of Exceptional Children, 890
Factors Influencing Decisions of Schoolteachers to Leave Education, 965
Factors Influencing Teacher Mobility in Nigeria, 979
Factors Involved in Burn-Out Among Teachers of Emotionally Disturbed and Other Types of Exceptional Children, 891
Factors Involved in Job Satisfaction Among Teachers in the Bureau of Indian Affairs System on the Navajo Reservation, 122
Factors of Emotional Exhaustion, Depersonalization, and Sense of Accomplishment Among Teachers of the Gifted, 889
Factors of Faculty Job Satisfaction as Related to Communication Satisfaction, 398
Factors Related to Burnout: A Review of Research, 799

Title Index

Factors Related to Teacher Morale in Selected Overseas and United States Schools, 261
Factors that Motivate Part-Time Faculty, 373
Factors Underlying the Measurement of Teacher Burnout, 848
Factors Which Motivate Job Acceptance and Profoundly Mentally Retarded Children, 526
Faculty Burnout, Morale, and Vocational Adaptation, 761
Faculty Dilemma: A Short Course, The, 456
Faculty Management: The Principal's Most Important Role, 663
Faculty Morale Study (1981). The Ohio State University at Lima Self-Study Report No. 1. Institutional Research Series 1981, 489
Faculty Perceptions of Institutional Quality and Vitality, 445
Faculty Satisfaction with Pay and Other Job Dimensions Under Union and Nonunion Conditions, 380
Faculty Self-Actualization: Factors Affecting Career Success, 339
Faculty Sex Composition and Job Satisfaction of Academic Women, 394
Faculty Under Stress, Person-Environment Fit Theory, 329
Faculty Work Orientations as Predictors of Work Attitudes in the Physical and Social Sciences, 428
Feasibility Studies of Teacher Core Job Characteristics. Final Report, 497
Field Guide to the Land of Teachers, A, 986
First Class, A Survey of Canadian Teachers in Their First Year of Service, 14
First Five Years of Teaching: Their Effect on Pupil Control Ideology and Commitment to Teaching, The, 30
First Year on the Faculty: Being There, 367
First Year on the Faculty: A Study of 100 Beginning College Teachers, 369
Five-Year Follow-Up Study of the Non-Teaching Agricultural Education Graduates--1968-73, A, 265
Flight from Physics Teaching, The, 308
Follow-Up of 1978/79 Graduates at the Ohio State University's College of Education Teacher Certification Program, 10
Follow-Up of a Random Sample of 1975/78 Graduates at The Ohio State University's College of Education Teacher Certification Program, 938
Formal Teacher Preparation, Job Performance, and Job Satisfaction of Allied Health Educators in Indiana, 457

Frozen and Forgotten: Stress Among Alaskan Bush Teachers, 758

Generalizing Personnel Training Models Used in Business and Industry to School Settings, 51
Generativity, Stuckness, and Insulation: Community College Faculty in Massachusetts, 335
Governance and Task Independence in Schools: First Report of a Longitudinal Study, 106

Happy, Healthy Teaching. A Teacher's Guide to Do-It-Yourself Renewal, 849
Herzberg's Theory Applied to Graduate Faculty in Departments of Physical Education Offering Doctoral Degrees, 424
Heuristicism of the Self-Actualized Teacher, The, 921
Higher Order Need Strength and Job Satisfaction in Secondary Public School Teachers, 172
How to Help Beginning Teachers, 607
Human Factor in Business--And in Schools, The, 543

"I Don't Get No Respect," 751
I Still Love to Teach; I just Hate Being a Teacher: An Investigation of the Relationship Between Life Cycle Theory and Dissatisfaction in Teaching, 955
Identification and Comparison of Factors Influencing Oklahoma Vocational Agriculture Instructors to Remain in the Profession, 551
Identification of Factors Influencing Vocational Agriculture Teachers to Leave Teaching, 941
Identification of Satisfying and Dissatisfying Factors in Staffs of Elementary and Secondary Public School Teachers from Two States, 504
Identification of Selected Factors Which Influence Job Satisfaction of Vocational Agriculture Teachers in Area VIII of Texas, 216
Identification of Skills and Characteristics Needed by Country School Teachers, The, 1
Impact of Changing Conditions of Service on the Recruitment of Teachers in Nigeria, The, 1026
Impact of Leadership Role Behavior on the Performance of Professionals as Subordinates: A Study of University Department Heads, The, 455
Impact of Self-Role Congruence, Length of Service, Job Satisfaction and Organizational Commitment on Propensity to Leave: A Study of Community College Instructors of Developmental/Remedial Courses, The, 393

Title Index

Impact of State Policy on Entrance into the Teaching Profession. Final Report, 960
Impact of the Steady State on the Professional Lives of Academics, The, 441
Impact of a Substantial Pay Raise on Teacher Performance and the Job Satisfaction in Region IX Service Center Area of Texas, 272
Implementation and Assessment of a School Staff Development Model for Changing School Climate and Teacher Stress. Revised, 754
Implementation of Pilot Middle Schools in Unified School District 501 Topeka, Kansas, and a Comparison of Teacher Perceptions in Middle Schools and Junior High Schools, 163
Implementation of Planned Educational Change: A Multivariate Analysis of the Decision Source for Change, Organizational Commitment, and Job Satisfaction Among Elementary School Teachers, The, 58
Importance-Weighted Approach to Overall and Job-Facet Satisfaction of Teachers, An, 259
Improving the Quality of Worklife for Teachers: A Contingency Approach, 525
Improving Teacher Professionalism, 179
Incentives to Increase the Number of Qualified Science Teachers in Precollege Institutions, 298
Increasing Job Satisfaction for Community College Faculty and Professional Staff Through a Stress Management Model, 341
Induction of Beginning Teachers in Australia, The, 45
Induction of Primary School Teachers. A Report, The, 49
Induction of Teachers: A Bibliography and Description of Activities in Australia and the U.K.; Research Report on Stage I of the Teacher Induction Project. Beginning to Teach, Vol. 1, The, 44
Influence of Quality of Worklife Variables on the Retention and Career Satisfaction of Science and Mathematics Teachers, 198
Influence of Students' Cultural Behaviors upon the Job Satisfaction of English as a Second Language (ESL) Teachers at the Defense Language Institute, Lackland Air Force Base, Texas, The, 229
Inner-City High School Teachers: The Relationship of Personality Traits and Teaching Style to Environmental Stress, 171
Inoculation Against Stress: A Technique for Beginning Teachers, 722

Inquiry into Teacher Stress: Symptoms, Sources and Prevalence in Public Schools, An, 689
Insights from Vocational Teachers of the Year, 208
Interactions Between Family and Day Care Systems. Final Technical Report, 287
Interpersonal Skills for Home Economics Educators: Four Strategies to Prevent Helper Burnout, 792
Interpersonal Trust and Personal Effectiveness in the Work Environment, 395
Intrinsic and Extrinsic Rewards: Teacher Satisfaction in Wyoming Public Secondary Schools, 134
Intrinsic Rewards of Teaching, 110
Investigation into the Relationship between Supervision of Student Teachers and Day Care Center Cooperating Teachers, An, 34
Investigation into the Sources of Job Satisfaction and Dissatisfaction as Perceived by Faculty Members and Administrators in Selected Private Higher Education Institutions in Thailand, An, 442
Investigation of Academic Job Satisfaction/Dissatisfaction in a Small Struggling Liberal Arts College, An, 420
Investigation of the Effects of Perceived Teacher Stress and Perceived Work Environment Complexity on Job Satisfaction of the Physical Education Faculty in Division I-AA Colleges and Universities, An, 371
Investigation of Eleven Job Satisfaction Variables as They Pertain to Full-Time Community College Faculty, An, 381
Investigation of the Extent to Which Members of a Single Occupation (Elementary Teacher) Show Different or Identical Interests Depending upon Whether They Are Male or Female or Members of Black or Caucasian Racial Groups, An, 114.
Investigation of the Factors Influencing Job Satisfaction-Dissatisfaction of Physical Education and Athletic Personnel in Selected Small Liberal Arts Colleges, An, 423
Investigation of Factors Related to Job Satisfaction and Dissatisfaction of Teachers in School Districts with Differing Labor Climates, An, 538
Investigation of Job Satisfaction Among Faculty Members of a Large Multi-Purpose University in the Dallas-Fort Worth Metroplex, 390
Investigation of Job Satisfaction Among Late Career Entry Teachers at the Elementary Level, The, 107
Investigation of Job Satisfaction Among Teacher Negotiation Team Chairpersons, An, 490

Title Index

Investigation of Job Satisfaction and Dissatisfaction Among the Teachers in Secondary Institutions in Kano State, Nigeria, An, 170
Investigation of the Job Satisfaction of Elementary and Junior High School Teachers in the Libyan Arab Republic, An, 197
Investigation of Job Satisfaction-Dissatisfaction Among Elementary School Teachers and Headteachers in Nairobi, Kenya, and a Comparison of Their Perceptions on Fourteen Selected Job Factors from Herzberg's Two-Factor Theory, An, 519
Investigation of Organizational Communication in Elementary Schools: A Field Study, An, 76
Investigation of the Personality Traits, Job Satisfaction Attitudes, Training and Experience Histories of Superior Teachers of Junior High School Instrumental Music in New York State, An, 210
Investigation of the Relationship Between Biographical Characteristics and Job Satisfaction Among Middle School Teachers in Four Suburban School Districts, An, 180
Investigation of the Relationship Between Certain Situational Variables, Personality Variables and Job Satisfaction Within the Path-Goal Model of Management Among Public School Teachers, An, 1008
Investigation of the Relationship Between Characteristics of Self-Actualization and of Job Satisfaction of Selected Faculty in Higher Education, An, 451
Investigation of the Relationship Between Job Satisfaction and Social Interaction for Professors of Educational Administration, An, 429
Investigation of the Relationship Between the Satisfaction with School Communication System and Teachers' Work Motivation, An, 553
Issues in Teacher Incentive Plans, 513
Is Teaching Hazardous to Your Health?, 610
It's a Good Job for a Woman (and a Man): Why males and Females Choose to Be Elementary School Teachers, 1031

Job and Retirement Satisfaction Among Faculty Members of Public and Private Universities, 473
Job Attitudes of Teachers with Coaching and Non-Coaching Responsibilities in Selected School Districts in the State of Illinois, 211
Job Involvement and Satisfaction as Related to Mental Health and Personal Time Devoted to Work, 73

Job Involvement of Teachers, 522
Job Performance and Job Satisfaction of Beginning Teachers, 28
Job Preparation and Turnover Among University Music Department Chairs and Band Directors, 443
Job Reinforcers and Job Satisfaction Among Public Secondary Industrial Arts Teachers in Minnesota, 301
Job Satisfaction and Need Importance: Race, Sex, and Occupational Group, 1004
Job Satisfaction and Teacher Absenteeism, 912
Job Satisfaction Among Academic Physicians: Attitudes Toward Job Components, 436
Job Satisfaction Among Faculty Members at Non-Metropolitan Teachers Colleges in Central Thailand, 409
Job Satisfaction Among Faculty Members in a Large Black Southern University, 388
Job Satisfaction Amongst Private and Public Secondary School Teachers, 182
Job Satisfaction and Burnout Among Minnesota Teachers, 687
Job Satisfaction and College Faculty in Two Predominantly Black Institutions, 355
Job Satisfaction and Conflict Among Public High School Teachers, 164
Job Satisfaction and Dissatisfaction of Teachers in Urban and Suburban Secondary Schools in Birmingham, Alabama, 168
Job Satisfaction and Faculty Motivation, 487
Job Satisfaction and the Impact of Individualized Contract Plans as a Method of Performance Evaluation for Allied Health Faculty, 422
Job Satisfaction and Job Dissatisfaction Experienced by Nurse-Faculty in Baccalaureate Nursing Programs, 425
Job Satisfaction and Level of Aspiration in Academic Employment, 336
Job Satisfaction and Perception of Teaching of High School Teacher/Coaches, 221
Job Satisfaction and Teacher Absenteeism, 55
Job Satisfaction and Teacher Attitudes of Regular Classroom and Special Education Teachers, 303
Job Satisfaction as It Relates to Professional Support of Teachers of the Emotionally Handicapped, 274
Job Satisfaction: A Comparative Study of Community College Faculty to Secondary School and Four-Year College Faculty, 450

Title Index

Job Satisfaction, Decisional Discrepancy, Academic Social Climate, and Academic Achievement in Selected Title I Elementary Schools, 96

Job Satisfaction Determinants Among Faculty and Administrators: An Application of Herzberg's Motivation-Hygiene Model in Higher Education, 432

Job Satisfaction Factors of School Administrators and Teachers, 614

Job Satisfaction Factors of Special Education Teachers Employed in Residential Institutions for the Mentally Handicapped in New Mexico, 219

Job Satisfaction in the Education Industry: A Case Study of Teachers' Interaction with Work Conditions in High School, 167

Job Satisfaction in Relatively Closed and Open Schools, 930

Job Satisfaction--Its Impact upon Teacher Attendance, 1030

Job Satisfaction Level of New Brunswick's French Business and Trade and Industrial Education Teachers in Relation to Attitudes and Other Demographic Variables, The, 290

Job Satisfaction of Canadian University Physical Education Faculty: The Influence of Work Orientation, Career Stage, Role Conflict, and Role Ambiguity, 391

Job Satisfaction of Community College Faculty, 401

Job Satisfaction of Elementary and Secondary Teachers, 901

Job Satisfaction of Engineering Teachers: A Cross-Cultural Study, 404

Job Satisfaction of Faculty Members at Selected Southern Universities, 402

Job Satisfaction of Faculty Members at Srinakharinwirot University, Thailand, 479

Job Satisfaction of the Faculty Members of the Schools of Education in Three Universities Granting Doctor of Philosophy Degrees in the State of Michigan, 314

Job Satisfaction of First-Year Teachers: A Study of Discrepancies Between Expectations and Experiences, 3

Job Satisfaction of Full-Time Faculty in the Community Colleges and Area Post-Secondary Vocational-Technical Schools of Arkansas: An Analysis Based on Herzberg's Motivator-Hygiene Theory, 414

Job Satisfaction of School Teachers in the Republic of China as Related to Personal and Organizational Characteristics, The, 923

Job Satisfaction of Staff Members of Umm Al Qura University in Makkah, Saudi Arabia, 315
Job Satisfaction of Substitute Classroom Teacher, 236
Job Satisfaction of Teacher Educators in Agriculture, 331
Job Satisfaction of Teachers and Organizational Effectiveness of Elementary Schools, 91
Job Satisfaction of Teachers: The Impact of Rational Beliefs and Life Stress, 879
Job Satisfaction of Teachers in a Selected County as Measured by the Purdue Teacher Opinionaire, 926
Job Satisfaction of Teachers in the Portland Metropolitan Area: An Examination of Differing Factors and Their Relationship to Herzberg and Lortie Theories, 537
Job Satisfaction of Teachers in Selected Extended School Year Program, 933
Job Satisfaction of Transferred and Reassigned Teachers, 190
Job Satisfaction of University Faculty in the United States, 485
Job Satisfaction of Vocational Agriculture Teachers in Louisiana, 230
Job Satisfaction of Vocational Agriculture Teachers in the Southeastern United States, 193, 253
Job Satisfaction, Professional Concerns, and Communication Patterns of Teachers: Differences along the Professional Continuum, 12
Job Satisfaction Related to Tested Congruence and Differentiation, 1057
Job Satisfaction Survey Study for Nursing Educators in Baccalaureate Nursing Programs, A, 338
Job Satisfaction/Dissatisfaction and the Motivation to Work of Full-time University Teaching Faculty: An Analysis, 389
Job Sharing in Education, 932
Job-Stress and Burnout of the Venezuelan Teachers: Related to Educational Systems Change (Educacion Basica), 780
Job Stress and Coping Behavior of Married Male and Female University Faculty Members, 332
Joys of Teaching, The, 430

Kansas Survey Regarding Attrition of Special Education Personnel. Kansas Regent Institution Special Project. Summary Report, 247
K-12: What the Data Show About Public Education in Minnesota, 280

Leader Behavior and Its Relationship to Subordinate Job Satisfaction as Moderated by Selected Contingency Factors in Minnesota Public Schools: A Path-Goal Theory Approach, 628

Leadership Behavior of School Principals in Relation to Teacher Stress, Satisfaction, and Performance, 562

Leadership Style of the Quasi-Administrator and Teacher Job Satisfaction, 64

Leadership Styles, Maturity Levels, and Job Satisfaction in Elementary Schools, 78

Leadership Styles of Principals and Teachers' Job Satisfaction, Satisfaction with Supervision, and Participation in Decision Making, 605

Leadership Styles of School Principals as Predictors of Organizational Climate and Teacher Job Satisfaction, 568

Levels of Reported Stressors and Strains Amongst Schoolteachers: Some UK Data, 738

Life Experience Commonalities That Exist Among Successful Teachers: Implications for Burnout, 795

Life-Support System for Teachers, A, 757

Living with Your Job, 305

Local Teacher Organizations: The Relationship Between Teachers' Perceptions of Their Union and Job Satisfaction, 991

Look at the Life of an Outdoor Educator, A, 249

Management Implications of Team Teaching: Final Report, 105

Management Practices: A Major Cause of Stress Among Teachers, 803

Managing the Load, 772

Managing Teacher Stress and Burnout, 868

Maslach Burnout Inventory: Factor Structures for Samples of Teachers, 685

Matter of Degree: Faculty Morale as a Function of Involvement in Decisions During Times of Financial Distress, A, 483

Meaning and Value of Work, Job Satisfaction and Productivity of Vocational Teachers, Graduates, Seniors, and College Preparatory Seniors, The, 246

Measurement of Factors of Satisfaction and Dissatisfaction Which Affect Tennessee Teachers in Their Work, The, 511

Measures of Occupational Attitudes and Occupational Characteristics, Appendix A to Measures of Political Attitudes, 1040

Meta-Analysis of Bureaucratic Structure and Teacher Job Satisfaction, A, 1058
Mediating Role of Principals' Situational Favorableness on School Effectivenesss in Lebanon, The, 666
Mental Health Absences from Work, Stress and Satisfaction in a Sample of New Zealand Primary School Teachers, 746
Mentoring Among Special Education Teachers, 267
Mentoring Among Teachers, 17
Merging Access and Excellence: The Work of Community College Faculty, 458
Merit, Motivation, and Mythology, 501
Merit Pay for Teachers, 530
Merit Pay: The Impact on Teachers and Schools, 980
Merit Pay, Teacher Evaluation and Motivation, 542
Method for Assessing Teacher Motivation, A, 527
Mid-Career Malaise of Teachers: An Examination of Job Attitudes and the Factors Influencing Job Satisfaction in the Middle Years. Final Report, The, 1005
Middle School Reorganization--Conversion to Excellence, 586
Mid-Life Professional Crises: Two Hypotheses, 700
Minnesota Community College Faculty Activities and Attitudes, 1956-1980, 466
Mr. Chips Revisited, 760
Model for Understanding, Preventing and Controlling Burnout, A, 739
Moderating Effect of Role Ambiguity on the Relationship Between Leader Behavior and Teacher Satisfaction, 595
Moonlighting, Salary, and Morale: The Texas Teachers Story, 971
Moonlighting, Salary, Morale, and the Approaching Teacher Shortage: A Follow-up Study, 762
Morale Is Bad, 376
Morale Maladies in American and Foreign Higher Education: The Faculty Flameout Diagnosis, 400
Morale of Teachers of the Visually Handicapped: Implications for Administrators, 200
Morale-Affecting Stressors: An Analysis of Black, White, and Hispanic Elementary Schools, 691
Motivating and Dissatisfying Factors Among Professional Educators, 496
Motivating Teachers for Excellence, 502
Motivating Teachers for Vocational Curriculum Development of the Handicapped, 150

Title Index 277

Motivating Teachers with Nonfinancial Incentives: The Relationships of Compensatory-Time Jobs and the Need to Achieve to the Job Satisfaction of High School Teachers in New York City, 509
Motivation as a Consideration in Organizational Change and Staff Development Within a Peripatic Support Group, 517
Motivation, Central Life Interests, Voluntarism, and Demographic Variables as Predictors of Job Satisfaction and Perceived Performance of Teachers, 552
Motivation, Job Satisfaction, and Career Aspirations of Married Women Teachers at Different Career Stages, 550
Motivation of Secondary-School Teachers in the Lake Union Conference of Seventh-Day Adventists Based on Herzberg's Dual-Factor Theory of Job Satisfaction and Motivation, 521
Motivational Factors and Attitude Changes in Teachers, 524
Motivations for Teaching, 534, 535
Multivariate Analysis of Factors Affecting the Job Satisfaction of Engineering Teachers, 405
Music in Ohio Schools. Final Report, 215
Must Principals Choose Between Teacher Morale and an Effective School?, 579

National Conference on Professional and Personal Renewal for Faculty. Proceedings (Atlanta, Georgia, April 10-12, 1966), 407
National Job Satisfaction Study of Industrial Arts Teacher Educators, A, 410
National Study of University Faculty Work Satisfaction and Organizational Climate in Health Information Management Departments, A, 481
NEA Survey Investigates Teacher Attitudes, Practices, 1021
Need for Structure: Program Openness and Job Satisfaction among Teachers in Open Area and Self-Contained Classrooms, 52
Nevada Teachers' and Administrators' Perceptions of the Male Mid-Life Characteristics, 635
New Jersey Public Community College Professors: A Study of the Relationships Between Compensatory and Spillover Leisure Activities and Level of Job Satisfaction, 350

1978 Follow-Up Study of University of Maine at Orono College of Education Graduates 1975 to 1977, 13
NYSUT Teacher Stress Survey, 820

Observational Assessment of Stress-Related Behavior in Teacher Trainees: Development of an Instrument, 876
Occupational Adaptation Among Career Elementary and Secondary Teachers, 995
Occupational and Organizational Determinants of Behavior at Work, 541
Occupational Cognition, Experience, Satisfaction and Self: Teacher Trainees' Vocational Self Constructs, 25
Occupational Environments and Support Systems: Their Effects on Stress and Job Satisfaction of Home/Hospital Teachers, 781
Occupational Involvement and Alienation Among Adults: The Effects of Gender and Age, 183
Occupational Stress and Functioning Among Women Elementary School Teachers: A Model Including Personality Traits, Coping, Social Support and Life Stress, 720
Occupational Stress and the Teacher of Gifted Elementary Students: A Preliminary Investigation, 67
Occupational Stress of Regular and Special Education Teachers, 776
Occupational Stress of School Teachers in Four Rural Minnesota School Districts, 764
On Coping with the Stresses of Teaching, 838
One Point of View: So You Want to Be a Developmental Educator?, 306
On-the-Job Stress and Burnout: Contributing Factors and Environmental Alternatives in Educational Settings, 682
Open Space Elementary School: Effects on Teachers' Job Satisfaction, Participation in Curriculum Decision-Making, and Perceived School Effectiveness, 77
Opinions of the Intermediate Level Teachers in Montana Concerning Grades Five Through Eight, The, 174
Options in Education. Teacher Burnout, Parts One and Two. Programs No. 248-249, 823
Organizational and Personal Life Stress and the Role of Moderator Variables in the Prediction of Burnout, Performance and Serious Illness, 677
Organizational Change: Implications for Institutional Research, 397
Organizational Characteristics and Teacher Psychic Reward, 100

Organizational Climate and Job Satisfaction in Schools:
    A Relationship Study Conducted in Selected Schools
    in the Davis County School District, Utah, 644
Organizational Climate and Job Satisfaction of Independent
    College Faculty, 421
Organizational Climate of Public Schools: A Human Services
    Approach, The, 1052
Organizational Climate Related to Job Satisfaction and
    Loyalty of Teachers and Principals in Selected Rural
    and Urban High Schools in Punjab, India, 647
Organizational Development in Schools and Its Effects
    on Absenteeism, Job Satisfactions and Work Motivation,
    498
Organizational Model for Employee Job Satisfaction, An,
    539
Organizational Strategies to Reduce the Risk, 841
Organizational Stress Among Teachers, 880
Organizational Structure and Teacher Job Satisfaction,
    74
Organizational Structure, Climate and School Effectiveness,
    950
Organizational Structures and Processes, Perceived School
    Effectiveness, Loyalty, and Job Satisfaction, 1014
Organizationally-Based Stress: What Bothers Teachers
    (An End of Year Perspective), 807
Organizationally Based Stress: What Bothers Teachers,
    808
Organizing Management to Maximize Community College Impact,
    476
Overall Stress and Job Satisfaction as Predictors of Burn-
    out, 745

Paradox of "Making It": Teachers and Collective Bargaining,
    The, 1038
Participation and Decision-Making: Review of Researches,
    1049
Participation in Decision Making and Job Satisfaction:
    An Empirical Test of the Vroom and Yetton Model in
    Selected Secondary Schools, 177
Participative Decision Making for Teachers--Placebo or
    Panacea?, 596
Participative Management in a Developing Economy: Poison
    or Placebo?, 363
Part-Time Faculty: Gender Differences in Job Duties,
    Support, and Satisfaction, 370
Patterns of Job Satisfaction and Stress on High School
    Industrial Arts Teachers in the State of Iowa, 214

Peer Review Model for Managing a Career Ladder/Master Teacher/Performance Pay Program for Elementary and Secondary Schools, The, 903
Perceived and Experienced Stress of Teachers in a Medium Sized Local School District, 797
Perceived Family Emotional Relationships, Person Orientations, and Expected-Job-Satisfaction Among Teachers in Training in Mexico: A Test of Anne Roe's Theory of Vocational Interest and Choice with the General Culture Group, 1053
Perceived Job Satisfaction and Organizational Structure in School Districts with High and Low Declining Enrollment, 646
Perceived Job Satisfaction of Teachers in Individually Guided Education and Non-Individually Guided Education Schools, 125
Perceived Organizational and Personal Factors Related to Job Satisfaction in Public School Teachers, 943
Perceived Organizational Structure and the Pupil Control Ideology and Job Satisfaction of Elementary and Secondary School Teachers, 992
Perceived Principal Effectiveness as a Function of the Relationship Between Leadership Style and Job Related Maturity of Elementary Teachers, 641
Perceived Problems of Beginning Teachers, 46
Perceived Role Conflict, Role Ambiguity, and Burnout Among Special Education Teachers, 709
Perceived Role Conflict, Role Ambiguity, and Teacher Burnout, 853
Perceived Stress Events by Teachers, 802
Perceived Stress of Special Education Teachers and Regular Education Teachers Based on Task-Oriented, Role-Oriented, and Environment-Oriented Stress, 674
Perceptions of Autonomy and Job Satisfaction Among Elementary Teachers in Southern Maine, The, 75
Perceptions of Outstanding Elementary Teachers About Themselves and Their Profession, 62
Perceptions of Pay Satisfaction Among Vocational and Nonvocational Secondary Teachers in Wisconsin, 154
Perceptions of Special Education Teachers in Texas Regarding Selected Job Related Factors, 241
Perceptions of Urban Teachers About Specific Characteristics in Their Work Environment that Relate to Need Deficiencies, 155
Perfectionism: An Investigation of Its Construct Validity and Its Relationship to Job Satisfaction, 92

Personal and Professional Conflict: Stress for Teachers, 693
Personal Characteristics and Job Satisfaction Dimensions of Personnel Working with Severely or Profoundly Retarded Students, 248
Personal Demographic, Cultural Adaptation and Job Satisfaction Variables as They Relate to Teacher Retention of First Year Import Teachers in Binational Schools of the Latin American and Caribbean Area, 38
Personality and Situational Correlates of Teacher Stress and Burnout, 733
Personality Characteristics and Job Satisfaction Among Teachers on the Elementary, Middle, and Secondary Levels, 949
Personality Factors Related to Career Choice and Job Satisfaction Among Female Elementary and Secondary Teacher Education Alumni, 982
Personality, Subject Area, Time in Service, and Instructional Methods: A Test of Holland's Theory, 160
Personnel Training--Secondary Vocational Agriculture Teacher Education, 209
Pharmacy Faculty Job Satisfaction: Its Relationship to Environment, Rewards and Performance, 474
Phenomenological Study of Teacher Perceptions of Life Developmental Changes as Related to Inservice Behaviors and Needs, A, 26
Planning a Career in Business Teaching, 212
Power Strategies in Organizations: Communication Techniques and Messages, 640
Practical Observations Associated with Teacher Stress and Morale, 870
Practical Solutions for Administrators to Reduce Stress in the Classroom, 696
Precursors of Employee Turnover: A Multiple-Sample Causal Analysis, 359
Predicting Job Satisfaction of First Year Teachers, 40
Prediction of Job Satisfactoriness and Job Satisfaction of Secondary School Teachers, 139
Predictors of Job Satisfaction Among Elementary School Teachers in Southern Taiwan, the Republic of China, 131
Predictors of Overall Job Satisfaction Among Public School Physical Educators, 218
Preservice Training and Job Satisfaction Among Middle Grade Teachers, 173

Prestige, Work Satisfaction, and Alienation. Comparisons Among Garbagemen, Professors, and Other Work Groups, 478
Preventing Burnout in Teachers of the Gifted, 716
Preventing Teacher Burnout: Suggestions for Efficiently Meeting P.L. 94-142 Mandates and Providing for Staff Survival, 859
Pride and Prejudice in the Teaching Profession, 348
Principal and the Profession of Teaching, The, 558
Principal Leadership Behavior and Teacher Job Satisfaction in Public Elementary Schools in Columbus, 597
Principal Leadership Style and Its Relationship to Teacher Job Satisfaction and Moderated by Selected Contingency Factors, 624
Principal Leadership, Teacher Job Satisfaction and Student Achievement in Selected Korean Elementary Schools, 601
Principal Succession and Changes in School Coupling and Effectiveness, 625
Principals' Experience and Teachers' Satisfaction in Lebanese Secondary Schools, 667
Principal's Leadership Behavior, Teacher's Decisional Participation, Teacher's Job Satisfaction and Student Achievement, 617
Principals' Leadership in Inner-City Schools: A Comparative Study of Leadership Behavior, Job Satisfaction and Student Achievement, 574
Principal's Leadership Style and the Job Satisfaction of Teachers in a Selected Urban School District, The, 585
Principal's Leadership Style: Does It Affect Teacher Morale?, 560
Principal's Leadership Style, Situational Control and School Effectiveness, 659
Principals, Meet Maslow: A Prescription for Teacher Retention, 670
Proceedings of the Annual National Agricultural Education Research Meeting (9th, St. Louis, Missouri, December 3, 1982), 283
Procedures Used in Phase I of the IGE Evaluation to Scale the Variable Teacher Job Satisfaction, 111
Process of Deciding "Not" to Become a Teacher, The, 908
Professional Autonomy and the Work Satisfaction of Nursing Educators, 383
Professional Development as a Stressor, 6
Professional Discretion and Teacher Satisfaction, 186

Professional Negotiations and Teachers Decisional States, 1023
Professional Role Performance Difficulties Reported by First Year Home Economics Teachers in Illinois Public Schools, 15
Professional Socialization and Contemporary Career Attitudes of Three Faculty Generations. AIR 1983 Annual Forum Paper, 346
Profile of Female Agricultural Teachers in the Future Farmers of America Eastern Region and Their Job Satisfaction Level, A, 312
Profile of Job Satisfaction for Graduate Physical Education Faculty Members, A, 342
Providing for Job Tenure, Job Satisfaction and Productivity in Teachers, 1029
Psycho-Social Correlates of Teacher Burnout: A Study of Absenteeism, Job Satisfaction, Job Stress, and Locus of Control Among Special Education Teachers in Selected Counties of West Virginia, 782
P.L. 94-142 and Stress: An Analysis and Direction for the Future, 686
Public School as Workplace: The Principal as a Key Element in Teacher Satisfaction. A Study of Schooling in the United States, 627
Public School: A Source of Stress and Alienation Among Female Teachers, The, 698
Public School Teacher Attitudes Toward Unionization, 959
Pupil Control Ideology-Pupil Control Behavior Congruence and the Job Satisfaction of Public School Teachers, 969

Qualitative Evaluation of Teaching Service, Subject Teacher Line, KULT-A, 225
Qualitative Look at Black Female Social Work Educators, A, 351
Quality Circle in an Urban K-8 Public School, A, 953
Quality of Work Life as Perceived by Elementary School Principals and by Elementary School Teachers, 120
Quality of Working Life (QWL): Some Potential Applications to Education, 606
QUEST Concept: A Handbook on Planning and Implementation, The, 593

Reading Specialists 1974-1979 Graduates of Kean College: A Follow-up Study, 21
Reading Teacher Burnout: The Supervisor Can Help, 569
Reading Teachers' Perceptions of Individual Efficacy in Relation to Organizational Structure, 260

Recognizing Personality Differences Among Teachers Can
    Help Supervisors, 594
Recruitment and Preparation of Quality Teachers for Rural
    Schools, 238
Recruitment to the Teaching Profession, 911
Rediscovering the Joys of Teaching, 861
Reduction in Force and Teacher Burnout, 835
Reflections on Academic Burnout, 333
Reinforcement Density: A Theoretical Application to Job
    Satisfaction, 141
Rejuvenating Teachers, 902
Relation Between the Evaluation of Teachers and Job Satis-
    faction and Teachers' Views on the Evaluation of
    Teachers, The, 940
Relation of Home Economics Teachers' Professional Identifi-
    cation and Personal Characteristics to Job Satisfaction,
    The, 300
Relation of Job Satisfaction to Vocational Preferences
    Among Teachers of the Educable Mentally Retarded,
    The, 310
Relation of Organizational Structure and Leadership Style
    to the Job Dissatisfaction and Job Satisfaction of
    Teachers in Suburban Elementary Schools, The, 61
Relation of Organizational Structure and Personal Attri-
    butes to Work Satisfaction Among Public School Teachers,
    The, 117
Relation of Structure to Satisfaction, Stress, and Per-
    formance Among Athletic Directors in Senior Colleges
    of the National Collegiate Athletic Association, 318
Relation of Teacher Attitude to Major, Employment Status,
    Teaching Level, and Satisfaction with Teaching for
    First-Year Teachers, The, 47
Relation of Teacher Job Satisfaction to Participation
    in the Decision-Making Process in Mississippi, The,
    1013
Relationship Among Job Satisfaction, Attitudes Toward
    Collective Bargaining and Employment at Two- and Four-
    Year Institutions at the City University of New York
    and the State University of New York, The, 317
Relationship Among Selected Personal Variables and Job
    Satisfaction of College Business Teachers in Colorado,
    The, 366
Relationship Between Administrative Management System,
    Selected Demographic Variables and Level of Job Satis-
    faction: An Analysis of Principal-Teacher Perceptions,
    631

Title Index

Relationship Between Certain Personality Types and Level of Job Satisfaction for a Selected Group of Elementary, Middle, and Secondary Public School Teachers in the Northeast Texas Area, The, 945

Relationship Between College Department Chairperson's Leadership Style as Perceived by Teaching Faculty and That Faculty's Feelings of Job Satisfaction, The, 480

Relationship Between Faculty Expectations and Perceptions of the Department Chairperson's Role and Job Satisfaction of the Faculty, The, 344

Relationship Between First-Year Teachers' Morale and Behavior, 32

Relationship Between General Job Satisfaction and Specific Work-Activity Satisfaction of Community College Faculty, The, 375

Relationship Between Industrial Education Teachers' Voluntary In-Service Participation and Their Personality Characteristics, Job Satisfaction, and Locus-of-Control, The, 251

Relationship Between Intrinsic and Extrinsic Job Satisfaction and the Performance of Prospective Teachers, A, 36

Relationship Between Job Satisfaction and Life Satisfaction Among Faculty in Selected Oklahoma Junior Colleges, The, 328

Relationship Between Job Satisfaction and Life Satisfaction of Educators in an Urban Public School System, The, 968

Relationship Between Job Satisfaction and Needs Fulfillment Among Urban High School Teachers, The, 157, 158

Relationship Between Job Satisfaction and Selected Factors of Teaching Workload, The, 399

Relationship Between Job Satisfaction and Teacher Performance of Vocational Agriculture Teachers in Louisiana, The, 231

Relationship Between Job Satisfaction and Vocational Preferences of Teachers of the Educable Mentally Retarded, The 311

Relationship Between Leadership of Elementary School Principals and Satisfaction of Elementary School Teachers During Declining Enrollment, The, 632

Relationship Between Leadership Style and Teacher Job Satisfaction, The, 582

Relationship Between Life Satisfaction and Job Satisfaction Among Teachers in Four Midwestern States, The, 907

Relationship Between Mississippi Public Junior College
   Instructors' Perceptions of Supervisory Behavior and
   Their Perceived Levels of Job Satisfaction, The, 462
Relationship Between Motivation of Wisconsin Elementary
   and Secondary School Teachers and Their Commitment
   to the Teaching Profession, The, 520
Relationship Between Organizational Climate and Mainstream-
   ing, The, 292
Relationship Between Organizational Climate and Teachers'
   Job Satisfaction in Iranian Middle Schools, The, 137
Relationship Between Part-Time Faculty Job Satisfaction
   and Perceptions of Division Chairpersons' Leadership
   Behavior in Community Colleges, 444
Relationship Between Perceived Leadership Style, Size
   of School and Non-Instructional Time on Teacher Job
   Satisfaction, The, 669
Relationship Between Personal Factors, Role Ambiguity,
   Role Conflict and Teacher Job Satisfaction, The, 1061
Relationship Between Personality Characteristics and Job
   Satisfaction of Secondary Marketing Education Teachers,
   The, 282
Relationship Between Principal's Leadership Style and
   Teacher Job Satisfaction, The, 603
Relationship Between Rate of Verbal Participation in Shared
   Decision Making and Teacher Job Satisfaction, The,
   922
Relationship Between School Calendar and Teacher Job Satis-
   faction, The, 1033
Relationship Between School Principal Leadership Behavior
   and Teacher Stress, Satisfaction, and Performance
   in the Schools of Incheon, Korea, The, 602
Relationship Between Secondary School Supervisors and
   Teacher Job Satisfaction, The, 637
Relationship Between Selected Demographic Variables, Job
   Satisfaction and Teacher Burnout, The, 765
Relationship Between Selected School Context and Support
   Variables and the Perceived Success and Satisfaction
   of Beginning Elementary Teachers, The, 7
Relationship Between Sex and Intrinsic Job Satisfaction
   of Adult Educators, The, 973
Relationship Between Some Personal Traits, Job Satisfaction
   and Job Performance of Employees, 897
Relationship Between Stress, Job Satisfaction, and Teaching
   Assignments Among Music Educators in the State of
   Michigan, The, 871
Relationship Between Teacher Absenteeism and Selected
   Personal, Status, and Situational Factors, The, 946

Relationship Between Teacher and Decisional Status and
    Loyalty, 600
Relationship Between Teacher Brinkmanship and Teacher
    Job Satisfaction, The, 655
Relationship Between Teacher Career Aspirations, Job Satis-
    faction and School Socioeconomic Status, The, 910
Relationship Between Teacher Job Satisfaction and Student
    Reading Achievement, Time Off-Task, and Teacher Plan-
    ning Time, The, 68
Relationship Between Teacher Perception of Elementary
    School Organizational Climate and Student Achievement,
    The, 102
Relationship Between Teacher Perceptions of the Principal
    Leader Behavior and Teacher Attitudes Toward Evaluation
    in Kentucky Public Schools, 612
Relationship Between Teachers' Attitudes Toward Educational
    Change and Their Job Satisfaction in Sudan, The, 1042
Relationship Between Union Effectiveness and the Quality
    of Members' Worklife, The, 917
Relationship Between University Faculty Job Satisfaction,
    Role Conflict, Task Clarity and Productivity, The,
    321
Relationship of Attitudes of Vocational Student Teachers
    to Their Plans to Teach, 1018
Relationship of Decision Involvement and Principals' Leader-
    ship to Teacher Job Satisfaction in Selected Secondary
    Schools, The, 615
Relationship of Expectancy Work Motivation, Selected Situa-
    tional Variables and Locus of Control to Teacher Job
    Satisfaction, 491
Relationship of Individual Needs and Perceived Organiza-
    tional Stress to Job Satisfaction in a Comparative
    Study of Elementary School Principals and Teachers
    in New York City, The, 777
Relationship of Job Preview to Absenteeism, Turnover, and
    Job Satisfaction of Public School Teachers, The, 970
Relationship of Job Satisfaction and Selected Demographic
    Variables with the Desire to Change Careers of Voca-
    tional Teachers, The, 957
Relationship of Job Satisfaction, Job Satisfactoriness
    and Personal Characteristics of Secondary School
    Teachers in Georgia, The, 153
Relationship of the Job Satisfaction of Classroom Teachers
    to Student Perceptions of Classroom Satisfaction,
    The, 978
Relationship of Job Satisfaction to Values Consensus of
    an Organization and Its Members, The, 977

Relationship of the Leadership Behavior of Nursing Educational Administrators and Job Satisfaction of Nursing Faculty Members in Korea, 411

Relationship of Need Fulfillment to Job Attitudes of Faculty in Higher Education, The, 396

Relationship of Organizational Structure and Leadership Behavior to Staff Satisfaction in IGE Schools, 623

Relationship of Personality Traits to Job Satisfaction of Teacher Education Majors Who Chose Teaching or Non-Teaching Careers, The, 1032

Relationship of the Principal's Communication Behavior to the Teacher's Perceived Job Satisfaction, The, 589

Relationship of the Principal's Leadership Style and Job Satisfaction of Teachers, The, 556

Relationship of Principals' Sense of Humor and Job Robustness to School Environment, The, 567

Relationship of Reduction in Force to Motivation and Aspects of Job Satisfaction of Teachers, The, 518

Relationship of Role Conflict and Role Ambiguity to Job Satisfaction Among College-Level Nursing Faculty, The, 439

Relationship of Role Perceptions of the Secondary School Music Educator and the Resultant Effect on Job Satisfaction, The, 268

Relationship of Satisfaction Level and Content of Job Satisfaction Questionnaire Items to Item Sensitivity, The, 379

Relationship of Selected Mississippi Public School Teachers' Locus of Control to Their Perceptions of Job Satisfaction, The, 1037

Relationship of Selected Personal Attributes of Business Teacher Educators to Job Satisfaction, 468

Relationship of Selected Variables to Teacher Absenteeism, The, 944

Relationship of Special Education Teacher Job Satisfaction and the Implementation of Public Law 94-142, The, 204

Relationship of Teacher Facilitation of Self-Directed Learning to Job Satisfaction of Secondary Home Economics Teachers, The, 206

Relationship of Teacher Morale and Zones of Indifference, The, 561

Relationship of Teacher Morale to the Racial Composition of the Student Bodies in Selected Elementary Schools in Metropolitan Atlanta, The, 85

Relationship of Teacher Motivation to Innovativeness and Job Satisfaction, 534
Relationship of Teacher Perceptions of Organizational Climate to Job Satisfaction in the Elementary Schools of a Metropolitan School District, The, 101
Relationship of Teachers' Job Satisfaction and Teachers' Job Dissatisfaction to Teachers' Union Attitudes, The, 948
Relationship of the Views Women Elementary Teachers Have of Their Work and Their Attitudes Toward the Feminist Movement, The, 94
Relationship of Work Values to Job Satisfaction in the Maryland Cooperative Extension Service, 266
Relationships Among Educational Needs, Educational Opportunities, and Job Satisfaction for Indiana Secondary English Teachers, The, 205
Relationships Among Esteem, Autonomy, Job Satisfaction and the Intention to Quit Teaching of Downstate Illinois Industrial Education Teachers, 313
Relationships Among Performance Ratings, Job Satisfaction Perceptions, and Preferred Non-Monetary Rewards for Elementary School Teachers, The, 112
Relationships Among Teachers' Satisfaction/Dissatisfaction Levels, Teacher Motivation, and Student Achievement, 515
Relationships Among Trust, Job Satisfaction, and Teacher Perceptions of Principal Effectiveness, The, 620
Relationships Between Elementary School Teacher Perceptions of Principal Leadership Style/Style Adaptability and Teacher Job Satisfaction/Satisfaction with Supervision, The, 673
Relationships Between Job Satisfaction and Self-Actualization Among Teachers in the San Diego City Schools, 1046
Relationships Between the Number of Sources of Attachment to Work and Elementary Teachers' Total Satisfaction, 118
Relationships Between Perceived Stress and Job Satisfaction, Locus of Control, and Length of Teaching Experience, The, 869
Relationships Between Selected Faculty Characteristics and Teaching Effectiveness, The, 418
Relationships Between Selected Personal Characteristics of Special Education Teacher Educators and Their Job Satisfaction, 488

Relationships Between Teacher Perception of Job Satisfaction and Specific Factors of Teacher Effectiveness as Perceived by the Principal and the Teacher, 577

Relationships Between Teacher Perception of Managerial Behavior, Teacher Satisfaction, and Teacher Absenteeism, The, 648

Relationships Between Teacher Stress, Attitudes Toward the Profession and Organizational Climate, The, 789

Relationships of Role Conflict and Role Ambiguity to Job Satisfaction of Nebraska Public School Administrators and Teachers, The, 1039

Relationships of a Quality Circle Process on Job Satisfaction and Organizational Commitment in Elementary Schools, 63

Relationships of School Bureaucratization, Elementary School Teachers' Professional and Bureaucratic Orientation, Conflict, and Job Satisfaction in a Selected School District, 88

Relationships of Selected Variables to Job Satisfaction of Recent Graduates in College of Education at Mississippi State University, The, 35

Relationships of Teacher Militancy to Organizational Structure and Job-Satisfaction, The, 985

Reported Stress and Well-Being in Teachers and Student Teachers, 830

Research Study About Teachers' Perceptions of Job Satisfaction, A, 621

Retesting Fiedler's Contingency Theory in Islamic Schools, 124

Rewarding Teachers: Issues and Incentives, 533

Rewards of Teaching, The, 549

Role Conflict and Its Correlates in an Educational Setting. Final Report, 914

Role Conflict Concerning Teachers of the Mentally Retarded and Its Relationship to Confidence in Leadership, Effectiveness, and Satisfaction, 285

Role of Noneconomic Factors in Faculty Union Voting, The, 385

Role Orientation of Community College Occupational Faculty, 374

Role Strain, Job Satisfaction, and Career Experiences of Working Mothers in Academia at Various Stages of the Family Life Cycle, The, 448

Satisfaction and Dissatisfaction Among Judaic Studies Teachers in Midwestern Jewish Day Schools, 256

Satisfaction of Community College Faculty: Exploding a Myth, 449
Satisfaction of Hygiene and Motivation Needs of Teachers Who Resigned from Teaching, 508
Satisfaction of Job Related Needs of Nursing Faculty, 406
Satisfaction of Teachers in Alberta with Their Work and Working Conditions. Report of a Study, 974
Satisfaction with Teaching as a Job and as a Career, 1015
Satisfying Teachers' Needs: It's Time to Get Out of the Hierarchical Needs Satisfaction Trap, 523
Satisfying/Dissatisfying Factors of California Mentor Teachers, 2
Science and Mathematics Teacher Shortage: A Study of Recent Graduates, The, 1027
School as a Workplace: The Realities of Stress. Volume I, Executive Summary; Volume II, School Site Case Studies and the Role of the Principal; Volume III, Methodology and Instrumentation, 856
School Climate and Teacher Stress, 850
School Teachers: Job Satisfaction vs. Extraversion and Neuroticism, 133
Secondary School Newspaper Advisor's Job Satisfaction: A Factor in Press Freedom, 581
Secondary School Principals' Leadership Behavior and the Atmosphere of the School as Perceived by Teachers, Principals, and Superintendents, 565
Secondary Schools' Management Systems and Relationship to Teacher Absenteeism, 162
Secondary Teacher Satisfaction-Dissatisfaction: A Symbolic Interactionist Analysis, 144
Secondary Teachers' Responses to Organizational Incentives, 166
Selected Middle School Teachers' Perceptions of Their Principals' Leadership as Related to the Years of Experience of Both, 583
Selected Personal Characteristics Related to Job Satisfaction of Public High School Business Teachers, 233
Selected Self-Perceptions of Secondary Student Teachers as They Relate to Self-Initiated Experiences with Children and Youth, 39
Self-Actualization Attitudes of Faculty and Their Perceptions of Their Career Success, 340
Self-Esteem as a Moderator in Vocational Choice: A Test of Korman's Hypothesis, 1056

Self-Esteem of Regular and Special Education Elementary Teachers as Related to Job Satisfaction, The, 84
77 Ways to Prevent Burnout, 857
Sex Differences in the Job Satisfaction of University Professors, 464
Sex Role Preference and Job Satisfaction Among Secondary Home Economics Teachers, 307
Situational Factors Affecting Teaching, The, 368
Six Teachers' Beliefs and Attitudes and Their Curricular Time Allocations, 119
Snows of Yesteryear, The, 161
Social Climate and Its Relationship with Principal's Effectiveness and Teacher Satisfaction, 650
Social Support and Occupational Stress in Special Education, 734
Socialization of Teachers: Career Rewards and Levels of Professional Concern, The, 11
Socioeconomic Status Relationship of Teacher and Student, and Teacher Behavior, The, 126
Some Attitudes That Indicate Job Satisfaction in Vocational Home Economics Teachers Graduated from Two Different Curriculums at Michigan State University, 302
Some Effects of Role-Value Congruence on Job Satisfaction, 913
Some Potential Effects of RIF-Related Job Actions on Public School Teachers, 712
Some Relationships Between Administrators' Opinions and Teachers' Quitting Behavior in an Urban Public School System, 573
Some Relationships Between Teacher Morale and Teacher Behavior, 963
Sources of Motivation Among College Music Faculty, 326
Sources of Satisfaction and Dissatisfaction for New Zealand Primary School Teachers, 72
Sources of Stress and Dissatisfaction in Experienced High School Teachers, 791
Sources of Teacher Job Satisfaction and Dissatisfaction for Senior High School Teachers, 142
Sources of Teacher Satisfactions, Stress and Burnout in a Suburban School District, 717
Stability and Reliability of a Modified Work Components Study Questionnaire in the Educational Organization, The, 532
Staff Development Curricula for Australian High School Teachers: Validation of a Theory Based Generation of Preferred Learning Profiles, 156

Title Index

Staff Development: Design, Implementation, and Assessment of a Comprehensive Program, 1051
Staff Development: Fine and Fit, 813
State Agency Involvement in Teacher Induction, 27
Statistical Analysis of Educator, Drop Out in Illinois Public Schools, A, 721
Status of the American Public School Teacher, 1975-76, 1036
Status of Vocational Agriculture and the Changing Roles of Teachers of Vocational Agriculture in North Carolina. Final Report, 299
Strategies for Change, 80
Strategies for Dealing with Burnout Among Special Educators, 860
Stress Among Accounting Educators in the United States, 460
Stress and the Boarding School Teacher, 705
Stress and Burnout in Suburban Teachers, 725
Stress and Burnout: A Primer for Special Education and Special Services Personnel, 858
Stress and the Classroom Teacher. What Research Says to the Teacher, 873
Stress and Its Relationship to the Educational Environment and Administration of Randomly Selected Wisconsin Public Schools, 866
Stress and the Professional Educator, 676
Stress and Teaching, 703
Stress as Perceived by Teachers of Hearing Impaired Children and Youth, 773
Stress in Female Secondary Classroom Teachers, 881
Stress in Teachers' Midcareer Transitions: A Role for Teacher Education, 819
Stress in Teaching, 718
Stress in Teaching: A Comparison of Perceived Stress Between Special Education and Regular Teachers, 811
Stress Management for School Personnel, 862
Stress-Management Training: Evaluation of Effects on School Psychological Services, 741
Stress Reduction: Techniques for Teachers, 736
Stress Stories of School Teachers and Administrators, The, 845
Structural Coupling and School Outcomes: Job Satisfaction Student Attitudes and Perceptions of School, Student Achievement in Reading, Student Achievement in Mathematics, and Perceived Organizational Effectiveness, 1007

Structural Coupling and Teacher Job Satisfaction in Preschools and Day Care Centers, 286
Structure Coupling in Schools, 626
Student Teacher Morale: A Comparison of Morale Among Four Groups of Student Teachers, 33
Study Designed to Investigate the Relationship Between the Strength of the Professional Employee's Contract and the Degree of Teacher Job Satisfaction, A, 997
Study of an Administrator's Use of Authority as It Relates to Teacher Loyalty, Job Satisfaction, and Alienation in the Public Schools of Guam, A, 613
Study of the Comparison of Job Satisfaction and Professional Preparation of Selected Junior and Senior High School Teachers in Colorado, 192
Study of Commitment to the Work Organization Among Community College Teachers of Developmental/Remedial Courses, A, 392
Study of Competencies Related to Stress Management and Ecological Concerns of Special Education Personnel, 778
Study of the Correlation Between Job Satisfaction and Values for Public and Non-Public School Teachers Currently Teaching in South Florida Schools, A, 1003
Study of Differential Perceptions of Leadership Behaviors of Community College Deans of Instruction and Their Relationship to the Job Satisfaction of Division/Department Chairpersons in Texas, A, 484
Study of Dissonance in the Classroom Setting: Its Relationship to Teacher Job Satisfaction, Student Achievement and School Satisfaction, A, 916
Study of Educators' Perceptions Concerning Teacher Education in Selected Institutes in Thailand, A, 434
Study of Effective and Ineffective Supervisory Behavior in Special Education, A, 514
Study of the Effects of Participation in Decision Making by Adjunct Faculty in Continuing Education, A, 416
Study of the Elementary Principal's Use of Formal and Informal Authority as It Relates to Teacher Loyalty, Job Satisfaction, and Sense of Powerlessness, A, 651
Study of Elementary Teacher Job Role as Perceived by Elementary Teachers and Their Principals, A, 54
Study of the Factors Contributing to Job Satisfaction of Female Teachers, A, 506
Study of Factors Measuring Faculty Job Satisfaction at Selected Universities in Thailand, A, 471
Study of Faculty Perceptions of Selected Morale Variables, A, 349

Title Index

Study of Five Aspects of Job Satisfaction Among Teacher Resignees, A, 1011
Study of Herzberg's Motivation-Hygiene Theory of Job Satisfaction as It Relates to Academic Personnel in Selected Small Liberal Arts Colleges, A, 417
Study of Higher Order Need Strength and Job Satisfaction in Secondary Public School Teachers, A, 536
Study of the Interaction of High School Principals' Leader Behaviors and the Locus of Control and Role Ambiguity of Teachers in Determining Their Job Satisfaction, A, 643
Study of Job Satisfaction Among Secondary School Teachers, A, 152
Study of Job Satisfaction and Burnout of Special-Education Teachers in Selected Areas of Rural Kansas, A, 779
Study of Job Satisfaction and Dissatisfaction Among Faculty Members in Teacher Training Institutions in Thailand, A, 477
Study of Job Satisfaction as Measured by the Minnesota Satisfaction Questionnaire as Applied to Selected Male and Female Vocational and Technical Teachers of Esfahan, Iran, A, 288
Study of Job Satisfaction as Perceived by the Certified Staff in Florida Public Elementary Schools, A, 546
Study of the Job Satisfaction of Elementary Teachers in Open-Space and Traditional Schools, A, 57
Study of Job Satisfaction of Rural and Urban Elementary School Teachers in Thailand, A, 90
Study of Job Satisfaction of Selected Parochial High School Teachers in Kansas, A, 159
Study of Job Stress in Police Officers and High School Teachers, A, 755
Study of Morale of Teachers of the Visually Handicapped in the Rocky Mountain High Plains Region--Implications for Administrators Regarding Teacher Burn-Out and Attrition, A, 201
Study of the Organizational Climate in High Schools of the District of Columbia and the Effect It Has on Selected Variables of Students and Teachers, A, 148
Study of Personal and Job Facets as Determinants of Job Satisfaction for Public Senior High School Teachers in the Commonwealth of Pennsylvania, A, 132
Study of Preferred Environment and Job Satisfaction of Special Intermediate School District 916 and Component District Faculty, A, 293
Study of Professional Attitudes of Teachers in Five Public School Systems in Tennessee and Michigan, A, 639

Study of the Relationship Among (1) Job Satisfaction and (2) Teacher Attitude and Involvement in a Teacher Center, A, 918

Study of the Relationship Between Job Satisfaction, Job Values and Need-Achievement, A, 529

Study of the Relationship Between Job Satisfaction/ Dissatisfaction of Assistant Principals and Secondary School Teachers and Their Perceptions of the Bases of Power of Principals, A, 633

Study of the Relationship Between Job Security, Feelings of Security, Job Satisfaction and Role Involvement of Teachers in Selected Public Secondary Schools in New York State, A, 176

Study of the Relationship Between the Leadership Behavior of Instructional Supervisors and the Job Satisfaction of Teachers in Texas, A, 662

Study of the Relationship Between Leadership Behavior of Principals in the Public Schools in East Tennessee and Job Satisfaction of the Teachers, A, 557

Study of the Relationship Between Motivator and Hygiene Variables and the State of Satisfaction/Dissatisfaction of Teachers in the Howard County School System, A, 547

Study of the Relationship Between Organizational Climate and Job Satisfaction of Teachers in Selected Schools in the District of Columbia, The, 1002

Study of the Relationship Between Organizational Climate and Teacher Morale, A, 191

Study of the Relationship Between Organizational Climate, Job Satisfaction, and Educational District Size, and the Differences in Their Perception by Male Administrators and Teachers in Saudi Arabia, A, 958

Study of the Relationship Between a Participatory Management Model and Selected Variables, A, 994

Study of the Relationship Between Teacher Morale and Perceived Needs Deficiency of Maslow's Needs Hierarchy, A, 548

Study of the Relationship Between Teachers' Attitude Toward Professionalism and Teachers' Satisfaction/ Dissatisfaction with Their Jobs, A, 1024

Study of the Relationship Between Teachers' Perceptions of Job Satisfaction and Their Perceptions of the Level of Implementation of Eighteen Basic Middle School Characteristics, A, 145

Study of the Relationship Between Teachers' Perceptions of Self-Actualization Needs and the Perceptions of Satisfaction with the Teaching Profession, A, 984

Title Index

Study of the Relationship of Teacher Job Satisfaction and the Level of Implementation of Recommended Middle School Practices, A, 175
Study of the Relationships Among Teacher Job Satisfaction, Teacher Militancy, and School District Conflict, A, 934
Study of the Relationships Among Job Satisfactoriness, Occupational Competency, Job Satisfaction, and Demographic Characteristics for Beginning Trade/Industrial and Technical Education Teachers in Georgia, A, 41
Study of the Relationships Between Leader Behavior of Private Secondary School Principals and Teacher Morale in Bangkok, Thailand, A, 653
Study of the Relationships Between Participation in the Decision-Making Process and Job Satisfaction Among the Faculty of a Midwestern Regional State University, A, 412
Study of the Relationships Between Perceived and Reported Supervisory Intervention Behavior and Faculty Job Satisfaction, A, 463
Study of the Relationships Between Self-Actualization and Job Satisfaction in Teaching, A, 1034
Study of the Relationship of Self-Actualization and Job Satisfaction of Certain Categories of Secondary School Teachers in the Nigerian States of Ondo, Oyo and Ogun, A, 136
Study of School Organizational Climate Variables Associated with Teacher Morale, A, 629
Study of Schooling: Adult Experiences in Schools, A, 905
Study of Selected Attitudes of Superintendents, Principals, and Teachers and Their Relationship to the Job Satisfaction of Principals and Teachers, A, 661
Study of Sex-Role Attitudes, Job-Involvement and Job-Satisfaction of Women Faculty at the University of Puerto Rico, Rio Piedras, A, 433
Study of Socialization and Job Satisfaction of Faculty at an Urban Two-Year Community College, A, 427
Study of Teacher Burnout at the Junior High School Level, A, 934
Study of Teacher Job Satisfaction in Kuwait, A, 196
Study of Teacher Motivation in Five Selected Seventh-Day Adventist Colleges in the United States, A, 467
Study of Teacher Participation in Curriculum Development and Teacher Job Satisfaction, A, 1001

Study of Teachers' Job Satisfaction in Iran and the Relationships Between the Dimensions of Teachers' Job Satisfaction and the Patterns of Principal's Management Behavior as Perceived by the Teachers, A, 590
Study to Determine Influencing Factors for Selecting Agricultural Education as a Career. Final Report, 972
Study to Determine Relationships Between Job Satisfaction of Lawson State Community College Instructors and Their Teaching Effectiveness as Perceived by Students, A, 472
Subjective Expectations and Job Facet Predictability in Job Satisfaction, 189
Subjective Warrant and Recruitment into Physical Education, The, 939
Substitutes for Principal Leader Behavior: An Exploratory Study, 634
Suggestions from Student Teachers, 50
Supervisor's Challenge: Changing the Teacher's Work Environment, The, 588
Supervisory Behavior and Teacher Satisfaction, 587
Support for Educational Change: Its Forms, Functions, and Sources, 9
Support for Parents and Professionals: A Key Issue for the Field of Deaf Education in the 1980's, 801
Support for Teachers in Stress: The Principal's Role, 888
Survey Feedback as an Organization Development Strategy in a Public School District, 645
Survey of Attitudes, Perspectives, and Job Satisfaction Among Selected Community College Academic Faculty, A, 446
Survey of Classroom Teachers of the Emotionally Disturbed: Attrition and Burnout Factors, A, 786
Survey of Factors Affecting Job Satisfaction and Dissatisfaction of Public Educators in High Schools and Junior High Schools in Idaho, A, 281
Survey of Salaries and Working Conditions of Vo-Ag Teachers in the U.S., A, 250
Survey of Texas Public School Teachers, A, 1006
Synthesis of Research on Teacher Motivation, 540

TAFE Project: The Teaching Functions and Activities of Technical College Teachers in Western Australia, The, 377
Take These Six Steps to Save a Troubled School, 694

Title Index

Teacher Absenteeism: A Study of the Association of Selected Teacher-Reported Job Attributes and Frequency of Absence, 69
Teacher Absenteeism at the Secondary School Level: An Investigation of Work-Related Attitudes and Demographic Correlates, 184
Teacher Attitude Toward Early Retirement Incentive Plans, 956
Teacher Brinkmanship, 657
Teacher Brinkmanship and Job Satisfaction, 656
Teacher Burnout, 678, 804, 874
Teacher Burnout: An Analysis, 701
Teacher Burnout: Assumptions, Myths, and Issues, 724, 726
Teacher Burnout: Diagnosis, Prevention, Remediation, 784
Teacher Burnout--A Failure of the Supervisory Process, 839
Teacher Burnout in Special Education--Myth or Reality?, 832
Teacher Burn-Out: An Investigation of the Relationship Among Locus of Control, Job Satisfaction, Self-Esteem and Depression of Teachers of the Emotionally Disturbed, 730
Teacher Burnout and Extinguishing of Civic Education, 788
Teacher Burnout in Special Education: The Personal Perspective of a Classroom Teacher, 769
Teacher Burnout Issue, The, 680
Teacher Burnout: Moving Beyond "Psychobabble," 852
Teacher Burnout: A Psychoeducational Perspective, 727
Teacher Burnout/Stress Management: An Exploratory Look in an Urban School System in Alabama, 846
Teacher Burnout/Stress Management Research: Implications for Teacher Preparation/Personnel Selection/Staff Development, 847
Teacher Burnout: Stylish Fad or Profound Problem, 711
Teacher Burnout: Will Talking About It Help?, 756
Teacher Centering to Reduce Burn-Out and Isolation, 732
Teacher Certificate Recipients at the University of Michigan 1946 Through 1976: A 1980 Follow-Up Study, 1050
Teacher Compensation and Career Ladders, 1041
Teacher Decision Involvement and Job Satisfaction in Wisconsin High Schools, 147
Teacher Development: A Study of Factors Related to Teacher Concerns for Pre, Beginning, and Experienced Teachers, 895

Teacher Dissatisfaction and Alienation as Related to Mainstreaming in Education, 291
Teacher Dissatisfaction on the Rise: Higher Level Needs Unfulfilled, 185
Teacher Education Graduates: Sex, Career Plans, and Preferences for Job Factors, 983
Teacher Enthusiasm Reaches Epidemic Proportions, 664
Teacher Involvement in Decision Making: Zones of Acceptance, Decision Conditions, and Job Satisfaction, 178
Teacher Job Satisfaction and Job Stress of Urban Secondary School Physical Education Teachers, 836
Teacher Job Satisfaction: An Application and Expansion of the Job Characteristics Model of Work Motivation, 512
Teacher Job Satisfaction: A Framework for Analysis, 243
Teacher Job Satisfaction and Dissatisfaction, 503
Teacher Job Satisfaction and Modern Language Curricular Variables in Alberta, 271
Teacher Job Satisfaction and the Personal Need for Control by Principals and Teachers, 658
Teacher Moonlighting: An Unstudied Phenomenon, 1060
Teacher Morale and Perceptions of Organizational Characteristics in Public Schools Serving Handicapped Children, 768
Teacher Morale: What Builds It, What Kills It, 566
Teacher Motivation, 507
Teacher Motivation: A Study to Determine the Motivating Potential of the Elementary and Secondary Teaching Job in Chester County, 495
Teacher Motivation, Job Satisfaction, and Alternatives--Directions for Principals, 505
Teacher Need-Satisfaction, Importance, and Control: A Comparative Analysis Between Principals' and Teachers' Perceptions, 563
Teacher Opinion Inventory. Instructions for Use. Part A. Part B. 1020
Teacher Participation in Decision-Making and Its Relationship to the Variables, Job Satisfaction, Organizational Commitment, Job Tension, and Attitudinal Militancy, 937
Teacher Participation in Decision Making: An Investigation of Staff Development and Job Satisfaction, 988
Teacher Perceptions Associated with Occupational Stress, 878

Title Index

Teacher Perceptions for Increasing Staff Stability at Difficult to Staff Schools in a Large Urban School District: Analysis of Pecuniary and Nonpecuniary Benefits, 1022
Teacher Personality Characteristics in Selected Open and Non-Open Elementary Schools, 79
Teacher Personality Type and Job Satisfaction, 993
Teacher Professionalism and Decision-Making Modes in Selected Elementary Schools as Determinants of Job Satisfaction, 97
Teacher Recruitment and Retention in a Rural School District: A Case Study, 931
Teacher Satisfaction in Georgia and the Nation: Status and Trends. Teacher Burnout: Causes and Possible Cures, 875
Teacher Socialization: The First Five Years, 31
Teacher Stress, 809
Teacher Stress and Burnout: Implications for School Health Personnel, 684
Teacher Stress: A Descriptive Study of the Concerns, 715
Teacher Stress: The Elementary Teacher's Perspective, 113
Teacher Stress in the Middle Years: Crisis vs. Change, 885
Teacher Stress: Measurement and Management, 812
Teacher Stress: Perceived and Objective Sources, and Quality of Life, 815
Teacher Stress: Phase II of a Descriptive Study, 759
Teacher Stress: Selected ERIC Resources, 855
Teacher Stress: Sources and Consequences, 816
Teacher Stress: Sources, Symptoms and Job Satisfaction, 731
Teacher Stress: A Workshop Approach, 840
Teacher-Student Relations as a Predictor of Teachers' Job Satisfaction, 138
Teacher Transfers: A Survey of Teachers' Opinions on Factors Influencing Their Period of Stay in Schools with a Low Staff-Retention Rate, 500
Teacher Voluntary Absenteeism and Perceptions of the Professional Environment, Job Satisfaction and Impact of Collective Bargaining, 1048
Teachers and Stress. Final Report, January 1981-May 1982, 747
Teacher's Counselor, 665
Teachers for the Social Studies, 263

Teachers in Stress: A Study of the Relationship Between Job Importance Perceptions of Stress and Life Satisfaction Among Selected Urban High School Teachers, 763
Teachers in Their Fifth Year: An Analysis of Teaching Concerns from the Perspectives of Adult and Career Development, 966
Teachers in Transition: Study of an Aging Teaching Force, 1012
Teacher's Perception of the Principal's Leadership Behavior and Faculty Morale: Their Impact on Student Achievement, The, 649
Teachers' Perceptions of the Principal's Power Sources and Their Relationship to Selected Organizational Variables, The, 592
Teachers' Perceptions of Their Personal and Professional Development, 56
Teachers' Satisfaction with Teaching, 920
Teaching Coping and School Principal Behaviors, 688
Teaching: An Endangered Profession. Response to Donna Kerr, 961
Teaching Events Stress Inventory, The, 704
Teaching: How to Handle the Pollution, 697
Team-Teaching Practices and Job Satisfaction in Open-Space Schools, 123
Tell the Tomatoes to Get Along Without You, 865
Test of Expectancy Work Motivation Theory in Educational Organizations, A, 531
Test of the Path-Goal Theory of Leadership in Educational Organizations, A, 576
Test of Path-Goal Theory: Work Values as Moderators of Relations of Leaders and Subordinates, A, 413
Thank God It's Monday, 353
There Is Life After Burnout, 774
They Don't Have to Be Futile, 578
This Good-Health Regimen Keeps Employes Fit--And School Budgets Trim, 707
Those Forgotten Motivators, 571
Time for a Change: Theory X or Theory Y--What Is Your Style?, 618
Tips for Coping: The Music Educator and Stress, 833
Toward More Realistic Teacher Education, 20
Toward a New Sense of Vocation, 851
Transition from Education Student to Beginning Teacher: Personality, Self-Perceptions, Vocational Characteristics, Commitment, and Work Satisfaction, The, 37

Trust and Participation in Organizational Decision Making as Predictors of Satisfaction, 361
Twelve Steps Toward Revitalization for Teachers, 817
Twelve Terrific Teacher-Boosting Tips, 622
Twelve Years On--A Longitudinal Study of Teacher Behaviour Continued, 8
208 English Teachers. A Study of Schooling in the United States, 276
Types of Intrinsic Rewards of Teaching and Their Relation to Teacher Characteristics and Variables in the Work Setting, 109

Understanding Student and Faculty Life. Using Campus Surveys to Improve Academic Decision Making, 324
Understanding Teacher Stress, 753
Unit of Analysis in the Study of the Relationship of Teacher Stress to School Variables, The, 766
University Music Faculty: Work Attitudes, Recognition, and Satisfaction, 447

Validating Measures of Teacher Stress, 828, 829
Validation Study of the Theory of Work Adjustment: The Prediction of Teacher Satisfaction, A, 510
Values as a Predictor of Job Satisfaction of Business Technology Faculty Among Selected Community Colleges, 337
Variables Associated with Stress and Burnout of Regular and Special Education Teachers. Final Report, 767
Variables Related to Stress and Burnout in Special Education Teacher Trainees and First-Year Teachers, 737
Variation in Job Satisfaction and Dissertation Among Missouri's Beginning, Mid-Career, and Retired Elementary and Secondary Public School Teachers, 975
Vocational Instructor's Survival Guide, 18
Vocational Satisfaction in Holland's Theory of Careers, 1019
Vocational Stability and Job Satisfaction Characteristics of Postsecondary Technology Instructors, 278
Vocational Teacher Perceptions of Their Locus of Control, Job Satisfaction, and Superintendent Leader Behavior in Central Ohio Joint Vocational Schools, 252

Warning to Principals: You May Be Hazardous to Your Teachers' Health, 611
What Makes Ms. Johnson Teach? A Study of Teacher Motivation, 544
What Teachers Like and Dislike About Teaching, 1054

What Teaching Does to Teachers: The Teacher as Worker, 952
When Faculty Zeal Sputters, Here's How to Rekindle Enthusiasm Among Teachers, 516
When the Morale Really Slips, 296
When Teachers Give Up: Teacher Burnout, Teacher Turnover and Their Impact on Children, 719
Who Are Our Burned Out Teachers?, 854
Who Speaks for Teachers? A Commentary on Teaching, 831
Who Will Teach in High School?, 900
Why College Students Choose to Teach: A Longitudinal Study, 981
Why Teachers Quit, 796
Why Teachers Resign, 951
Why Vocational Agriculture Teachers in Ohio Leave Teaching, 989
Why Vocational Agriculture Teachers Leave the Profession: A Comparison of Perceptions, 1016
Women Administrators and Women Teachers: A Comparative Study, 1025
Women and Work in Saudi Arabia: A Study of Job Satisfaction in Higher Education, 323
Women Elementary-School Teachers and the Feminist Movement, 93
Work Adjustment of Vocational Education Teachers, 269, 270
Work as an Information Environment, 386
Work Experience of American College Professors: Some Data and an Argument, The, 415
Work of Community College Faculty: A Study Through In-Depth Interviews, The, 459
Work Perceptions and Job Satisfaction of Vocational Home Economics Teachers in Missouri, 220
Work-Related Value Systems and Teacher Morale, 570
Work Stress and Satisfaction of Comprehensive School Teachers: An Interview Study, 814
Work Values and Job Attitudes Held by New Teachers in Vocational Education in Mississippi, 234
Work Values and Job Satisfaction of Principals and Teachers of Nigerian Secondary Schools, 149
Working Conditions and Career Options Lead to Female Elementary Teacher Job Dissatisfaction, 127

SUBJECT INDEX

Academic ability 936
Academic social climate 96
Accounting teachers 440, 460
Achievement motivation 529
Adaptation-Innovation Inventory 554
Adjective Check List 1056
Adjective Self Description 982
Administration support 274
Administrator role 555, 558, 564, 578, 611, 630, 634, 654, 663, 696, 757, 859, 888
Adult educators 226, 893, 973
Age 26, 67, 72, 183, 854, 924, 990, 1012
Allied health faculty 422, 457
American Indian teachers 122
Androgyny 454
Anxiety 19, 395, 676, 678, 680, 692, 711, 785, 797, 804, 807, 819
Art teachers 851
Aspirations 336, 372

Assistant principals 633, 745
Assistant professors 372, 454
Athletic coaches 207, 211, 221
Athletic directors 318
Attitude change 753, 996
Attitudes Toward Women Scale 433
Attitudinal Militancy Scale 985
Audit of Administrator Communication 589
Australian teachers 31, 37, 44, 45, 49, 156, 377, 441, 500, 559, 744, 870
Authoritarianism 59, 1028
Authority 613, 962
Autonomy 75, 313, 575, 579, 962
Auxiliary Experiences Survey 39

Balanced F-Scale 59, 1008
Band Director Job Satisfaction Questionnaire 232
Band directors 232, 443
Beginning teachers 1-51, 209, 262, 367, 368, 369, 564, 596, 607, 722, 887

Behavior Pattern Observation Scale for Teachers 876
Behavioral Morale Checklist 658
Black schools 60, 171, 351, 355, 388
British teachers 8, 44, 187, 403, 404, 517, 731, 738, 911
Bureaucracy 20, 88, 116, 559, 1058
Bureaucratic Orientation Scale 130
Burnout-Tedium Measure 848
Business education teachers 199, 202, 212, 222, 233, 244, 255, 270, 290, 337, 366, 451, 468, 469

California Personality Inventory 965
California Psychological Inventory 79
Canadian teachers 1, 14, 91, 235, 271, 290, 391, 522, 614, 745, 845, 880, 882, 1012, 1045
Career aspirations 910
Career change 104, 140, 199, 308, 313, 753, 819, 847, 941, 954, 957, 965, 989, 1009, 1016
Career Change Scale 957
Career choice 22, 25, 37, 127, 196, 199, 203, 226, 276, 456, 461, 534, 810, 911, 919, 925, 935, 938, 939, 972, 981, 982, 983, 1018, 1026, 1031, 1041, 1056, 1062

Career development 448, 469, 550, 701, 966, 1041
Career ladders 903, 1041
Career orientation 357
Career Orientations Inventory 935
Career satisfaction 1015
Career success 339, 340
Career Survey Form 448
Catholic high school teachers 962
Central life interests 275, 531, 552
Change strategies 694, 727, 753, 757, 774, 784, 817, 986
Chinese teachers 599, 923
Class size 798
Classroom Environment Scale 978
Classroom techniques 62
Cognitive style 426
Collective bargaining 317, 360, 466, 906, 909, 959, 1038, 1048; see also unionism
College environment 324, 327, 339, 340, 356, 360, 366, 371, 372, 387, 395, 400, 419, 435, 441, 456, 474, 478, 489
College teachers 314-489, 531, 861; see also community college teachers, junior college teachers
Collegial supervision 929
Commitment to teaching 30, 37, 63, 129, 520
Communication problems 744, 758
Communication satisfaction 76, 222, 242, 258, 273,

Subject Index

398, 475, 553, 581, 589, 640, 1059
Communication Satisfaction Questionnaire 222, 242, 258, 273, 398, 553, 1059
Community college teachers 316, 317, 319, 327, 328, 335, 341, 349, 350, 364, 373, 374, 375, 376, 381, 382, 392, 393, 398, 399, 401, 414, 427, 438, 444, 445, 446, 449, 450, 452, 458, 459, 461, 462, 465, 466, 472, 476, 482, 484; see also college teachers, junior college teachers
Competence 119, 260
Conceptual Systems Test 52
Conflict 164, 260
Conflict Assessment Questionnaire 88
Conflict management 135
Conflict resolution 736, 825, 976
Coping 332, 419, 460, 678, 680, 688, 693, 695, 697, 705, 718, 720, 725, 731, 736, 739, 742, 747, 749, 758, 770, 784, 785, 793, 804, 818, 821, 825, 833, 838, 846, 849, 862, 867, 887
County Extension Agents' Job Satisfaction Inventory 309
Creativity 99
Creativity Battery 99
Cultural adaptation 38
Cultural/behavioral influences 229
Culture conflict 758

Curriculum 119, 150, 156, 239, 271, 302, 1001

Day Care Cooperating Teachers Questionnaire 34
Decision Involvement Analysis Questionnaire 147, 188, 1013
Decision making 77, 86, 96, 97, 128, 147, 177, 178, 181, 188, 207, 324, 361, 385, 395, 412, 416, 465, 483, 578, 596, 598, 600, 605, 615, 616, 617, 619, 922, 937, 943, 988, 1013, 1023, 1028, 1044, 1047, 1049; see also teacher participation
Decision Mode Index 97
Decision Participation Analysis Questionnaire 181, 617, 623
Decisional Condition Instrument 77
Decisional Participation Scale 465
Declining enrollment 646, 712
Delegation 598
Depression Adjective Check List 730
Developmental stages 6, 26, 56, 156, 700, 966, 995
Diagnostic Survey for Leadership Improvement 583
Differentiated staffing classrooms 87, 961
Discipline problems 820, 823
Dissonance theory 916
Distinctive teachers 224

Early childhood teachers 243, 1045
Educational administration teachers 429
Educational Attitude Survey 768
Educational change 58, 71, 80, 397, 780, 831, 1042
Educational Change Scale 1042
Educational environment (teaching environment) 23, 66, 241, 807, 850, 856, 866, 943, 1035; see also school environment, work environment
Educational Forces Inventory 1035
Educational improvement 4, 113, 654, 967
Educational needs 205
Educational opportunities 205
Educational practices 53
Educational problems 14, 53
Educational quality 280
Educational Work Components Study 219, 325, 532, 542, 547, 550, 633
Edwards Personal Preference Schedule 40
Elementary School Substitute Questionnaire 108
Elementary teachers 7, 8, 11, 12, 42, 49, 52-131, 197, 279, 499, 515, 519, 524, 546, 553, 574, 597, 616, 617, 624, 631, 682, 641, 651, 665, 668, 673, 743, 746, 752, 776, 783, 789, 805, 806, 807, 808, 831, 877, 879, 910, 918, 963

999, 1001, 1019 1031
Embedded Figures Test 426
Employment opportunities 348
Engineering teachers 403, 405
English as a Second Language teachers 229
English teachers 205, 276, 296, 304, 348, 728, 865
Environmental Assessment Technique 327
Equity theory 154
Evaluation of Practices in Individualized Schooling 111
Executive Professional Leadership Questionnaire 580, 617
Expatriate teacher 169
Expectancy theory 491, 492, 531, 553, 554, 563
Experienced Role Conflict Index 289
Extended school year 933
Extension Workers Job Satisfaction Inventory 266
Extraversion 133

Faces measure 219
Faculty college relationship 324, 330, 333, 334, 346, 347, 356, 360, 368, 369, 373, 376, 392, 397, 401, 419, 438, 456, 458, 459, 476, 483, 489
Faculty development 373, 452
Faculty Environmental Preference Scale 293

Subject Index

Faculty Job Attitude Survey 365
Faculty Job Satisfaction Instrument 463
Faculty Job Satisfaction Survey 420
Faculty Job Satisfaction/ Dissatisfaction Scale 477
Faculty mobility 392
Faculty Satisfaction with Rewards Instrument 321
Faculty vitality 346, 347, 353
Female teachers 70, 73, 93, 94, 127, 129, 310, 311, 312, 323, 351, 394, 433, 448, 506, 550, 720, 740, 881, 963, 1019; see also gender differences
Feminist Scale 94
Fiedler's theory 659, 666, 667
Field instructors 453
Foreign language teachers 271
Former teachers 954, 965
Friedlander Instrument 293
Fundamental Interpersonal Relations Orientation-Behavior Instrument 668

Gender differences 114, 167, 183, 370, 372, 464, 486, 698, 715, 854, 898, 973, 983, 1004; see also female teachers, male teachers
General Affective Tone Score 189
General Health Questionnaire 746, 814
General Well-Being Schedule 783

Geography teachers 367, 368
Gifted students 67, 716, 743, 889
Global Rating of Job Satisfaction 713
Graduate surveys 10, 13, 21, 22, 265, 908, 925, 936, 938, 941, 973, 1050
Group dynamics 20

Headmasters 652
Health teachers 408
Hebrew school teachers 284
Heni Faculty Attitude Survey 381
Herzberg's theory 2, 61, 131, 142, 170, 197, 256, 266, 314, 315, 317, 326, 331, 338, 381, 389, 414, 417, 423, 424, 425, 431, 432, 442, 467, 471, 487, 490, 493, 499, 504, 506, 508, 509, 511, 514, 515, 519, 520, 521, 528, 532, 537, 538, 545, 546, 547, 563, 616, 637, 948, 973, 1010; see also intrinsic and extrinsic rewards
High school teachers 132, 133, 134, 135, 139, 141, 142, 146, 147, 148, 150, 153, 155, 156, 157, 158, 159, 164, 167, 178, 185, 190, 195, 202, 207, 217, 221, 269, 304, 307, 493, 509, 580, 638, 643, 755, 763, 766, 791, 886, 904, 1052; see also secondary teachers

Higher Order Need Strength
  Measure B 172, 505,
  536
Holland's theory 37, 160,
  251, 925, 1019
Home economics teachers
  15, 206, 220, 237, 270,
  300, 302, 307, 792,
  1063
Home/hospital teachers
  781
Human Services Survey
  877
Humanities teachers 316

Import teachers 39
Incentives 89, 109, 166,
  513, 524, 530, 533,
  549, 954, 1022; see
  also rewards
Index of Activity Inventory
  934
Index of Job Satisfaction
  48, 135, 158, 221, 331,
  384, 480, 529, 557,
  597, 783, 969, 1034
Index of Organization
  Reaction 177
Index of Organizational
  Effectiveness 950, 1014
Indian teachers 133, 152,
  403, 404, 682, 1049
Individual Characteristics
  Scale 284
Individual development
  335
Individually Guided Education 58, 111, 125, 181,
  295, 623
Industrial arts teachers
  203, 214, 240, 245,
  251, 270, 301, 313,
  410
Industrial Relations Center
  Union Attitude Scale
  948
Industrial training 51

Inservice education 49,
  17, 18, 26, 46, 51,
  115, 150, 244, 251,
  283, 593, 741, 754,
  816, 840, 850, 865,
  929
Institutional Functioning
  Inventory 465
Institutional identification 322
Instructional improvement
  588
Instructional Leadership
  Behavior Scale 601
Instructional Systems
  Effectiveness Scale
  601
Interests 156, 352, 1053,
  1057
Intermediate school
  teachers 277; see also
  junior high school
  teachers, middle school
  teachers; secondary
  teachers
Internal-External Scale
  252, 396, 643, 712,
  730, 782, 844, 877,
  965, 990, 1037
Interpersonal relationships
  96, 138, 902
Interpersonal Trust Scale
  395
Interruptions 81
Intolerance of Ambiguity
  Scale 146
Intrinsic and extrinsic
  rewards 36, 109, 110,
  134, 142, 202, 301,
  391, 453, 502, 544,
  901; see also Herzberg's
  theory
Inventario de Extenuacion
  Personal 750
Inventory of School Openness 74
IPAT Anxiety Scale 867

Subject Index

Iranian teachers 137, 288
Irrational Beliefs Test 879
Islamic teachers 124
Israeli teachers 99, 121, 1062
Itinerant teachers 517, 714, 779

Job acceptance 526
Job attributes 69
Job characteristics 132, 512
Job Characteristics and Job Satisfaction Questionnaire 284
Job Descriptive Index 55, 58, 66, 74, 78, 97, 101, 112, 146, 173, 189, 190, 193, 195, 205, 219, 227, 244, 252, 253, 272, 277, 307, 315, 319, 325, 327, 337, 342, 344, 371, 386, 387, 390, 396, 398, 411, 412, 421, 429, 439, 457, 464, 465, 473, 481, 485, 486, 509, 568, 590, 612, 621, 624, 631, 643, 644, 648, 662, 673, 695, 755, 777, 782, 869, 871, 898, 927, 928, 944, 947, 968, 970, 987, 992, 1008, 1019, 1032
Job Diagnostic Survey 495, 498, 512, 646, 712, 848, 1008
Job enrichment 497
Job Episodes Questionnaire 515
Job facet predictability 189
Job-facet satisfaction 259, 384, 409, 479, 643
Job in General 970
Job involvement 73, 118, 120, 129, 178, 207, 211, 403, 455, 522, 541, 943
Job Involvement Scale 433
Job Involvement Survey 1008
Job performance 28, 36, 112, 143, 231, 272, 318, 352, 367, 386, 387, 455, 457, 470, 474, 493, 562, 602, 635, 642, 677, 841, 897
Job reinforcers 301
Job related maturity 641
Job-Related Stress Scale 836
Job related tension 207, 211, 289, 318, 937, 994
Job-Related Tension Index 289, 395
Job role perception 54
Job Satisfaction Among Allied Health Faculty Scale 422
Job Satisfaction Blank 37, 310, 311, 448, 781, 925, 982, 1053
Job Satisfaction Continuum Scale 284
Job Satisfaction Index 52, 64, 163, 289, 403, 408
Job Satisfaction Inventory 401, 404, 589, 613, 651, 656
Job Satisfaction Measure 1059
Job Satisfaction Questionnaire 90, 304, 554, 623, 771
Job Satisfaction Rating Scale 12

Job Satisfaction Scale
220, 575, 636, 836,
1039, 1042
Job Satisfaction Survey
63, 147, 181, 188, 595,
603, 922
Job Satisfaction/
Dissatisfaction Scale
364, 409, 425
Job satisfactoriness 139,
153
Job security 176, 751
Job sharing 932
Job Stress Scale 782
Job Stress in the School
Setting 674
Judaic Studies teachers
256
Junior high teachers 134,
153, 163, 181, 188,
192, 197, 223, 224,
239, 510, 752, 834;
see also intermediate
school teachers, middle
school teachers, secondary teachers

Kenyan teachers 519
Korean teachers 411, 601
Kuwaiti teachers 196

Labor climates 538
Leader Behavior Description
Questionnaire 64, 102,
131, 218, 252, 277,
411, 444, 480, 557,
565, 570, 572, 574,
582, 590, 599, 605,
612, 624, 632, 641,
643, 648, 649, 653
Leader Effectiveness and
Adaptability Description
78, 195, 603, 673
Leadership behavior 102,
143, 218, 275, 277,
285, 411, 413, 444,
455, 462, 463, 514,
557, 562, 565, 570,
574, 583, 584, 590,
595, 597, 599, 601,
605, 612, 615, 617,
619, 623, 624, 628,
631, 632, 634, 637,
643, 649, 653, 662;
see also leadership
style, principals
Leadership Opinion Questionnaire 662
Leadership style 61, 64,
78, 124, 131, 195, 345,
480, 484, 556, 560,
568, 576, 580, 581,
582, 585, 591, 602,
603, 636, 641, 642,
648, 659, 666, 667,
669, 673; see also leadership behavior, principals
Least Preferred Co-Worker
Scale 568, 580, 667
Lebanese teachers 666,
667
Leisure activities 350
Leisure Activities Questionnaire 350
Liberal arts teachers
358
Liberian teachers 297
Libyan teachers 197
Life satisfaction 328,
763, 877, 907, 955,
968
Likert's theory 143, 162
Locus of control 82, 251,
252, 341, 491, 545,
643, 712, 730, 733,
782, 799, 844, 869,
990, 1037, 1047
Locus of Control instrument
869
Lortie's theory 537

Mainstreaming 291, 292
Mainstreaming Planning
Inventory 292

Malaysian teachers 384
Male administrators 635
Male teachers 98, 195,
   545, 635, 955, 1045;
   see also gender differences
Management Appraisal Survey
   556
Management of Differences
   Exercise 135
Management Style Diagnosis
   Test 591
Marital Adjustment Scale
   1063
Marital satisfaction 1063
Marketing teachers 282
Maryland Cooperative Exten-
   sion Service teachers
   266, 309
Maslach Burnout Inventory
   682, 685, 687, 714,
   740, 745, 752, 765,
   766, 770, 771, 798,
   799, 832, 848, 854,
   889
Maslow's theory 155, 176,
   186, 317, 508, 509,
   548, 670, 973, 1034;
   see also needs
Master teachers 903
Mathematics teachers 198,
   1027
Maturity Scale 78
Meaning and Value of Work
   Scale 220
Measure of Self-
   Actualization 102
Measure of Sex Role Prefer-
   ence 307
Mental health 73
Mentor teachers 2, 17,
   24, 267
Merit pay 501, 513, 530,
   533, 542, 980
Mexican teachers 1053,
   1055

Middle school characteristics 145, 175, 187
Middle School Practices
   Index 175
Middle School Questionnaire
   145
Middle school teachers
   137, 145, 146, 163,
   173, 174, 175, 180,
   181, 187, 188, 224,
   515, 583, 586, 879;
   see also intermediate
   school teachers, secondary teachers
Midlife transitions 700,
   790, 885, 955, 1005,
   1012
Minnesota Anticipated
   Satisfaction Question-
   naire 3
Minnesota Importance Questionnaire 65, 269
Minnesota Job Description
   Questionnaire 54, 301,
   510
Minnesota Satisfaction
   Questionnaire 3, 41,
   65, 84, 86, 87, 88,
   100, 115, 118, 125,
   131, 136, 137, 139,
   142, 145, 148, 149,
   153, 202, 206, 210,
   228, 231, 233, 237,
   240, 248, 251, 268,
   269, 274, 279, 282,
   286, 288, 290, 294,
   300, 301, 303, 312,
   350, 366, 402, 426,
   427, 433, 444, 451,
   468, 474, 485, 510,
   511, 542, 556, 572,
   580, 599, 608, 628,
   647, 661, 668, 672,
   687, 714, 730, 901,
   909, 913, 918, 923,
   934, 945, 949, 957,

993, 1002, 1003, 1024, 1033, 1037, 1061
Minnesota Satisfactoriness Scale 41, 153, 272
Minnesota Teacher Attitude Inventory 290, 303, 789
Model Organizational Orientation Rating Scale 461
Modified Friedlander Scale 358
Motivation Feedback Opinionnaire 542
Motivation and Reward Scale 554
Motivation techniques 516, 543, 549, 566, 579, 618
Motivation to Teach Survey 39
Multiple employment 762, 971, 1006, 1060
Multiunit schools 105, 295
Music Educator Describer 268
Music teachers 210, 215, 268, 281, 326, 443, 447, 833, 871

National Job Satisfaction Study Instrument 245, 410
Need Satisfaction Questionnaire 608, 766
Need-Satisfaction in Work Survey 158
Needs 65, 108, 155, 157, 158, 172, 185, 343, 354, 396, 505, 508, 510, 523, 536, 538, 540, 544, 548, 550, 563, 668, 777, 852, 861, 862, 935, 1004; see also Maslow's theory

Needs Hierarchy Questionnaire 343, 548
Neuroticism 133
New York State United Teachers Stress Survey 237
New Zealand teachers 72, 746, 747
Nigerian teachers 104, 136, 149, 169, 170, 363, 431, 979, 1026, 1029
Nominal Group Technique 373
Nonfinancial incentives 509, 513
Noninstructional responsibility 18, 772
Norwegian teachers 814, 815
Nursing teachers 338, 344, 358, 383, 406, 411, 425, 439, 463

Occupational Interest Survey 114
Occupational orientation 151
Occupational Stress, Coping and Health Problems of teachers 764
Ohio Inventory of Employee Morale 649
Open classrooms 52, 57, 79, 103, 105
Open space schools 77, 123
Organizational change 517
Organizational characteristics 100
Organizational climate 82, 101, 102, 137, 143, 148, 163, 164, 165, 191, 195, 218, 292,

Subject Index

304, 330, 353, 376,
383, 421, 435, 461,
465, 475, 481, 538,
565, 567, 568, 572,
588, 606, 629, 644,
645, 647, 650, 754,
757, 789, 793, 805,
808, 850, 880, 958,
1002, 1052
Organizational Climate
Description Questionnaire
101, 102, 137, 148,
163, 191, 195, 218,
292, 481, 565, 568,
572, 591, 597, 644,
647, 650, 789, 958,
1002
Organizational commitment
359, 937
Organizational Commitment
Questionnaire 58, 63,
931
Organizational effectiveness 492, 1007, 1014
Organizational Inventory
88
Organizational Leadership
Stress Questionnaire
789
Organizational structure
61, 74, 117, 130, 260,
286, 318, 354, 403,
541, 625, 646, 930,
950, 985, 992, 1014
Outdoor teachers 249
Outstanding teachers 62
Overall Job Satisfaction
Instrument 632
Overseas teachers 261

Parental support 274,
726
Parochial school teachers
159, 258
Part time teachers 370,
373, 416, 438, 444

Participation in Decision
Making Scale 1008
Pay satisfaction 154,
250
Pay Satisfaction Questionnaire 154
Peer evaluation 672, 903
Peer relationship 735
Perceived Equity Scale
132
Perceived Needs in Stress
Counseling 881
Perceived Stress Questionnaire 881
Perceived Work Environment
Measure 371
Perfectionism 92
Performance evaluation
422
Person-environment fit
theory 327, 329
Person Interest Inventory
1053
Personal Interview Questionnaire 210
Personal life stress 677
Personal Lifestyle Survey
846, 847
Personal Opinion Questionnaire 877
Personal Orientation Inventory 136, 248, 451,
1034, 1046
Personal Reaction Survey
491
Personal Report of Communication Apprehension
1059
Personal satisfaction
296
Personality Indicator
282, 945, 993
Personality Inventory
133
Personality needs 40
Personality traits 103,
160, 171, 210, 248,

251, 282, 327, 354, 460, 594, 676, 811, 863, 945, 949, 982, 993, 1028, 1032, 1057, 1062
Personality Scales 949
Pharmacy teachers 474
Physical and social science teachers 428
Physical education teachers 195, 218, 224, 342, 371, 391, 423, 424, 836, 939
Physical health 674, 677, 680, 684, 703, 720, 867, 878
Physical Symptoms Inventory 712
Physician teachers 436
Physics teachers 308
Post secondary vocational teachers 319
Power 164, 385, 592, 633, 640, 651
Power Scale Index 633
Preference for Instructional Methods Scale 160
Preschool and day care center teachers 286, 287
Preservice teacher education 1, 29, 42, 50, 173, 908
Principal Behavior Check List 585
Principal effectiveness 620, 641, 650
Principal Effectiveness Scale 641
Principal perceptions 54
Principal succession 625
Principals 97, 124, 149, 153, 505, 507, 556, 557, 558, 562, 563, 567, 579, 594, 605, 607, 610, 615, 618, 627, 634, 639, 655, 661, 663, 665, 670, 747, 777, 856; see also leadership behavior, leadership styles
Principal's Questionnaire 632
Principal-Staff Authority Inventory 613, 651
Private colleges 385
Private school teachers 182, 653, 705, 761, 872
Productivity 246, 321, 346, 560, 1029
Productivity Index 321
Professional and Bureaucratic Orientation Scale 88
Professional development 43, 267, 341, 407, 692, 693, 748, 841, 864, 995
Professional growth 14
Professional identification 300
Professional life 964
Professional negotiations 1023
Professional Orientation Scale 66, 97, 130
Professional preparation 192
Professional recognition 179, 186
Professionalism 66, 97, 151, 179, 263, 408, 1024, 1025
Professionalism Scale 218, 300, 408, 1024
Profile of Organizational Characteristics 631, 646, 768
Profile of a School 87, 162, 950, 1014

Subject Index 317

Project Teacher Activities 289
Psychic reward 100
Psychological Participation Index 86
Public Law 94-142 204, 291, 686
Pupil Control Behavior Form 969
Pupil control ideology 30, 31, 82, 671, 969, 992
Pupil Control Ideology Form 671, 969, 992
Purdue Student-Teacher Opinionaire 5, 1018
Purdue Teacher Evaluation Scale 577
Purdue Teacher Opinionaire 7, 35, 57, 59, 60, 68, 85, 86, 95, 103, 123, 130, 159, 167, 175, 180, 191, 192, 200, 201, 223, 236, 254, 362, 462, 472, 548, 561, 570, 577, 582, 601, 609, 653, 671, 740, 765, 899, 904, 926, 999, 1046, 1055

Quality circle process 63, 953
Quality of Employment Job Satisfaction Survey 608
Quality of Employment Survey 474
Quality of Work Life 120, 198, 606
Quality of worklife 525, 693, 814, 917, 1005
Questionnaire for Secondary Teachers 152

Racial composition 85, 114, 690, 691, 1004

Reading teachers 21, 115, 223, 260, 569, 748, 842, 864
Reduction in force 95, 518, 712, 723, 835
Reinforcement theory 141
Remedial teachers 306
Research teachers 345
Resource room teachers 67, 217, 779
Resource Specialist Role Agreement Questionnaire 228
Resource specialists 228
Retention Factor Questionnaire 203
Retirement 357, 473, 956, 1044
Retirement Descriptive Index 473
Retrenchment 441, 452, 483
Revitalization 817
Rewards 112, 260, 298, 345, 349, 437, 474, 476; see also incentives
Robustness 567, 899
Robustness Semantic Differential Scales 899
Roe's theory 1053
Role ambiguity 146, 391, 439, 470, 595, 643, 781, 853, 1039, 1061
Role conflict 146, 207, 285, 289, 321, 391, 439, 470, 796, 853, 914, 1039, 1061
Role Conflict and Ambiguity Scale 146, 439, 595, 643, 768, 777, 877, 1039, 1061
Role expectations 217, 344, 345, 576, 1000; see also role perceptions
Role involvement 176
Role models 760

Role perception 228, 268, 374, 393, 709; see also role expectations
Role strain 448
Role Strain Interview Schedule 448
Roman Catholic teaching sisters 213
Rural teachers 1, 4, 90, 235, 238, 242, 262, 758, 764, 779, 803, 931, 935

Satisfaction with Teaching Questionnaire 746
Saudi Arabian teachers 315, 323, 958
School calendar 1033
School change 9
School Climate Profile 304
School counselors 692, 741, 793, 882
School effectiveness 566, 579, 586, 588, 618, 625, 626, 665, 950
School environment 143, 155, 179; see also educational environment, work environment
School Environmental Complexity Scale 66
School location 132
School management system 162
School newspapers 581
School size 75, 491, 669
School Structure and Climate Survey 491
Science teachers 198, 298, 827, 1027
Second career or late entry teachers 107
Secondary teachers 132-192, 198, 199, 205, 206, 209, 230, 232, 237, 242, 268, 270, 281, 301, 449, 450, 521, 531, 576, 581, 593, 595, 598, 615, 619, 637, 640, 646, 650, 653, 665, 666, 723, 748, 828, 829, 836, 881, 900, 952, 1009; see also high school teachers, intermediate school teachers, middle school teachers
Self actualization 136, 339, 340, 451, 545, 753, 761, 862, 921, 984, 1034, 1046
Self concept 25, 29, 62, 104, 116, 117, 728, 752, 771, 838, 895, 899
Self congruence 164, 392, 393
Self contained classrooms 52, 57, 87, 103, 714, 779
Self directed learning 206
Self Directed Search 1019
Self esteem 84, 296, 313, 363, 683, 692, 701, 730, 738, 764, 852, 1056
Self Perception Inventory Teacher Form 730
Self Perception Self-Rating Scale 39
Self Report Inventory 982
Sense of humor 567
Sex-Role Inventory 898
Shared governance 994
Situational Leadership theory 78
Sixteen Personality Factor Questionnaire 79, 103, 210, 913, 1032
Social Desirability Scale 913, 1056

Subject Index

Social interaction 429
Social Readjustment Rating
  Scale 879
Social studies teachers
  263
Social support system
  71
Socioeconomic status 126
Sources of Stress Inventory
  843
Special education teachers
  64, 84, 146, 150, 194,
  200, 201, 204, 219,
  241, 247, 248, 254,
  267, 274, 277, 279,
  285, 292, 294, 303,
  310, 311, 488, 514,
  526, 660, 674, 681,
  682, 683, 686, 695,
  702, 709, 734, 735,
  737, 742, 750, 767,
  768, 769, 771, 773,
  776, 778, 779, 782,
  786, 787, 798, 800,
  801, 811, 822, 826,
  832, 837, 858, 859,
  860, 872, 890, 891,
  892
Staff development 83,
  156, 353, 543, 593,
  654, 754, 790, 813,
  988, 1051
Stages of Concern 11
Stanford Teacher Competence
  Appraisal Guide 36
State Anxiety Scale 713
State departments of education 27
State-Trait Anxiety Inventory 713, 783
State Trait Personality
  Inventory 755
Stress management 341,
  713, 718, 722, 741,
  772, 778, 793, 805,
  806, 812, 813, 816,
  837, 838, 841, 846,
  862, 882
Stress Profile for Teachers
  682, 740, 872
Stress-Related Questionnaire 871
Stress-Satisfaction Questionnaire 755
Structural coupling 286,
  626, 1007
Structural Dimensions
  Questionnaire 623
Structural Properties
  Questionnaire 61, 130,
  950, 985, 992, 1014
Student achievement 68,
  96, 102, 110, 239, 275,
  304, 492, 515, 574,
  601, 617, 625, 649,
  659, 665, 916, 931, 1007
Student Achievement Diagnostic Questionnaire
  for Administrators 527
Student behavior 802
Student motivation 81
Student Opinion Inventory
  148
Student teachers 5, 19,
  25, 29, 33, 39, 40,
  42, 43, 50, 830, 1018
Study of Values Scale
  1003
Subject area teachers
  193-313; see also high
  school teachers, intermediate school teachers,
  junior high teachers,
  middle school teachers,
  secondary teachers,
  vocational education
  teachers
Subjective expectation
  189
Substitute teachers 236
Suburban school teachers
  168, 180, 717, 725,
  952

Sudanese teachers 1042
Supervision 34, 48, 75, 362
Supervisory Behavior Description Questionnaire 462, 662
Supervisory Intervention Behavior Instrument 463
Supportive Activities Questionnaire 274
Survey of Administrator's Use of Authority 613
Survey of Principal Attitudes 937
Survey of Teacher Opinion and Behavior 176
Survey of Teacher Satisfaction/Dissatisfaction 975
Swedish teachers 225
Symptom Checklist 776

Taiwanese teachers 131, 294
Task clarity 321
Task Clarity and Role Conflict instrument 321
Teacher absenteeism 55, 69, 162, 165, 184, 491, 498, 642, 648, 689, 782, 912, 944, 946, 947, 970, 987, 994, 1030, 1048
Teacher administrator relationships 70, 260, 330, 333, 356, 370, 376, 445, 476, 494, 507, 508, 540, 555-673, 688, 691, 696, 718, 719, 726, 735, 820, 839
Teacher alienation 183, 291, 333, 400, 478, 561, 573, 604, 613, 656, 679, 698, 703, 706, 711, 718, 727, 732, 762, 796, 824, 831, 834, 855, 864, 875, 915
Teacher Alienation Inventory 613, 651, 679
Teacher Attitude Checklist 295
Teacher Attitude Survey 717, 768, 886
Teacher attitudes 12, 15, 42, 47, 53, 56, 65, 69, 70, 72, 80, 92, 94, 98, 119, 122, 144, 185, 208, 215, 226, 234, 382, 401, 415, 436, 437, 441, 445, 446, 458, 466, 507, 524, 587, 604, 611, 639, 655, 664, 681, 693, 702, 710, 723, 733, 738, 751, 753, 759, 772, 784, 786, 787, 798, 800, 801, 802, 810, 811, 815, 823, 824, 840, 842, 845, 851, 857, 859, 864, 868, 880, 896, 905, 906, 918, 919, 920, 933, 938, 959, 966, 986, 996, 1000, 1014, 1021, 1031, 1040, 1042, 1045; see also work attitudes
Teacher Attitudes Toward Supervision Instrument 672
Teacher attrition 140, 201, 241, 247, 265, 308, 313, 393, 786, 787, 1011; see also teacher turnover
Teacher background 369, 459, 737, 854
Teacher behavior 32, 126, 217, 655, 656, 772, 824, 841, 963, 1006
Teacher brinkmanship 655, 656, 657

Subject Index

Teacher Brinkmanship Inventory 656, 657
Teacher burnout 17, 23, 144, 157, 185, 316, 333, 419, 508, 535, 569, 573, 674-894; see also teacher stress
Teacher Burnout Inventory 729
Teacher centers 732, 918
Teacher certification 960
Teacher characteristics 8, 10, 53, 56, 62, 108, 109, 132, 203, 276, 377, 488, 520, 544, 573, 591, 723, 799, 874, 895, 936, 1011, 1036, 1040, 1062
Teachers' Characteristics Questionnaire 499
Teacher Concerns Checklist 12, 895
Teacher conflict 88
Teacher Description Questionnaire 641
Teacher education 20, 21, 23, 27, 33, 35, 37, 47, 49, 51, 174, 225, 238, 257, 265, 434, 788, 825, 858, 887, 900, 911, 960, 986, 1043
Teacher effectiveness 62, 91, 110, 368, 369, 418, 472, 513, 523, 552, 558, 562, 577, 663, 665, 710, 749, 823, 902, 920, 1060
Teacher Effort Index 515
Teacher employment 13, 530, 551, 1050
Teacher evaluation 513, 896, 940
Teacher Evaluation Satisfaction instrument 612

Teacher Facilitation of Self-Direction Inventory 206
Teacher Human Relations Questionnaire 585
Teacher improvement 774, 839, 902, 986
Teacher induction 7, 24, 44, 45, 49
Teacher influence 600, 895, 972
Teacher innovativeness 554
Teacher Job Descriptive Index 928
Teacher Job Satisfaction Questionnaire 958, 998
Teacher longevity 134
Teacher loyalty 598, 600, 613, 636, 647, 651
Teacher Loyalty Inventory 613, 636
Teacher militancy 934, 985
Teacher mobility 979, 989, 996
Teacher morale 5, 6, 24, 32, 33, 81, 84, 95, 110, 111, 113, 116, 122, 127, 161, 186, 191, 208, 223, 238, 239, 261, 264, 280, 283, 296, 305, 308, 333, 347, 356, 360, 363, 376, 392, 400, 430, 438, 452, 456, 483, 489, 494, 502, 503, 516, 543, 548, 549, 555, 560, 561, 564, 566, 571, 578, 579, 584, 586, 593, 607, 619, 622, 627, 629, 630, 649, 652, 658, 663, 664, 670, 676, 678, 680, 681, 683, 688, 690, 691,

694, 697, 703, 705,
706, 710, 711, 718,
722, 724, 725, 726,
727, 728, 732, 736,
739, 742, 749, 751,
756, 757, 760, 761,
769, 774, 778, 790,
791, 793, 797, 800,
801, 803, 804, 808,
809, 810, 813, 814,
816, 817, 819, 821,
823, 824, 825, 826,
831, 832, 834, 835,
839, 841, 847, 849,
855, 857, 858, 860,
862, 863, 864, 867,
868, 870, 873, 875,
883, 885, 887, 888,
891, 892, 902, 904,
963, 971, 996, 999,
1017, 1035, 1054
Teacher motivation 89,
104, 120, 150, 172,
325, 352, 389, 417,
432, 467, 487, 490–554,
618, 645, 728, 790,
883, 902, 935, 965
Teacher Occupational Stress
Factor Questionnaire
371, 743, 776, 846,
847
Teacher Opinion Inventory
1020
Teacher Opinion Survey
150
Teacher Opinionnaire 948,
985, 1017
Teacher orientation 27,
218, 564, 607
Teacher Orientation Study
103
Teacher participation
186; see also decision
making
Teacher Perception Questionnaire 729

Teacher Performance Assessment Instrument 112,
931
Teacher persistence 247,
719, 721, 739, 758,
760, 791, 908, 954,
961, 966, 1027, 1050
Teacher placement 262
Teacher planning time
68
Teacher Preparation Evaluation Inventory 896
Teacher promotion 516,
903
Teacher qualifications
986, 1043
Teacher Questionnaire
52
Teacher quitting behavior
573, 915
Teacher recruitment 238,
931, 939, 961, 967, 1026
Teacher retention 203,
241, 334, 430, 500,
551, 931
Teacher Reward and Satisfaction Scales 134
Teacher role 15, 16, 130,
291, 299, 686, 709,
711, 792, 829, 880
Teacher Role Perception
Scale 916
Teacher salaries 96, 272,
348, 380, 501, 533,
544, 762, 971, 1006,
1060
Teacher Satisfaction Scale
574
Teacher Satisfaction/
Compatibility Questionnaire 79
Teacher selection 936
Teacher shortage 1006,
1027
Teacher socialization
11, 30, 31, 43, 44,
346, 427

Subject Index

Teacher stress 19, 67, 113, 121, 171, 214, 237, 267, 329, 330, 332, 371, 454, 460, 562, 602, 611, 642, 674-874; see also teacher burnout
Teacher Stress Inventory 734, 755, 812, 854
Teacher Stress Survey 702
Teacher-student relationship 109, 110, 138, 418, 683, 711, 718, 719, 760, 902, 999
Teacher supervision 564, 569, 587, 588, 594, 621, 839, 924
Teacher thrust 620
Teacher training 210, 212, 240; see also teacher workshops
Teacher transfer 500
Teacher turnover 164, 359, 443, 453, 951, 970, 994; see also teacher attrition
Teacher View of the School Organization 937
Teacher welfare 50, 407, 756, 1026
Teacher workshops 813, 840, 865, 882; see also teacher training
Teacher's Job Satisfaction and Dissatisfaction Inventory 499
Teacher's Need Satisfaction Questionnaire 637
Teacher's Perception of Supervisor Questionnaire 637
Teacher's Work Motivation Questionnaire 553
Teaching 10, 23, 46, 56, 93, 415, 430, 435, 437, 441, 459, 502, 530, 534, 535, 536, 549, 551, 759, 762, 763, 780, 788, 789, 797, 802, 803, 815, 819, 838, 861, 895-1063
Teaching Anxiety Scale 39
Teaching Clarity Index 48
Teaching conditions 27, 53, 70, 109, 122, 306, 368, 558, 566, 588, 627, 670, 682, 690, 691, 719, 721, 725, 726, 727, 797, 803, 807, 808, 809, 814, 819, 823, 831, 849, 856, 873, 883, 893, 971; see also working conditions
Teaching Events Stress Inventory 675, 703, 704, 803
Teaching experience 70, 253, 271, 288, 737, 869, 895, 896, 966
Teaching Likes and Dislikes Survey 1054
Teaching methods 377, 748
Teaching skills 29
Teaching styles 109, 171
Team teaching 59, 103, 105, 106, 123
Team Teaching Questionnaire 123
Tel-Aviv Educational Incidents Test 99
Tendency to Act Collectively Scale 151
Tennessee Self-Concept Scale 34, 84, 148, 771
Test of Imagination 74
Thai teachers 90, 434, 442, 471, 479, 653

Title I elementary teachers 96, 275, 289
Traditional schools 77
Training and Experience Questionnaire 210
Transferred teachers 190
Trust 385, 395, 638, 1028

Unionism 151, 320, 380, 385, 917, 942, 948, 959, 991; see also collective bargaining
Urban teachers 90, 155, 157, 158, 168, 171, 273, 427, 585, 690, 748, 763, 845, 846, 856, 886, 894, 915, 953, 1004, 1022

Value Survey 337
Values 337, 908, 977, 1003
Values for Working 266, 309
Venezuelan teachers 780
Vocational adjustment 46, 56, 415, 761, 887
Vocational agriculture teachers 193, 209, 216, 230, 231, 250, 253, 257, 264, 265, 283, 299, 305, 312, 331, 551, 796, 818, 941, 972, 989, 1016
Vocational education teachers 18, 32, 41, 48, 154, 208, 227, 234, 246, 252, 269, 288, 290, 293, 374, 377, 434, 459, 551, 957
Vocational maturity 6, 56
Vocational Preference Index 278

Vocational Preference Inventory 160, 251, 310, 311, 327, 1057
Vocational stability 278
Voluntarism 531, 552

White schools 60
Work adjustment 269, 270, 510
Work attitudes 127, 185, 347, 428, 447, 604, 851, 905, 939, 941, 952, 989, 1005; see also teacher attitudes
Work environment 500, 503, 541, 606, 611, 645, 676, 699, 715, 739, 796, 820, 884, 905, 1057; see also educational environment, school environment
Work Environment Preference Schedule 403, 404
Work Environment Scale 978
Work schedules 364
Work values 149, 220, 234, 246, 266, 309, 413, 570, 913, 930
Work Values Inventory 149, 234, 363, 913
Work Values Questionnaire 570
Working conditions 225, 241, 250, 386, 475, 538, 544; see also teaching conditions
Workload 329, 356, 399, 415, 435, 437, 441

You and Your Job Instrument 141

Zones of Indifference Instrument 561